Hiking and Exploring Utah's
Henry Mountains
and Robbers Roost

Michael R. Kelsey

Including The Life and Legend of Butch Cassidy

S HANKSVILLE 5MI, LEFT. FOLLOW
SHORT ORANGE POSTS.

BLM HANKSVILLE
801 542-3461
P.O. BOX 99
HV UTAH
84734

Kelsey Publishing
456 E. 100 N.
Provo, Utah, USA, 84601
Tele. 801-373-3327

SUE
MAPS $2.50

First Edition April 1987

Copyright ©1987 Michael R. Kelsey All Rights Reserved

Library of Congress Catalog Card Number--86-083281
ISBN Number 0-9605824-6-0

List of Distributors for Kelsey Publishing

Write to one of these companies when ordering any of Mike Kelsey's books. His books are listed at the back of this book.

Alpenbooks, P.O. Box 27344, Seattle, Washington, 98125
Banana Republic, 175 Bluxome Street, San Francisco, California, 94107
Bookpeople, 2929 Fifth Street, Berkeley, California, 94710
Canyon Country Publications, P.O. Box 963, Moab, Utah, 84532
Gordons Books, 5450 N. Valley Highway, Denver, Colorado, 80216
Many Feathers--Southwestern Books, 5738 North Central, Phoenix, Arizona, 85012
Quality Books(for Libraries), 918 Sherwood Drive, Lake Bluff, Illinois, 60044
Mountain 'n Air Books, 3704 1/2 Foothill Blvd., La Crescenta, Calif., 91214.
Recreational Equipment, Inc.(R.E.I.), P.O. Box C-88126, Seattle, Washington, 98188
Wasatch Publishers, Inc., 4647 Idlewild Road, Salt Lake City, Utah, 84124

For the **UK** and **Europe,** and the rest of the world contact:
CORDEE, 3a De Montfort Street, Leicester, England, UK, LE1 7HD

Printed by Press Publishing, 800 N. 1600 W., Provo, Utah

All fotos by the author, unless otherwise stated.
All maps, charts, cross sections drawn by the author.

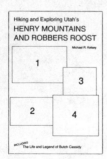

Front Cover Fotos
1. Larry Canyon
2. Mt. Ellen
3. Buffalo, Henry Mountains (Larry Sip foto)
4. Butch Cassidy's, "Wild Bunch"

Back Cover Fotos
5. The Crack, Robbers Roost Canyon
6. Star Mine, Mt. Hillers
7. Mt. Ellen, from Stair Canyon Rim
8. Reconstructed Wolverton Mill, Hanksville
9. Autumn Scene, Stair Canyon
10. South Face of Mt. Hillers

Table of Contents

Map Symbols

Town or Community............................ o□□	Peak and Prominent Ridge..............
Buildings or Homes............................ o●	Stream or Creek, Desert.................
Back Country Campsite.......................... ▲	Stream or Creek, Mountain..............
Campsite.. ●	River, Large....................................
Campgrounds..	Stream or Creek, Intermittent or Dry..
Church..	Canyon Narrows......................... (N)
Cemetery or Grave Site....................... †	Lake or Pond..................................
Ranger Station......................................	Mine, Quarry, Adit, Prospect............
Airport or Landing Strip...........	Water or Dry Falls...........................
Railway...	Spring or Seep................................
U. S. Highway................................ (89)	Radio Transmitter...........................
Utah State Highway....................... (24)	Pass..
Road-Maintained................................	Natural Arch.......................... (A)
Road-4 Wheel Drive(4WD)..........	Geology Cross Section...................
Track-Road, Unusable........................	Pictograph........................... (PIC)
Trail, Foot or Horse...........................	Petroglyph........................... (PET)
Route, No Trail................................ ●●●●●	Cowboy Glyph...................... (CG)
Peak or Summit................................... ✗	Fremont Indian Ruins.............. (R)

Abbreviations

Canyon...................C. or Can.		Campground....................................C.G.	
Lake.................................L.		Ranger Station................................R.S.	
River.................................R.		4 Wheel Drive Vehicle 4WD	
Creek.................................Ck.		High Clearance Vehicle.......................HCV	

4

ACKNOWLEDGMENTS

It's impossible to recall all the many people who helped me with information for this book. Special thanks should go to the following people. The one who helped most was Larry Gearhard, the recreation specialist for the BLM in Hanksville. Larry discussed roads, trails, and hikes with the author many times, and always had lots of good information. In the same Hanksville BLM office were several other employees who helped out as well. Barbara Ekker, writer and historian living in Hanksville, also contributed much information, as well as reading part of the manuscript. Pearl Baker, who grew up on the Biddlecome Ranch, and who now lives in Green River, contributed her time and visited with the author on several occasions. She allowed the author to quote from three of her books. Twice the author had good visits with long time cattleman and resident of Hanksville, Horace Ekker. His brothers Riter and Darys, also gave their time. Dora Flack allowed the author to quote from her book, *Butch Cassidy, My Brother*(Lula Betenson). Garth Noyes of the Cat Ranch, spent one afternoon with the author discussing the ranches of the Henry Mountains.

As usual, my mother, Venetta Kelsey, helped proof read the manuscript, on more than one occasion. She also helps out with the small publishing business while I'm gone to the mountains or canyons.

THE AUTHOR

The author experienced his earliest years of life in eastern Utah's Uinta Basin namely around the town of Roosevelt. Then the family moved to Provo, where he attended Provo High School, and later Brigham Young University, where he earned a B.S. degree in Sociology. Soon after he discovered that was the wrong subject, so he attended the University of Utah, where he received his Masters of Science degree in Geography, finishing in June, 1970.

It was then that real life began, for on June 9, 1970, he put a pack on his back and started traveling for the first time. Since then he has traveled to 129 countries and island groups. All this wandering has resulted in several books written and published by the author:*Climbers and Hikers Guide to the Worlds Mountains(2nd Ed.); Utah Mountaineering Guide, and the Best Canyon Hikes(2nd Ed.); China on Your Own and the Hiking Guide to China's Nine Sacred Mountains(3rd Ed); Canyon Hiking Guide to the Colorado Plateau;* and finally, *Hiking Utah's San Rafael Swell.*

Introduction to Hiking

This book covers the Henry Mountains Region of southeastern Utah. It's not a big land, but it's an area with many contrasts, so there's lots to see. This region extends from Hanksville and State Highway 24 in the north, to Lake Powell on the southeast. On the west is the Waterpocket Fold and Capitol Reef National Park. On the east, the arbitrary boundary for this book are the Orange Cliffs, which look down on the Maze District of Canyonlands National Park.

Inside these boundaries lay some of the most desolated deserts in the state, but also, some of the deepest, most isolated, and beautiful canyons in Utah. In contrast to the arid canyonlands, there are also the Henry Mountains. This group of relatively high peaks offers a cool retreat from the summer heat, in the middle of an otherwise rather inhospitable wasteland.

Also included within the boundaries of the region, is the relatively high mesa land known as the Robbers Roost Country. In about a 15 to 20 year period beginning in the early 1880's, this country with its wild and wooly canyons, offered hiding places for men who were always looking over their shoulder. It was the part-time home of Robert LeRoy Parker, otherwise known as Butch Cassidy. This land lies to the east of Hanksville, and between the Dirty Devil River and the eastern escarpment known as the Orange Cliffs. On early day maps of the United States, this was the last blank spot to be filled in. That was done by John W. Powell after he made his 1869 float trip down the Colorado River.

Perhaps the picture already painted seems a bit too much for the city kid who drives a car, but that's not quite so. In recent years, and with the building of the dam and rising waters of Lake Powell, there have been more and more people getting into these mountains and canyons. The cattlemen and miners first built roads, then came the BLM and recreationists or tourists. Through more and more use, and with the help of the country road crews, many of these roads today can be traveled by the average car. Of course there are many that still only qualify as 4WD tracks. Look at the *Reference Map of Hikes*. Almost all the backcountry roads shown on that map can be traveled by the average highway automobile.

Whether you plan to get off the main track or not, here are some helpful hints. Always have a full tank of fuel. Best place to fill up the tank is Hanksville, but Hite has a gas station-store(with diesel fuel available at the marina only). Bullfrog has very good services as well, but as you might expect, costs are high.

Besides plenty of fuel, carry more water, food, and tools than you think you'll need. The author carries 4 to 5 jugs full of water at all times, especially if he's out in the drier areas, and it's hot weather. For everyone, especially those with cars, take a shovel for smoothing out small gullies, or filling in deep ruts. Often times there are only one or two rough spots between you and your destination.

Another item to carry is a battery jumper cable. For the serious backcountry traveler, and those who might be going into the higher country, either early or late in the season, tire chains can be handy. The author drives a VW Rabbit, with cargo coils, gas shocks, and oversized tires, which have raised the body up about 6 to 8 cms(2.5" to 3"). He now goes almost everywhere in it.

Even though this country looks rather bleak to some, especially as one drives along the paved highways, there is water in almost every major canyon. Remember, the Henry Mountains rise to 3512 meters, and are covered with a pine-spruce-fir forest. Because these mountains pierce the sky, heavy precip falls, even though it may be only on the higher summits. Because of the mountains, there are many springs and seeps in the canyons surrounding the Henrys.

Rainfall often comes in heavy downpours. The month with the heaviest precip is August, followed closely by September, with July and October next, having about the same amounts. The driest months for Hanksville, are from January through March, in contrast to the northern part of the state along the Wasatch Front. Hanksville receives about 15 cms of moisture annually, compared to about 38 cms for Salt Lake City. The greatest amount of precip falls on the higher slopes of Mt. Ellen, which amounts to about 75 cms a year(75cms ÷ 2.5cms = 30 inches).

To the hiker, this suggests the best time to hike in the canyons is in the fall, because he has a better chance to find good pothole water for drinking. But it also means that roads have a better chance of being washed out at that time. However, washed-out roads don't occur that often. On average, any one area may have water in an otherwise dry wash, only once or twice a year. Every time there's water in a gully, it doesn't necessarily means it's a big "gully washer".

A word should be mentioned about the threat of flash flooding in the canyons. For the most part, the danger of being caught in any of these canyons at the time of a cloudburst, is very slim. True, there are some narrow canyons in these parts, but they don't compare with the Buckskin Gulch of the Paria River, or the Zion Narrows. For the most part, the narrows you'll find in these canyons are short, so high spots out of the way of rising waters, aren't far away.

Because the area has high mountains, and low altitude canyonlands, one cannot generalize and say this or that month is the hiking season. For the low lands, the very best time to hike or travel, is in the spring, from late March through May, with April generally being ideal. In late May, and in the areas around lake Powell, you'll begin to be bothered by those little gnats or midges, which get in your hair and bite. They are especially bad in June. Later in summer these insects become less numerous, and slowly die off as the fall season approaches.

In summer the temps are very high in the canyons, and this is not a good time to hike there. By September, the temperatures drop and the insects leave, and it becomes more liveable. October is the ideal month in the fall, perhaps in the whole year.   The first part of November is often a good time to hike, but the days become very short then. Remember, on November 21, the amount of daylight is about the same as on January 21. March 21 and September 21 have the same amount of daylight as well. Spring time is nice because the days are longer than in the fall.

The coldest 90 day period in Utah is from November 23, until February 22. Any precip falling in this time frame will surely fall as snow, making life miserable for those unprepared. However, the well prepared hiker can enjoy winter in the lower canyons, if he has planned for cold temps. During stable weather conditions, as when the valleys around Salt Lake City are fog-bound, it's usually nice in the canyonlands. The best part of winter hiking is, there are no insects and few if any other hikers. On the other hand, if you get stuck, you may have a long wait for help.

In the high country, the reverse is true. Summer is the time to climb the peaks, and escape the heat of the lowlands. The best time to climb in the high country is from about June 1 through the end of October, but early winter storms can come, and cause great concern for travel on the back roads, especially in areas with clay soils. On the lower mountains, Holmes and Ellsworth for example, the hiking season would be extended, perhaps to a year-round basis in some years.

Here's a health problem you should be aware of. It's an intestinal disorder called Giardiasis, caused by the microscopic organism, Giardia Lamblia. Giardia are carried in the feces of humans and some domestic and wild animals. The cysts of Giardia may contaminate surface water supplies. The symptoms usually include diarrhea, increased gas, loss of appetite, abdominal cramps, and bloating. It is not life threatening, but it can slow you down and make life miserable. BLM and national park rangers constantly harangue hikers about its deathly possibilities, so here's what you do. If on a short hike, carry your own water. On longer trips, take water from a spring source out of reach of animals, especially cattle. Or boil water for one minute, or treat with iodine. Iodine, is the recommended treatment. Until the last few years, one had to have a doctors prescription to buy iodine tablets, but today you can buy them easily, especially in stores which specialize in backpacking supplies. Remember, the biggest polluters are cattle. So when you see cattle tracks right in the creek bed or seep, take care, and head up-stream to the spring source.

Included under each hike, is information about water in the area. For the most part you can take water right from the small stream, seep or spring, in the smaller side canyons, and drink it. Again, look for sign of cattle before drinking. There are less cattle in the canyons today than there have been in years past. In a discussion with one of the local cattlemen in Hanksville, the topic of whether or not to drink water in the canyons was brought up. He flatly stated, that most of the water you'll find out there, especially in places like the Roost Canyon, is the best water in the world. He's been drinking it for years and hasn't suffered. The same is true of this author, who has never had a problem when drinking water in the backcountry, whether it's been in the high mountains or the desert canyons.

Here are some more tips about water. Because the area is generally arid, water isn't everywhere. If you're out on an overnight hike, take along an extra empty jug or two, of the one gallon(3.75 liters) size. This will allow you to carry water from a spring or stream, to your campsite, which sometimes will be away from the water source.

Many visitors to these canyons, hike without a tent. Because it's generally dry, and because there are many natural alcoves or sandstone caves or ledges in each canyon, you can often get by without a tent. But this author prefers a tent no matter what. There are always insects, unless it's the colder time of year, and it's easier to keep things clean while using a tent. Of course, you can't see the stars when sleeping in a tent.

For those who are uncertain what to wear, here are some ideas. In winter of course, you'll need to bundle up a bit, at least for the morning or evening hours, but around midday, one can often shed a coat, for just a long sleeved shirt. At night, you'll likely want to keep a small camp stove going in the tent, so take large quantities of fuel. It's true, some winter weather can be unpleasant, but it can also be one of the best times to hike in the canyons.

In spring or fall, the author prefers to begin the day with long pants and a long sleeved shirt, but usually later on, these are discarded for a pair of shorts and T-shirt. In summer, when temperatures are very warm throughout much of the region, you'll want to get out and hike in the morning hours as much as possible, and of course you'll want the lightweight clothing.

For we fair-haired folk, sun protection is a must. Some kind of broad brimmed hat is good, but it can be miserable in the wind. The author has rigged up an adjustable baseball type cap, with a "cancer curtain" around the back side, like the French Foreign Legion caps. This prevents skin deterioration and possibly skin cancer.

Most hikes in the Henry Mountains Region are day-hikes, so you'll need a small day-pack. With one you can carry a lunch, water, a camera, map and extra clothing you'll shed from the morning hours.

The author has done his best to make the maps in this book as accurate as possible, but they are no substitute for the real thing. Buy the maps recommended below. This author generally carries but two maps, both of which are metric and both are at the scale 1:100,000. Those maps are the USGS maps *Hanksville* and *Hite Crossing,* which cover all hikes in this book. Some readers will automatically hate the metrics involved, but these maps are much newer and updated than the older 1:62,500 scale maps. Read in the back of this book under topo maps, for more information.

A word to those with the ORV's(Off Road Vehicles). Because of the increased use of these vehicles in recent years, some areas are becoming terribly scarred with the tracks of these man-made "animals". It is the opinion of this writer that it's primarily the overuse and abuses of these machines, that has led the opposition, in this case the so-called *environmentalists,* to unite and begin legislation to set aside wilderness areas on the Colorado Plateau. If the abuses continue, the opposition will become stronger, and one day this nation will surely ban the use and importation of such machines. A word to the wise.

And speaking about keeping the place pristine and beautiful, why can't we all pitch in a help collect our own garbage and take it home and dispose of it properly. Each trip the author makes to the outback, he comes home with a garbage can liner full of soda pop and beer cans. Only if we all help, can we preserve the wilderness character of our land.

This book uses the metric system. Most of the complaints the author has received in the past concerning its use has come because automobile odometers use miles and his books use kilomage. But once you get used to it, it's easy to convert. Remember, two miles are about three kms, and 60 miles are about the same as 100 kms. The ratio is about 2 to 3. See the metric conversion table in the front of the book(page 8).

The reason for using metrics is simple; the USA, Burma, and Brunei(on the northwest coast of the island of Borneo), are the only three countries in the world which still use the outdated English System of measurement. Sooner or later we too must change over. This is a start. Other helpful hints are: 10 inches of rain is equal to about 25 cms, or one inch equals about 2.5 cms. Five thousand feet is about the same as 1500 meters. Remember, one meter is just a little more than one yard. Three feet then are very close to one meter. Once you understand some of the basics, it's easy to use.

METRIC CONVERSION TABLE

1 Centimeter = .39 Inch	1 Mile = 1.609 Kilometers	1 Quart (US) = .946 Liter
1 Inch = 2.54 Centimeters	100 Miles = 161 Kilometers	1 Gallon (US) = 3.785 Liters
1 Meter = 39.37 Inches	100 Kilometers = 62 Miles	1 Acre = 0.405 Hectare
1 Foot = 0.3048 Meter	1 Liter = 1.056 Quarts (US)	1 Hectare = 2.471 Acres
1 Kilometer = 0.621 Mile		

METERS TO FEET (Meters x 3.2808 = Feet)

100 m = 328 ft.	2500 m = 8202 ft.	5000 m = 16404 ft.	7500 m = 24606 ft.
500 m = 1640 ft.	3000 m = 9842 ft.	5500 m = 18044 ft.	8000 m = 26246 ft.
1000 m = 3281 ft.	3500 m = 11483 ft.	6000 m = 19686 ft.	8500 m = 27887 ft.
1500 m = 4921 ft.	4000 m = 13124 ft.	6500 m = 21325 ft.	9000 m = 29527 ft.
2000 m = 6562 ft.	4500 m = 14764 ft.	7000 m = 22966 ft.	

FEET TO METERS (Feet ÷ 3.2808 = Meters)

1000 ft. = 305 m	9000 ft. = 2743 m	16000 ft. = 4877 m	23000 ft. = 7010 m
2000 ft. = 610 m	10000 ft. = 3048 m	17000 ft. = 5182 m	24000 ft. = 7315 m
3000 ft. = 914 m	11000 ft. = 3353 m	18000 ft. = 5486 m	25000 ft. = 7620 m
4000 ft. = 1219 m	12000 ft. = 3658 m	19000 ft. = 5791 m	26000 ft. = 7925 m
5000 ft. = 1524 m	13000 ft. = 3962 m	20000 ft. = 6096 m	27000 ft. = 8230 m
6000 ft. = 1829 m	14000 ft. = 4268 m	21000 ft. = 6401 m	28000 ft. = 8535 m
7000 ft. = 2134 m	15000 ft. = 4572 m	22000 ft. = 6706 m	29000 ft. = 8839 m
8000 ft. = 2438 m			30000 ft. = 9144 m

CENTIMETERS / INCHES scale

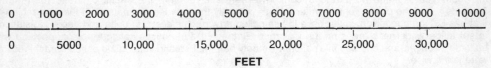

METERS / FEET scale

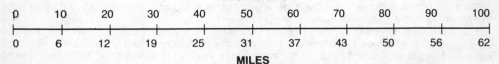

KILOMETERS / MILES scale

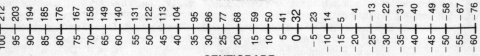

FAHRENHEIT / CENTIGRADE scale

REFERENCE MAP OF HIKES

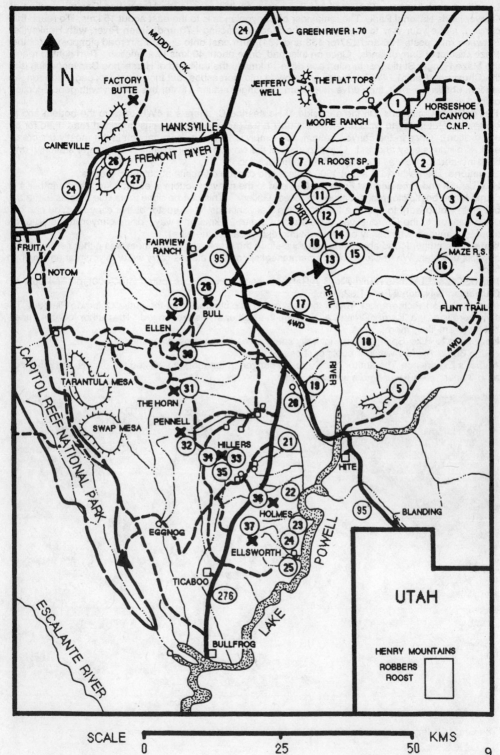

N

MUDDY CK.

GREEN RIVER I-70

FACTORY BUTTE

JEFFERY WELL

THE FLAT TOPS

MOORE RANCH

HANKSVILLE

CAINEVILLE

FREMONT RIVER

FRUITA

NOTOM

FAIRVIEW RANCH

95

R. ROOST SP.

HORSESHOE CANYON C.N.P.

DIRTY

DEVIL

MAZE R.S.

FLINT TRAIL

4WD

RIVER

BULL

ELLEN

TARANTULA MESA

THE HORN

SWAP MESA

PENNELL

HILLERS

HITE

HOLMES

EGGNOG

ELLSWORTH

TICABOO

276

CAPITOL REEF NATIONAL PARK

POWELL

95

BLANDING

LAKE

BULLFROG

ESCALANTE RIVER

UTAH

HENRY MOUNTAINS
ROBBERS ROOST

SCALE   KMS

0   25   50

Horseshoe Canyon

Location and Access The small bordered area on this map is the Horseshoe Canyon section of Canyonlands National Park. The remainder of Canyonlands is to the east about 15 kms. To reach this canyon, make your way to Highway 24, the road connecting I-70 and Green River, with Hanksville. Between mile posts 136 and 137(or 133 and 134), turn east onto a good dirt road signposted for the Maze District of Canyonlands. Once on this road, drive about 40 kms to a junction. Turn right to reach the Maze Ranger Station, or turn left and drive 11 kms to the trailhead of Horseshoe Canyon(which is at the Chuchuru Cabin). 4WD vehicles are allowed into Horseshoe, but they must proceed to the ranger station, obtain a permit, then drive north from the ranger station. Enter this country with good supplies of food and fuel.

Trail or Route Conditions On the east side of Horseshoe C., there's a 4WD track to the bottom and a campsite. But from the west side there is only a trail(actually the remains of an old road used for oil exploration). Once in the canyon bottom, you simply walk up or down canyon in the mostly dry creek bed. Walking is easy and fast. One can walk all the way up canyon(south) to the ranger station, if one is so inclined, or walk all the way to the Green River(north).

Elevations The trailhead is about 1600 meters; the canyon campsite about 1425 meters.

Hike Length and Time Needed From the trailhead to the canyon bottom is about 2 kms, and another 4 or 5 kms to the best pictographs, called the "Great Gallery". This can be done in as little time as half a day, but most would want to spend a full day in the Canyonlands N. P. sector of this canyon. You can hike down canyon to the Green River, a distance of about 25 kms one way, or up canyon to some of the tributary canyons, which may be the most interesting part of the hike.

Water The author found about three sections along the creek bed where there was either flowing water or pools of water. Water Canyon has a permanent spring, but always carry water in your car and in your pack.

Map USGS or BLM map Hanksville(San Rafael Desert for the access route)(1:100,000), or The Spur or Canyonlands National Park(1:62,500).

Main Attraction Pictographs! This is the best group of pictographs on the entire Colorado Plateau. The style here is called "Barrier Creek", against which all other styles are judged. The author found 4 panels, but there are likely more.

Ideal Time to Hike Spring, fall or winter dry spells; or early mornings in summer.

Hiking Boots Any dry weather boots or shoes.

Author's Experience The author hiked into the canyon in the morning, visited the panels and returned, all in 3 hours. You'll want more time than that.

The Great Gallery; a panel of pictographs in Horseshoe Canyon.

MAP 1, HORSESHOE CANYON

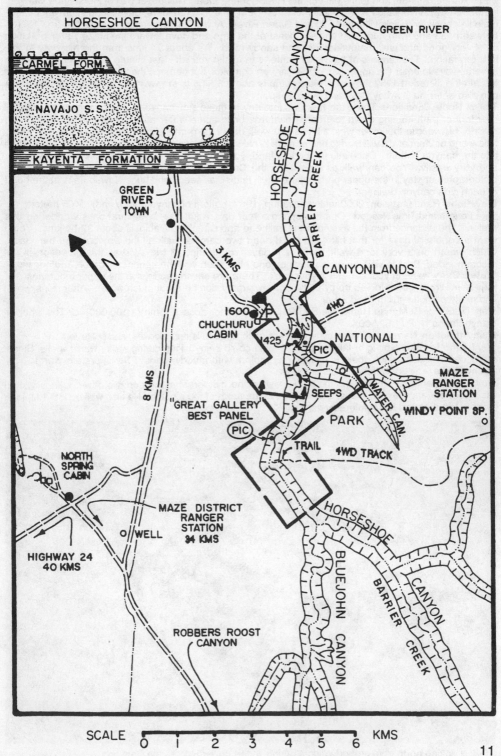

HORSESHOE CANYON

CARMEL FORM.

NAVAJO S.S.

KAYENTA FORMATION

GREEN RIVER TOWN

N

GREEN RIVER

HORSESHOE CANYON

BARRIER CREEK

3 KMS

CANYONLANDS

4WD

1600 P
CHUCHURU CABIN

1425

PIC

NATIONAL

MAZE RANGER STATION

8 KMS

"GREAT GALLERY" BEST PANEL

PIC

SEEPS

WATER CAN.

WINDY POINT SP.

PARK

TRAIL

4WD TRACK

NORTH SPRING CABIN

MAZE DISTRICT RANGER STATION 34 KMS

WELL

HORSESHOE

HIGHWAY 24 40 KMS

ROBBERS ROOST CANYON

BLUEJOHN CANYON

BARRIER

CANYON

CREEK

SCALE   0 1 2 3 4 5 6   KMS

Upper Horseshoe Canyon

Location and Access The upper part of Horseshoe Canyon is located just north and northwest of the Maze Ranger Station, and to the east of the Roost Spring area. This upper part of Horseshoe Canyon is not part of Canyonlands N. P., but is mostly on BLM land. To get there, drive along Highway 24, the main link between Hanksville, and I-70 and Green River. At a point between mile posts 136 and 137(or between 133 and 134), turn east and southeast at the sign and drive toward the Maze Ranger Station on a very good and well maintained dirt and sandy road. It's about 74 kms from the highway to the ranger station. The rangers at the visitor center can assist you with last minute questions. There are several ways to enter the upper part of this canyon complex, but perhaps the best place is to enter from the airstrip, listed at 1952 meters. This air strip is about 8 kms to the west of the ranger station. You can also enter via Cowboy Cave and Burro Seep.

Trail or Route Conditions There are few trails into any of these side canyons, but there is an occasional cow trail or path leading down to greener pastures or to some water hole. Walk due north from the airstrip, but veer to the left or west a bit as you walk down the gentle slope. When you see cow trails, follow one of them and it will lead to one or more breaks in the Navajo Wall where you can then get down into the canyon bottom. Once into the bottom land, you can walk up or down canyon in the dry creek bed very easily. You can walk all the way to the Canyonlands sector of this canyon and view the pictographs, or stay in the upper parts, where you'll find small seeps and huge Navajo Falls at the head of each side canyon drainage.

Elevations Ranger station, 2000 meters; air strip, 1952; bottom of canyon(north end), 1425 meters.

Hike Length and Time Needed One can spend a half day, a full day, or several days wandering this region. The distance from the airstrip to the trailhead and Chuchuru Cabin, is about 32-34 kms. You'd want a couple of days for that hike, but you'd need two cars; or walk all the way back on the roads, which would be a very long walk, perhaps 4 days, round-trip. A trip such as this however, is not recommended. Best to visit the pictographs on one hike, then visit the upper canyon on another trip.

Water Carry water in your car and in your pack. There are several springs in the upper tributaries, but they sometimes get muddied up by cattle or they simply don't put out much water. After rains, you'll find many potholes full of good water.

Map USGS or BLM map Hanksville(San Rafael Desert for access route)(1:100,000), or The Spur or Canyonlands N. P.(1:62,500).

Main Attraction Narrow and deep canyon heads, with huge falls and alcoves, and solitude.

Ideal Time to Hike Spring or fall, but some people could enjoy hiking during winter warm spells. Since the access road is sandy, there is usually no problem with muddy roads. Summers are warm.

Hiking Boots Any dry weather boots or shoes.

Author's Experience On one trip the author visited the pictographs, then on two other outings visited the Spur Fork and Cowboy Cave, and the area to the north of the air strip. He also walked into Bluejohn Spring, but that part is not interesting.

12   Looking north from around Wildcat Spring, in the upper Horseshoe Canyon.

MAP 2, UPPER HORSESHOE CANYON

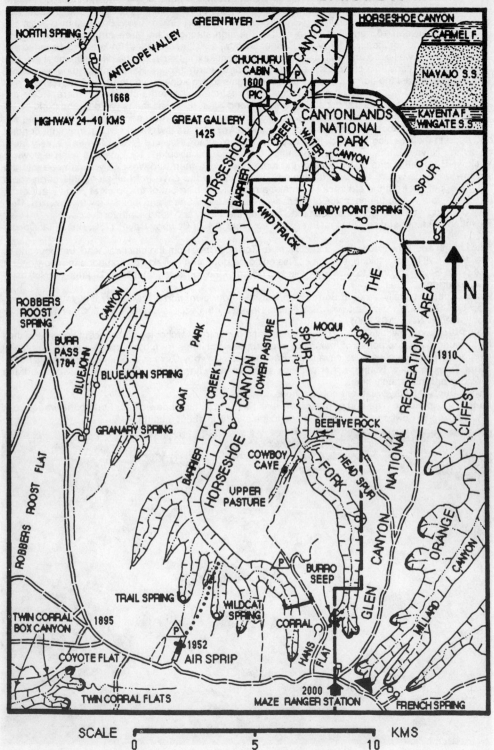

SCALE

0   5   10   KMS

Cowboy Cave and Spur Fork

Location and Access The canyon featured on this map is Spur Fork, one of several tributaries to the upper Horseshoe Canyon complex. Cowboy Cave is in one of the drainages of Spur Fork. To get there, drive along Highway 24, the road linking Hanksville, with I-70 and Green River. Between mile posts 136 and 137(or between 133 and 134), turn east at the sign stating, "The Maze of Canyonlands N. P." Proceed east and southeast to the Maze Ranger Station, a distance of about 74 kms. This road to the ranger station is well used and well maintained, and because it's sandy, can be driven in about any kind of weather conditions. To get to the main trailhead, drive north through Hans Flat, to about two or two and a half kms past the corral. Park as the road begins to drop down over the top of the Navajo, and look for a faint old wagon road running to the northwest(the author left a stone cairn there). One can also head off north from the ranger station toward Head Spur. Drive as far as you can and park.

Trail or Route Conditions From the car-park at 1850 meters, walk the sandy old track heading for Upper Pasture, but about 150 meters after dropping down over the low Navajo Bluffs, turn right or north, and head in the direction of a rock feature called by the author, *Beehive Rock*. The trail is very faint below the Navajo Bluffs. This is a very sandy track and you shouldn't try to take a vehicle down it. Walk NNE to within one or two kms of the main Spur Fork, then turn west 'till you can see into the shallow drainage where the cave is located. You can see the cave from all along this north-south drainage, but not from the old track. To make a nice all day hike out of this, park at Hans Flat Corral, and make your way to the east side of the canyon above Burro Seep, and look for a way down in. Then walk down canyon to where the wagon road crosses the wash, and head south for the cave.

Elevations Ranger station, 2000 meters; main trailhead, 1850; Cowboy Cave, 1750; Hans Flat Corral, 1925 meters.

Hike Length and Time Needed It's about 5 kms to Cowboy Cave from the main trailhead, or about one or one and a half hours walking, one way. This could be done in a half day by someone in a hurry. The hike down Spur Fork, then to Cowboy Cave and return to the corral, is about 18 to 20 kms, or a full days hike, round-trip.

Water There's usually water at Burro Seep, but take your own, and always carry it in your car.

Map USGS or BLM map Hanksville(San Rafael Desert for the access route)(1:100,000), or The Spur or Canyonlands N. P.(1:62,500).

Main Attraction Cowboy Cave. This cave has been dug Into by archeologists in recent years, and they have found dung and bones of mammoth and camels, and items from other species in the one meter deep manure which covers the cave floor. See more on Cowboy Cave in another section of this book.

Ideal Time to Hike Spring, fall or perhaps some winter warm spells. Summers are warm, but the altitudes are moderately high.

Hiking Boots Any dry weather boots or shoes.

Author's Experience The author parked at Hans Flat Corral, hiked down Spur Fork to the wagon road crossing, up to Cowboy Cave, and returned to the car, all in about 6 hours.

Cowboy Caves, or Cave. Located in upper Spur Fork.

MAP 3, COWBOY CAVE AND SPUR FORK

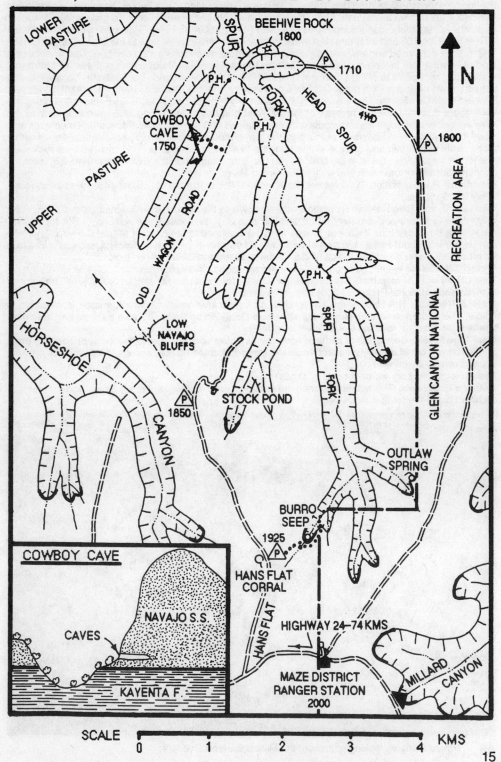

LOWER PASTURE

SPUR

FORK

BEEHIVE ROCK
1800

P 1710

4WD

HEAD SPUR

P 1800

RECREATION AREA

GLEN CANYON NATIONAL

P.H.

COWBOY CAVE
1750

P.H.

PASTURE

UPPER

OLD WAGON ROAD

LOW NAVAJO BLUFFS

P.H.

SPUR FORK

HORSESHOE

CANYON

P 1850

STOCK POND

OUTLAW SPRING

BURRO SEEP

1925 P

HANS FLAT CORRAL

HANS FLAT

HIGHWAY 24–74 KMS

MILLARD CANYON

MAZE DISTRICT RANGER STATION
2000

COWBOY CAVE

NAVAJO S.S.

CAVES

KAYENTA F.

SCALE 0 1 2 3 4 KMS

15

Millard Canyon

Location and Access The head of Millard Canyon is located just to the east of the Maze District Ranger Station, and just inside the Glen Canyon National Recreation Area, which borders Canyonlands National Park. This canyon runs north, then east, and into the Green River. To get there, drive along Highway 24, the main road linking Hanksville, with I-70 and Green River. Between mile posts 136 and 137(or between 133 and 134) turn east and southeast and drive the 74 kms to the Maze Ranger Station. This road is very good and well used by ranchers, rangers and tourists, and can be driven in about any kind of weather(but in long dry spells it does turn to washboard). About a km southeast of the ranger station is a viewpoint to Millard Canyon, one of the best sights around. Don't miss it. To get into the canyon, drive north from the ranger station 5 or 6 kms to a fork in the road. Park there, at 1850 meters.

Trail or Route Conditions There is no trail into this canyon; you simply route-find. From the car-park, walk about due east around the base of the hill, past one drainage running NNE, and then look for an easy way over and down an intermediate layer of Navajo S.S., which forms a low cliff. Once over and down through the Navajo, walk south along the Kayenta Bench(see geology cross section). Further along, walk east again and down over the Wingate Wall, which at that point is covered by a rock slide and some vegetation. Once at the bottom, you can turn south and visit the canyon headwall, which is very impressive; or turn north and walk to the Green River.

Elevations Ranger station, 2000 meters; trailhead, 1850; canyon bottom, about 1450; the Green River, about 1225 meters.

Hike Length and Time Needed From the trailhead down to the Green River is about 26 to 28 kms, one way. Strong hikers could make that distance in one day, then return the next day. But for some it might be a three day trip. It's about 10 kms from the trailhead to the head of Millard Canyon. This hike can be done in about half a day, by a strong hiker. If you have the time and inclination, you might look for a possible route down into the canyon from the area around Observation Rock.

Water Take all the water you'll need, as there are no springs in this canyon.

Map USGS or BLM map Hanksville(San Rafael Desert for the access route)(1:100,000), or The Spur or Canyonlands National Park(1:62,500).

Main Attraction The head of this canyon has an impressive headwall; whether seen from above or below. The entire scene is as nice as the view from Dead Horse Point. It's also isolated and unknown. It makes an easy route to the Green River as well.

Ideal Time to Hike Spring, fall or perhaps some winter warm spells. In winter, the lower or northern parts of this canyon could be very pleasant; while the mesa top could be cold and snowy. Summers are very warm down in the canyon.

Hiking Boots Any dry weather boots or shoes.

Author's Experience The author has seen the canyon from the viewpoint many times, and on one trip, he hiked down the route just described.

16   Millard Canyon, looking north from the Millard Canyon Overlook.

MAP 4, MILLARD CANYON

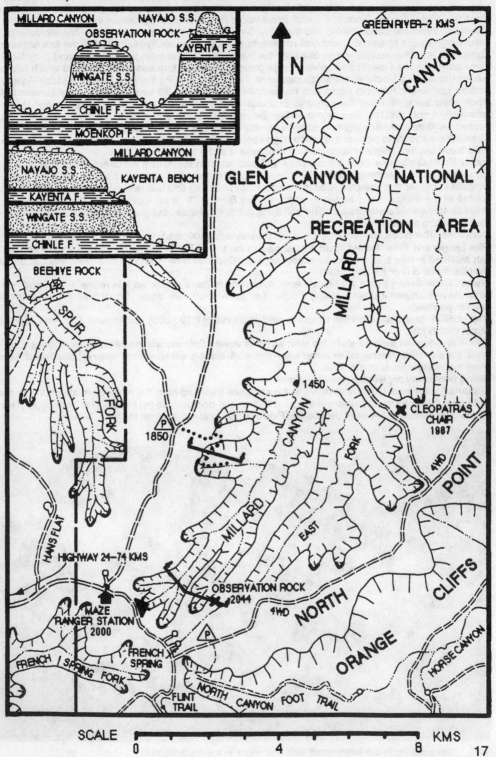

MILLARD CANYON   NAVAJO S.S.
OBSERVATION ROCK
KAYENTA F.
WINGATE S.S.
CHINLE F.
MOENKOPI F.

MILLARD CANYON
NAVAJO S.S.
KAYENTA BENCH
KAYENTA F.
WINGATE S.S.
CHINLE F.

N

GREEN RIVER – 2 KMS

CANYON

GLEN   CANYON   NATIONAL

RECREATION   AREA

MILLARD

BEEHIVE ROCK

SPUR FORK

1450

CLEOPATRAS CHAIR
1987

P
1850

4WD

POINT

CANYON

MILLARD

EAST   FORK

HANS FLAT

HIGHWAY 24 – 74 KMS

OBSERVATION ROCK
2044

4WD   NORTH   CLIFFS

MAZE RANGER STATION
2000

FRENCH SPRING

P

ORANGE

HORSE CANYON

FRENCH   SPRING FORK

FLINT TRAIL

NORTH   CANYON   FOOT   TRAIL

SCALE

0   4   8

KMS

The Block Trail

Location and Access The Block is a small mesa or large butte, which is the final remnant of a much bigger mesa or plateau, which is found further to the north around the Maze Ranger Station, the Island in the Sky part of Canyonlands N. P., and Dead Horse Point. It rises high above the area between the Colorado River(now Lake Powell) and the Dirty Devil River. From its top one has fine views in all directions. To get to an old sheep trail running to the top, drive along Highway 95, the link between Hanksville, and Hite and Blanding. Between the two bridges which span the Colorado and Dirty Devil River arms of Lake Powell, and between mile posts 46 and 47, turn east onto the road which heads toward the Sewing Machine, the Maze District of Canyonlands N.P., the Flint Trail, the Maze Ranger Station, and finally Robbers Roost and Highway 24. Drive about 30 kms along this very bumpy, but much used track, to Cove Canyon and to about a km past the corral shown on the map. Most vehicles(but not 4WD's), stop before exiting the narrow canyon and park at the trailhead-campsite marked 1600 meters. Any higher clearance vehicle can make it to the trailhead, but if you have a car, better take a shovel to smooth over some high spots, or fill in small gullies. The road is considered a 4WD track, but most higher clearance cars can make it to the trailhead OK.

Trail or Route Conditions From the campsite-trailhead, walk on the road in the direction of Cove Spring, but turn off to the northwest just before the spring, and walk this very old track to the base of the Wingate Cliffs. At that point the road fades into a cairned route and trail, which runs up the drainage to the top of the Wingate and Kayenta flat top of The Block. Once on top, you can then walk in any direction to view different places. The trail up is difficult to follow, but you can make it up the slope, whether you're on the trail or not.

Elevations The Block, just under 2100 meters; trailhead, 1600; and Lake Powell, 1128 meters.

Hike Length and Time Needed From the car-park to the top of The Block is only about 6 kms or so, and can be hiked in less than 2 hours by almost anyone. Depending on what you do on top, you can make the hike a half-day or full-day outing.

Water Cove Spring has a year-round flow, but ranchers have neglected it in recent years, and now cattle have stomped it down, making it difficult to get a good safe drink. So take all the water you'll need in your car.

Map USGS or BLM map Hite Crossing and Hanksville(1:100,000), or Browns Rim and Fiddler Butte(1:62,500).

Main Attraction An isolated mesa top hike, with fine views. Solitude with no camping restrictions.

Ideal Time to Hike Spring, fall or winter warm spells. Summers are very warm around Lake Powell, plus there are many insects at that time.

Hiking Boots Any dry weather boots or shoes.

Author's Experience The author drove to the campsite-trailhead from the highway in about one and a half hours, using a shovel to improve the road bed on one occasion, to get his VW Rabbit through. Next morning he walked to the point overlooking Fiddler Butte, and returned; all in about 3 hours.

Cove Spring in the foreground, with The Block in the background.

MAP 5, THE BLOCK TRAIL

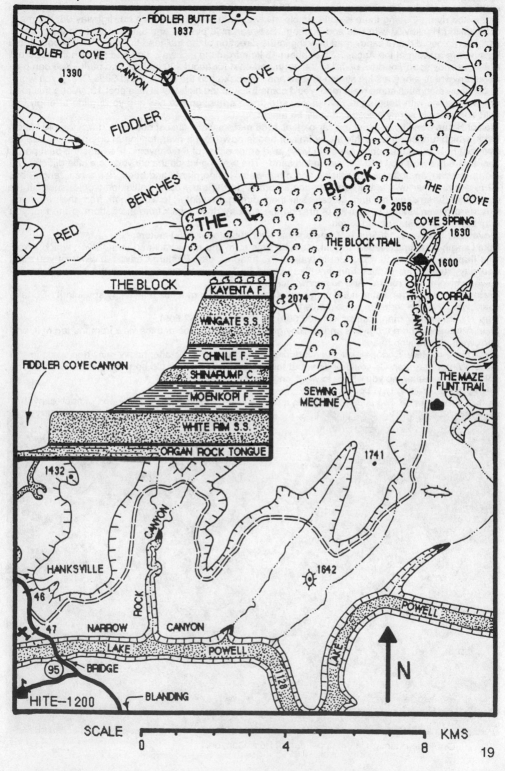

FIDDLER BUTTE
1837

FIDDLER   COVE
•1390

COVE

CANYON

FIDDLER

THE   BLOCK

•2058

THE   COVE

BENCHES

THE

THE BLOCK TRAIL

COVE SPRING
1630

RED

THE BLOCK

KAYENTA F.

•2074

P 1600

CORRAL

WINGATE S.S.

COVE CANYON

FIDDLER COVE CANYON

CHINLE F.

SHINARUMP C.

THE MAZE
FLINT TRAIL

MOENKOPI F.

SEWING
MECHINE

WHITE RIM S.S.

ORGAN ROCK TONGUE

•1432

•1741

CANYON

HANKSVILLE

1642

46

ROCK

POWELL

47   NARROW   CANYON

LAKE   POWELL

LAKE

95 BRIDGE

1128

N

HITE--1200   BLANDING

SCALE   0   4   8   KMS

19

Buck and Pasture Canyons

Location and Access These two canyons, plus the Lower Sand Slide are located about 15 kms south, southeast of Hanksville. They drain into the Dirty Devil River, just above where Robbers Roost Canyon meets the river. Getting there is quite simple. Drive south out of Hanksville on Highway 95, the main road linking Hanksville with Hite and Bullfrog. Between mile posts 5 and 6, turn east onto a good and well maintained dirt and sandy road heading in the direction of the trailhead to Angel Trail. About 4 to 5 kms before arriving at the Angel Trail, or about 15 kms from the highway, stop and park on the road(but not in a sandy spot!), or drive up hill to the north and east for about 200 meters, and park. You can park about anywhere along a 2 km stretch of road and still make it to the Lower Sand Slide OK. If you were to continue along this same main road, you'd come back to the highway at mile post 10. Along this road are two places with deep sand. When you see these spots, go like hell and you'll glide through OK. Just don't stop in sandy places and you'll be alright.

Trail or Route Conditions From the car-park at 1488 meters, walk almost due north down the old sandy track, which further on turns into a cow trail. It heads down to the river, forking at one point. Cross the river(but not during the spring run-off in May), and enter either of the canyons. Perhaps the best part of this hike is the walk down to the river in the sand. The walking inside the canyons is a little difficult. All along the canyon bottoms are willows and other water-loving plants and trees. It's a real tangle, but there are nice narrows at the head of each tributary. In the early days, cattlemen would fence off the mouths of these canyons, and run calves in them during the winter, to wean them from their mothers. But there doesn't seem to be a lot of grazing there today. If you walk from the bottom to the top, you may box in some deer ahead of you.

Elevations Trailhead, 1488(or 1450)meters; the river, just under 1250 meters.

Hike Length and Time Needed It's only about 2 kms from the main trailhead to the river, which takes less than half an hour to walk. But to walk to the head of say, Pasture Canyon, it will take you all of one day, round-trip. A nice half-day hike, would be to walk to the river, view the petroglyphs and cowboy glyphs, and return. And no bushwhacking!

Water There is some water in the canyons, but at least some of it has a swampy smell to it. So take your own. The river water must be purified.

Map USGS or BLM map Hanksville(1:100,000), or Hanksville(1:62,500).

Main Attraction The petroglyphs and cowboy glyphs, the sand slide and the view from the top of it, and narrows in the canyon heads.

Ideal Time to Hike Spring or fall, but not during high water, which is after heavy rains and sometime in May. Winter warm spells could be fine, but fording the river then would be tough! Hike the canyons only in cool weather, so you'll have to wear long pants.

Hiking Boots Wading type boots or shoes.

Author's Experience The author went down the slide twice and got into the lower end of each canyon.

One side drainage in the upper part of Buck Canyon.

MAP 6, BUCK AND PASTURE CANYONS

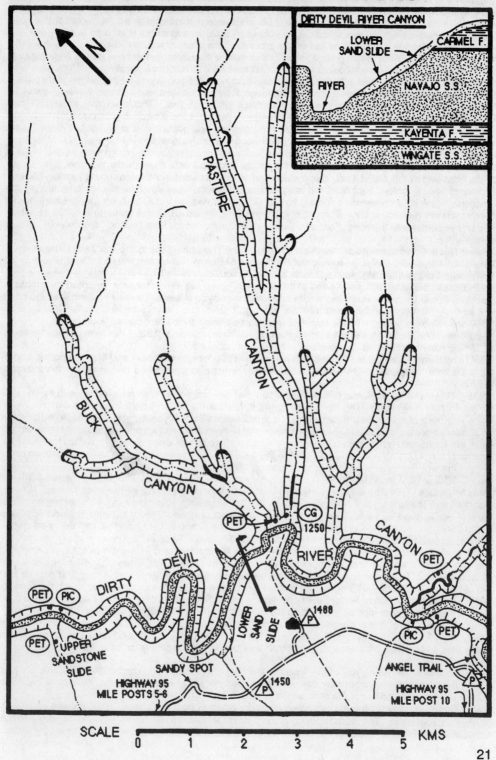

DIRTY DEVIL RIVER CANYON

LOWER SAND SLIDE

CARMEL F.

RIVER

NAVAJO S.S.

KAYENTA F.

WINGATE S.S.

N

PASTURE

CANYON

BUCK

CANYON

PET

CG
1250

CANYON

PET

RIVER

DEVIL

DIRTY

PET

PIC

LOWER SAND SLIDE

P 1460

PIC

PET

PET

UPPER
SANDSTONE
SLIDE

SANDY SPOT

P 1450

ANGEL TRAIL

P

HIGHWAY 95
MILE POSTS 5-6

HIGHWAY 95
MILE POST 10

SCALE

0 1 2 3 4 5

KMS

Robbers Roost Canyon

Location and Access Robbers Roost Canyon is located about 20 kms east of Hanksville. There are two ways to reach Roost Canyon, both involving the Angel Trail. The best way is to come in from the west. Drive south out of Hanksville on Highway 95. Between mile posts 5 and 6, turn east onto a good and well maintained dirt and sandy road. Drive about 18 to 20 kms to where you come to a junction, with a short, bright orange post sticking out of the ground. Turn east, or left, and drive 300 meters to the Angel Trailhead. Look at the map titled *Angel Trail* for more details on this access road. If you were to continue along this main road, you'd again reach Highway 95 at mile post 10. So you can make a loop of this road to the Angel Trail. On the access road map note the two sandy spots. When you come to these places, drive fast and you'll pass right through them, as the two worst places are only about 15 to 20 meters in length. You shouldn't have trouble if you drive fast. The other way to reach Roost Canyon is to drive to the eastern trailhead of the Angel Trail. Get there by driving along Highway 24, the road linking Hanksville, and I-70 and Green River. Between mile posts 136 and 137(or between 133 and 134) turn east and southeast and drive this good road to Burr Pass where is located a junction. It's at this junction you turn off to the Roost Spring; but instead of going to the spring, go straight and towards the Biddlecome-Ekker Ranch. Just before the ranch, turn west onto a unmaintained road, which ends at the east end of the Angel Trail. This last section of road has deteriorated in recent years. There are two more very remote possibilities for entry to Roost Canyon, but you'll have problems finding the locations. One is to come into the main fork of Roost Canyon via the Arch(A on map), where an old cattle trail was once constructed. Another route involves an old CCC trail made in the 1930's, which apparently comes into the North Fork somewhere. This author never found it, and no one could put it on a map.

Trail or Route Conditions At the west end of the Angel Trail, head out to the southeast and down a slickrock valley and minor ridge toward the confluence of Beaver Creek and the Dirty Devil River. Once down onto the intermediate Navajo Bench, turn north and bench-walk about one and a half kms, then drop down to the river. After one bend of the river, you cross the river once, and you're at the mouth of Robbers Roost Canyon. From the mouth and into the canyon system, it's easy walking and you can't get lost. At the upper end of each tributary are high barrier falls, always coming off the Navajo S.S. They are all box canyons, and you might push and trap deer in these canyons as you hike up.

Elevations The westside trailhead, 1500 meters; eastside trailhead, 1525; the canyon mouth, about 1225; the canyon bottom at the head of the North Fork, about 1500 meters.

Hike Length and Time Needed From the mouth of Roost Canyon to the upper end of North Fork is about 22 to 24 kms. If you want to visit all the tributaries, better plan on about 5 or 6 days, for the average person.

Water There's water in all reaches of the canyon and side canyons. It comes and goes in the Navajo Sands. The running water, as the author found it, is shown as heavy dark lines on the map. Since there is a herd of horses in the canyon(with a fence across the canyon mouth) you should try and get your water from a place where the water comes out of the sand or at a spring source. Take along an extra jug for hauling water from a spring to your camp. The author drank the water without purification, and had no trouble. One long time rancher in the area told the author, "the water in Roost Canyon is the best in the world, and it makes the best coffee you'll ever drink".

Map USGS or BLM map Hanksville(1:100,000) or Hanksville and Robbers Roost Canyon(1:62,500).

Main Attraction This entire canyon system is a box canyon, made up of the ever present Navajo Sandstone. These canyons resemble very much the Escalante River country, with narrow canyons, vertical walls, huge falls and alcoves, running water and solitude. The upper end of North Fork has some very good narrows. One canyon the author calls *The Crack*, is very good. It's in this part of the canyon a couple of tough hikers might find a way out. The *Great Falls* in the upper end of right fork of North Fork, is perhaps the biggest falls and alcove in the system and it would make a fine campsite. Along Middle Fork you'll find two alcoves with Douglas fir trees. This is the only place in the whole Robbers Roost Country where the author has seen these trees. White Roost is long and narrow and interesting. The South Fork begins just below Roost Spring, where you would have to have a rope to get in. There's a section of South Fork between the Roost Spring and the Kayenta Falls which you can't enter unless you have ropes or look for a log or build a pile of stones(just below the Kayenta Falls). South Fork is probably the deepest of the canyons. In the main fork, there's an arch. Walk up the sandy slope to it's base, then you can get to the rim by walking underneath it on an old and now unused cattle trail. There are also several petroglyph and pictograph panels at or near the mouth of Roost Canyon.

Ideal Time to Hike Since you'll have to cross the Dirty Devil River, you can't make it into this canyon during the high water period in May, but otherwise spring or fall are the best times. Summers are extra warm, and with that fording of the river, winter is all but out of the question.

Hiking Boots Waders for the river crossing, then dry weather boots or shoes in the canyon itself.

Author's Experience The author spent 3 long days and about 29 hours walking to all of these tributaries. He rates it as one of the best hikes in this book; and perhaps the *best* of the longer hikes.

MAP 7, ROBBERS ROOST CANYON

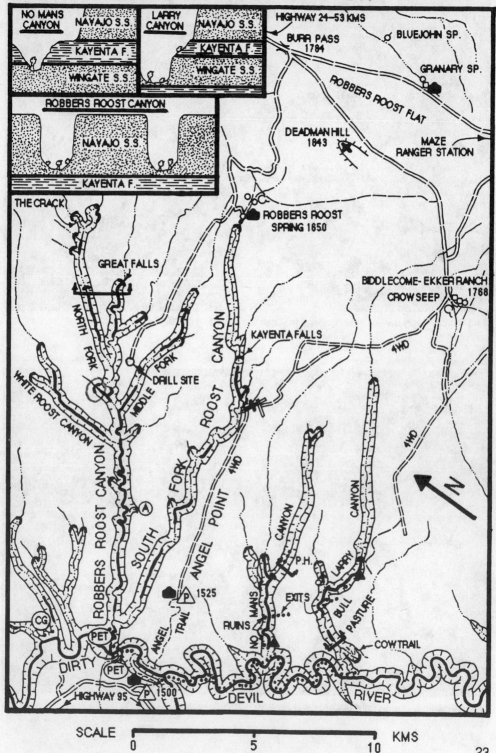

NO MANS CANYON
NAVAJO S.S.
KAYENTA F.
WINGATE S.S.

LARRY CANYON
NAVAJO S.S.
KAYENTA F.
WINGATE S.S.

ROBBERS ROOST CANYON
NAVAJO S.S.
KAYENTA F.

HIGHWAY 24—53 KMS
BLUEJOHN SP.
BURR PASS 1784
GRANARY SP.
ROBBERS ROOST FLAT
DEADMAN HILL 1843
MAZE RANGER STATION
THE CRACK
ROBBERS ROOST SPRING 1650
GREAT FALLS
BIDDLECOME-EKKER RANCH 1768
CROW SEEP
NORTH FORK
MIDDLE FORK
DRILL SITE
WHITE ROOST CANYON
KAYENTA FALLS
ROBBERS ROOST CANYON
4WD
4WD
ROBBERS ROOST CANYON
SOUTH FORK
ANGEL POINT
4WD
4WD
NO MANS CANYON
LARRY CANYON
P.H.
A
P 1525
EXITS
BULL
CG
ANGEL TRAIL
RUINS
PASTURE
PET
COW TRAIL
DIRTY
PET
DEVIL
RIVER
HIGHWAY 95
P 1500

N

SCALE
0   5   10   KMS

The Crack, a very narrow side drainage in upper Robbers Roost Canyon.

An old cattle trail runs right under Roost Arch, in Robbers Roost Canyon.

Typical scene in any of the upper parts of Robbers Roost Canyon.

The Great Falls, in the upper end of Middle Fork, Robbers Roost Canyon.

The Angel Trail

Location and Access The Angel Trail is located about half way between Hanksville and the Biddlecome-Ekker Ranch, which is in the middle of the Robbers Roost Country. This trail is one of the routes used by some of the outlaws in the 1880's and 1890's to travel between Hanksville and the Roost Spring area and other sites where the outlaws hid from the law. It runs east-west and crosses the Dirty Devil River. To get there, drive south out of Hanksville to between mile posts 5 and 6, and turn left or east and go about 20 kms. At a junction, where is found a low, bright orange post, turn east and drive about 300 meters to the trailhead. If you continue along this main road, it takes you back out to the highway, and to mile post 10. There are two sandy places along this road, as shown on the map. When in the area, travel as fast as your vehicle and road will allow, and don't stop in sandy places. When you see the deep sand ahead, drive fast, and you'll glide right through the 15 to 20 meter wide sand-traps. Remember, just keep momentum up and you'll be alright. The other route possibility, is to come in from near the Biddlecome-Ekker Ranch to the east side trailhead, but the last section of road is in bad condition. Most 2WD vehicles can make it however, if a shovel is taken, to fill in small gullies. The recommended entry point is from the west side.

Trail or Route Conditions From the west side trailhead, walk in a southeast direction, down a little valley and low ridge in the direction of the confluence of Beaver Creek and the river. When you reach the intermediate Navajo Bench, turn due north and walk about one and a half kms, then drop down into the river. Cross the river and just across from Angel Cove Spring, locate the trail again, going up and to the east. You can also make it down to the river from the Navajo Bench, right where Beaver Creek and the river meet. Hikers can do this, but horses can't. All along the way, look ahead for stone cairns marking the route. On the west side, hikers keep putting up carins, then someone else comes along and kicks then down. But surely you can find the way with little trouble. The campsite at Angel Cove Spring is perhaps the best on the Dirty Devil River.

Elevations The trailheads, 1500 and 1525 meters; the river, about 1225 meters.

Hike Length and Time Needed From trailhead to trailhead, it's only about 10 kms. The average hiker will want most of a day for this round-trip hike.

Water Good water at Angel Cove Spring, but treat the river water and that coming out of Beaver Creek. Best to take your own, if you're day-hiking.

Map USGS or BLM map Hanksville(1:100,000), or Hanksville and Robbers Roost Canyon(1:62,500).

Main Attraction Historic trail, Angel Cove Spring, the scenic river canyon.

Ideal Time to Hike Spring or fall, but not in the high water period during May. To do the entire trail, you'll have to wade the river. Without crossing the river, you could hike the western half of the trail in winter.

Hiking Boots Waders to cross the river, and then dry weather boots or shoes.

Author's Experience The author has been up and down this trail on the west side a dozen times, but only on one trip did he make it to the east side trailhead.

The Angel Trail and Henry Mountains. From East Side Trailhead.

MAP 8, THE ANGEL TRAIL

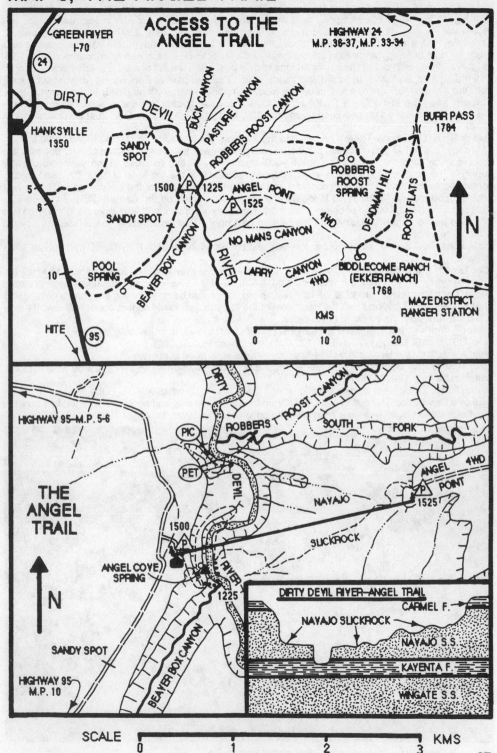

ACCESS TO THE ANGEL TRAIL

GREEN RIVER I-70

HIGHWAY 24 M.P. 36-37, M.P. 33-34

24

DIRTY DEVIL

BUCK CANYON

PASTURE CANYON

ROBBERS ROOST CANYON

HANKSVILLE 1950

SANDY SPOT

BURR PASS 1784

1500 P 1225

ANGEL POINT

P 1525

ROBBERS ROOST SPRING

DEADMAN HILL

ROOST FLATS

N

SANDY SPOT

5

6

NO MANS CANYON

RIVER

4WD

BEAVER BOX CANYON

LARRY CANYON

4WD

BIDDLECOME RANCH (EKKER RANCH) 1768

10

POOL SPRING

MAZE DISTRICT RANGER STATION

HITE

95

KMS

0   10   20

HIGHWAY 95—M.P. 5-6

DIRTY

ROBBERS ROOST CANYON

SOUTH FORK

PIC

PET

DEVIL

ANGEL 4WD

POINT

P 1525

THE ANGEL TRAIL

NAVAJO

1500

P

SLICKROCK

N

ANGEL COVE SPRING

RIVER

1225

SANDY SPOT

BEAVER BOX CANYON

HIGHWAY 95 M.P. 10

DIRTY DEVIL RIVER—ANGEL TRAIL

CARMEL F.

NAVAJO SLICKROCK

NAVAJO S.S.

KAYENTA F.

WINGATE S.S.

SCALE

KMS

0   1   2   3

27

Beaver Canyon

Location and Access Beaver Canyon, sometimes known as Beaver Box Canyon, or Beaver Creek, is located about 15 kms southeast of Hanksville. This short canyon runs parallel with one part of the road running to the Angel Cove Spring and Angel Trail. Beaver Canyon is only moderately deep, only moderately scenic, but it does have a permanent water supply, thus a rather unique live beaver population. One of the unique things about this canyon is that the beaver use various grasses and reeds for dam building, rather than the customary willows or limbs from aspen or cottonwood trees. To get there, drive south out of Hanksville 16 kms to mile post 10. Turn left or east and drive down a good, well maintained, and often used dirt and sandy road. You can park at Pool Spring, only about 3 kms from the highway, or continue further up the road, and park where you'll be closer to the canyon itself. You can also drive to the Angel Trailhead, but there's one sandy spot to pass enroute. When you see the sand ahead, speed up and keep up momentum, and you'll go through OK. Just don't stop in the sand!

Trail or Route Conditions There's no trail into this canyon, but there are in places, faded cattle tracks. This canyon is not all that much fun to hike, because of the way the canyon bottom alluvial deposits are eroding away, and the willows and brush you'll encounter. All this because of the year-round water supply. The down-cutting of these alluvial deposits started with the big flood of Sept. 22, 1897, and is continuing to this day. You might consider just visiting the upper part of the canyon and the falls and pool at 1350 meters. You'll have to locate and use a route down off the Carmel Cliffs, if you make a direct approach to it, instead of coming down the main canyon. You could also drive on to the west side trailhead of the Angel Trail, and visit the bottom part only. This would allow you to see the canyon without the tangle.

Elevations Pool Spring, 1425 meters; the falls and spring source, 1350; Dirty Devil River, about 1225 meters.

Hike Length and Time Needed To walk from Pool Spring to the river would be to walk about 15 kms. It's not recommended you walk the whole canyon, because of the brush and erosional features. It's only about 3 or 4 kms from the road to the falls and spring, which can be done in less than half a day. If you start at the Angel Trail, and visit the lower part of the canyon, you could do it in about half day. It's only a two km walk from the trailhead to the creek.

Water There's year-round water in Beaver C., but it's best to treat it, or just take your own.

Map USGS or BLM map Hanksville(1:100,000), or Hanksvllle(1:62,500).

Main Attraction Live beaver in a desert canyon; moderately good scenery.

Ideal Time to Hike Spring, fall or winter warm spells. Cool weather is best, so you'll be wearing long pants and a long sleeved shirt.

Hiking Boots Better have wading boots or shoes if you plan to do much walking in the canyon.

Author's Experience The author went down from the top, to the falls and pool, and returned in 3 hours or so. On another trip, he went in a ways from the bottom end and from the Angel Trail.

Beaver Dams, located in the lower end of Beaver Box Canyon.

MAP 9, BEAVER CANYON

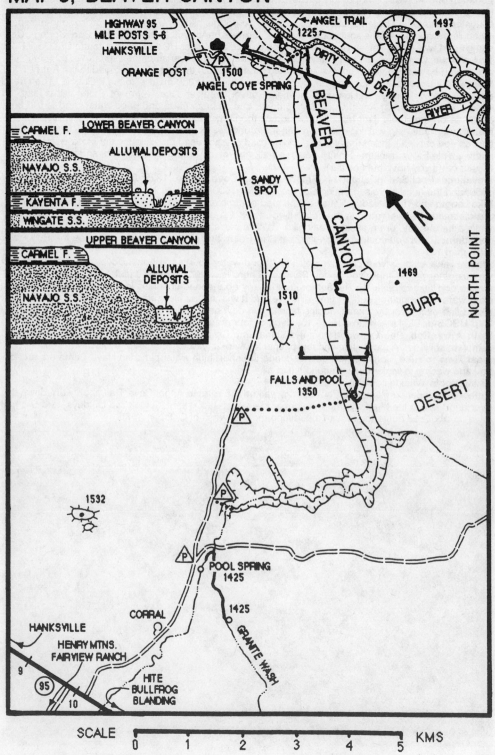

HIGHWAY 95
MILE POSTS 5-6
HANKSVILLE

ANGEL TRAIL
1225
1497

ORANGE POST

1500
ANGEL COVE SPRING

DIRTY

BEAVER

DEVIL

RIVER

CARMEL F.   LOWER BEAVER CANYON
ALLUVIAL DEPOSITS
NAVAJO S.S.
KAYENTA F.
WINGATE S.S.

UPPER BEAVER CANYON
CARMEL F.
ALLUVIAL DEPOSITS
NAVAJO S.S.

SANDY
SPOT

N

CANYON

NORTH POINT

1469

1510

BURR

FALLS AND POOL
1350

P

DESERT

P

1532

P

POOL SPRING
1425

CORRAL

1425

HANKSVILLE

HENRY MTNS.
FAIRVIEW RANCH

GRANITE WASH

9

95

HITE
BULLFROG
BLANDING

10

SCALE
0   1   2   3   4   5   KMS

29

Dirty Devil River

Location and Access The portion of the Dirty Devil River on this map is just to the southeast of Hanksville, and to the east of Highway 95. This is the part where the river cuts deep into the mostly sandstone strata to a depth of about 425 meters. To do this hike, you should first proceed to mile post 10 on Highway 95, 16 kms south of Hanksville. Turn east and park in the vicinity of Pool Spring. Cars can go part way down Poison Spring C., but you'd need a 4WD or HCV to make it to the Dirt Devil River.

Trail or Route Conditions Beaver Canyon is difficult to walk in because of the live beaver population in the canyon bottom, so you should walk the road running out to the westside trailhead to the Angel Trail. From this main road, look for the side road running to the east 300 meters to the trailhead. Then head down a shallow drainage and low ridge to where Beaver Creek and the river meet. Stone cairns lead you down. Plan a camp at Angel Cove Spring if you can; it has shade and good water, and is the best campsite on the whole river trip. Then it's down the Dirty Devil, crossing many, many times. Take a meter and a half long walking stick to probe the murky water for possible deep holes. Midway in the canyon you can walk faded remains of a mining road or track used for exploring the Moss Back Member of the Chinle F. for uranium. Finally, you can walk up Poison Spring Canyon road, and hitch hike back to your car(if you have but one car).

Elevations Pool Spring, about 1425 meters; Angel Cove Spring, 1225; Dirty Devil Gaging Station, 1150; and the head of Poison Spring Canyon is about 1500 meters.

Hike Length and Time Needed Notice on the map some black dots and circled numbers. The numbers are distances in kms between the dots. If you walk the entire circle, it's 104 kms. For most people that's a long 4 day, or an easier 5 day hike. With a car shuttle(two cars), you could shorten the hike considerably. Or you could exit(or enter?) at Burr Point, and shorten it even more. See the Burr Point Hike, map 13.

Water Take water in your car, then you'll find good water sources at Angel Cove, Wall Spring, and in various other places in Poison Spring Canyon. There is water year-round in the Dirty Devil, but most people don't like to drink it. The author found many abandoned channels in the river, where he found clear water not requiring settling time. He treated it with clorax bleach(but Iodine tablets are best). It tasted fine except for the clorax. Iodine tablets can now be found in backpacking stores.

Map USGS or BLM map Hanksville(1:100,000), or four maps at 1:62,500 scale.

Main Attraction Petrified wood from the Shinarump Con.; a deep "Grand Canyon" type gorge; and complete solitude. A great hike, and few people know of it, yet!

Ideal Time to Hike Spring or fall, but not during the short high water period in May. Summers are too hot, and wading in winter doesn't sound fun at all.

Hiking Boots Wading boots or shoes.

Author's Experience Parked at Pool Spring, walked the road to Angel Cove Trail, then went down the river and back to the highway where he got a ride for the last 6 kms. It took two full days, and two half days, or about 27 hours total walk-time, during the first week of October, 1985.

30   Looking down into the Dirty Devil River Gorge, and the mouth of Twin Corral Box Canyon(right).

MAP 10, DIRTY DEVIL RIVER

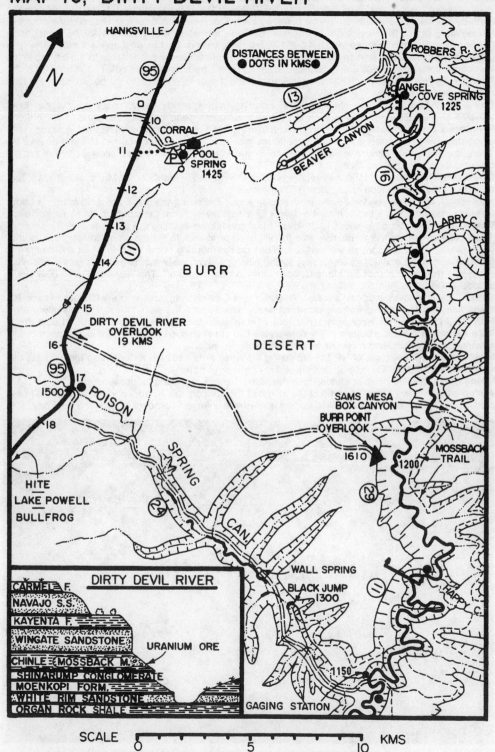

HANKSVILLE

95

DISTANCES BETWEEN
DOTS IN KMS

ROBBERS R. C.

13

ANGEL
COVE SPRING
1225

10
CORRAL

11
POOL
SPRING
1425

BEAVER CANYON

16

12

13

LARRY C.

BURR

14

15

DIRTY DEVIL RIVER
OVERLOOK
19 KMS

16

DESERT

95

17

1500

POISON

SAMS MESA
BOX CANYON
BURR POINT
OVERLOOK

18

1610

1200

MOSSBACK
TRAIL

29

SPRING

HITE
LAKE POWELL
BULLFROG

24

CAN.

WALL SPRING

BLACK JUMP
1300

11

HAPPY C.

DIRTY DEVIL RIVER

CARMEL F.
NAVAJO S.S.
KAYENTA F.
WINGATE SANDSTONE
CHINLE MOSSBACK M.
SHINARUMP CONGLOMERATE
MOENKOPI FORM.
WHITE RIM SANDSTONE
ORGAN ROCK SHALE

URANIUM ORE

1150

GAGING STATION

SCALE 0 5 10 KMS

31

No Mans Canyon

Location and Access No Mans Canyon is one of a number of major canyons flowing into the Dirty Devil River from the east. In this case, it flows from the Robbers Roost area, southwest. It's bounded on the north by Robbers Roost Canyon, on the south by Larry Canyon. This drainage like so many others in the region, cuts into the Navajo Sandstone, the dominant formation, thus making it for the most part, a box canyon. The author looked for, but didn't find, a route in from the top, so it appears the only way to get there is via the lower end and the Dirty Devil River. There is however, one route to the rim top in the lower end of the canyon. To get to No Mans Canyon, read the access route description on map 8, the Angel Trail. This will get you to the west trailhead to the Angel Trail, which is the beginning of the hike to No Mans Canyon

Trail or Route Conditions From the Angel Trail, head down river, which you will cross many times. Take a meter and a half long walking stick to probe for possible deep holes in the sandy river bottom. Sometimes you'll feel like you're starting to sink in the sand, but the author, who has walked many kms along this river, has never had a bad experience with quicksand. Once you get to the mouth of No Mans, the walking up canyon is easy. Sometimes you'll have old cow trails to follow, but there are not many cattle in the canyons today.

Elevations The trailhead, 1500 meters; Angel Cove Spring, 1225; mouth of No Mans, about 1215; and the mesa top at the canyon head, about 1700 meters.

Hike Length and Time Needed From the west side Angel Trailhead, to the mouth of No Mans, is about 10 kms or less. This is a two or three hour walk for most hikers. From the mouth of No Mans to the last falls in the upper canyon is about 12-13 kms. Most can hike to that point in 3 or 4 hours. This means that if you can get started at mid-day from the trailhead, and walk to the mouth of No Mans and camp, you can visit the entire canyon the next day. Then on the morning of the third day, you could return to the trailhead, or try something else. Very strong hikers, with an early morning start from the trailhead, could see the lower half of No Mans C. and return in one long day. This last suggested hike would include a visit to the Fremont Indian ruins.

Water Take plenty in your car, always. Also at Angel Cove Spring, and at many locations inside No Mans Canyon. The flowing water is shown as heavy dark lines on the map. You must purify river water.

Map USGS or BLM map Hanksville(1:100,000), or Hanksville and Robbers Roost Canyon(1:62,500).

Main Attraction Near the bottom of the canyon are two small alcoves with Fremont Indian ruins inside, several low waterfalls, and some moderately high canyon walls.

Ideal Time to Hike Spring or fall, but not during the week or two of high water during May. Fall is the very best, with the golden colored cottonwood leaves everywhere.

Hiking Boots Wading boots or shoes(inside No Mans Canyon, dry weather footwear).

Author's Experience From his camp at the mouth of the canyon, the author spent about 5 hours in the canyon, and saw it all, then he packed up and walked to the Angel Trailhead, all in a nine hour day.

A small alcove with Fremont Indian ruins, in the lower end of No Mans Canyon.

MAP 11, NO MANS CANYON

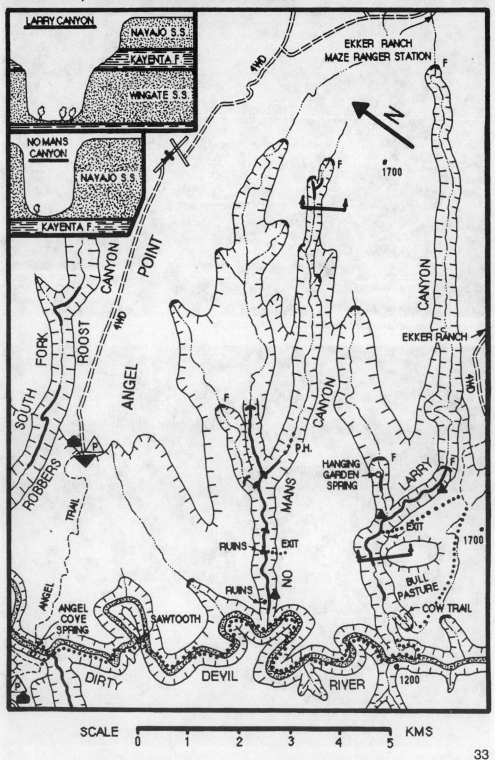

LARRY CANYON

NAVAJO S.S.

KAYENTA F.

WINGATE S.S.

NO MANS CANYON

NAVAJO S.S.

KAYENTA F.

4WD

EKKER RANCH
MAZE RANGER STATION

F

N

F

1700

F

ROOST CANYON POINT

4WD

ANGEL CANYON

SOUTH FORK

NO MANS CANYON

LARRY CANYON

EKKER RANCH

4WD

ROBBERS

TRAIL

P

F

P.H.

HANGING
GARDEN
SPRING

F

F

RUINS   EXIT

EXIT

1700

RUINS

BULL
PASTURE

COW TRAIL

Angel

ANGEL
COVE
SPRING

SAWTOOTH

P

DIRTY   DEVIL   RIVER   1200

SCALE
0   1   2   3   4   5
KMS

33

Autumn colors, deep inside Larry Canyon.

One of several deep pools and a waterfall in No Mans Canyon.

A short narrows section, a waterfall, and a pool, in Woodruff Canyon.

A narrows section in the upper end of Sams Mesa Box Canyon,

Larry Canyon

Location and Access Larry Canyon drains the area just to the north of the Biddlecome-Ekker Ranch, then flows southwest to the Dirty Devil River. Larry is very much a box canyon, with high Navajo and Wingate walls all around. This makes for very few access routes. One route, is to come in from the west side trailhead of the Angel Trail, and walk down the river. This has a certain appeal to some, but perhaps not for others. See map 8, the Angel Trail, for a description on how to get to that trailhead. Another entry possibility is to drive to very near the Ekker Ranch, but turn west just before the ranch, and proceed in a southwest direction on a never-maintained road(which gets worse each year). Carrying a shovel in your car can help. If you can't drive this road, you can walk it. Head in the direction of Bull Pasture, or the entry point just northeast of Bull Pasture. See map 7, Robbers Roost Canyon, for a better look at the access route.

Trail or Route Conditions There's a cow trail and another possible entry point, just north and just south, of the area known as Bull Pasture. The cow trail would be easier to find, if you're coming from the direction of the Ekker Ranch. Read the part on No Mans Canyon, about coming down the Dirty Devil. Once inside Larry Canyon, you can't go far, as there are blocking cliffs or large alcoves in each of the two major forks of the canyon. Inside Larry Canyon are many fine campsites, as there's water in many locations.

Elevations Angel Trailhead, 1500 meters; the mouth of the canyon, about 1200; the mesa rim, about 1700 meters.

Hike Length and Time Needed From the Angel Trailhead to the mouth of Larry C, is about 16 or 17 kms. About a half-day hike, with a pack. From the river to the upper parts of the canyon is only about 7 kms. So in about half a day you can go as far as is possible from the river to the upper parts, and return. Depending on how far you can drive your vehicle down from the ranch, it'll take two or three days round-trip, for the hike into Larry Canyon, and return. From the Angel Trailhead, about 3 days round-trip.

Water The upper half of the hikable part of Larry C. had running water during the authors visit. Purify the river water.

Map USGS or BLM map Hanksville(1:100,000), or Hanksville and Robbers Roost Canyon(1:62,500).

Main Attraction A very deep canyon, with interesting falls and narrows, water, and solitude.

Ideal Time to Hike Spring or fall, but you can't hike down the river during the spring runoff in May. If doing the ranch-Bull Pasture-cow trail route, it's possible to hike in winter warm spells. Summers are hot in the canyon bottoms.

Hiking Boots Waders for the river route, dry weather boots or shoes for the Bull Pasture route.

Author's Experience In three long days, the author did the entire Angel Trail, the hike to and into No Mans Canyon, the hike into Larry C., and the walk back up river to the trailhead.

Larry Canyon, and at the head of navigation, next to the Navajo Falls.

MAP 12, LARRY CANYON

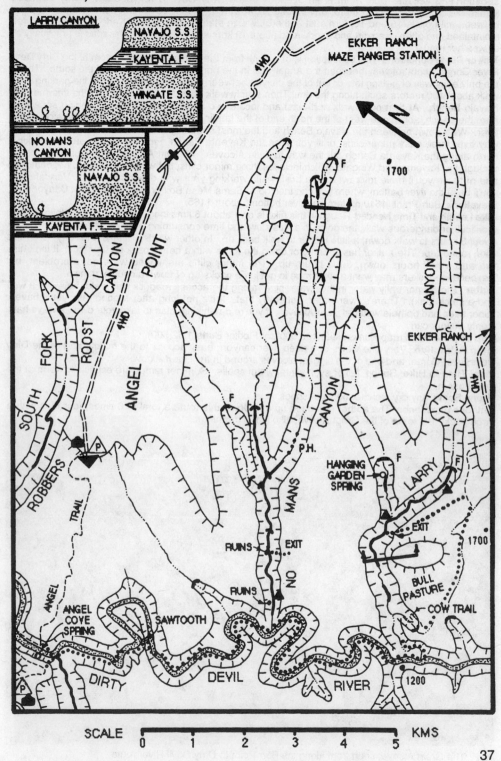

LARRY CANYON

NAVAJO S.S.

KAYENTA F.

WINGATE S.S.

NO MANS CANYON

NAVAJO S.S.

KAYENTA F.

EKKER RANCH
MAZE RANGER STATION

4WD

F

1700

N

F

EKKER RANCH

4WD

ROOST CANYON POINT

4WD

SOUTH FORK

ANGEL POINT

ROBBERS

TRAIL

P

F

F

P.H.

MANS

HANGING
GARDEN
SPRING

LARRY

F

F

EXIT

1700

RUINS

EXIT

NO

BULL
PASTURE

Angel

ANGEL
COVE
SPRING

SAWTOOTH

RUINS

COW TRAIL

P

DIRTY

DEVIL

RIVER

1200

Burr Point–Dirty Devil River Hike

Location and Access Burr Point is an overlook of the Dirty Devil River, about half way between Hanksville and Hite. To get there, drive along Highway 95. About 25 kms south of Hanksville, and between mile posts 15 and 16, turn east at the BLM sign stating, Burr Point Overlook. Drive this well maintained and often used dirt and sandy road about 19 kms to the overlook. This road is practically an all weather road.

Trail or Route Conditions This description is of a route from the mesa rim to the bottom of the Dirty Devil River Gorge, about midway between the Angel Trail in the north, and Lake Powell in the south. This is the only easy way of getting into or out of the canyon between those two points. From the parking spot, walk about 100 meters south along the rim. Then simply walk down the steep slope to the intermediate Navajo Bench. At that point walk northeast and locate two small Navajo Buttes standing separated from the bench, about due west of the north end of the landing strip you'll see on the other side of the river. Walk down between the Navajo Bench and the most southerly of the two buttes, and make your way over three easy minor cliffs, until you're on the Kayenta Bench. From there on you'll be walking north along the Kayenta Bench all the way to Twin Alcoves. At Twin Alcoves, you must drop down through the Kayenta and Wingate, which includes three minor cliffs, but which are easy to negotiate. At one of these you'll have to crawl over a bush while working your way down over a cliff. Very shortly, you'll be at the river bottom, where you can then go to Sams Mesa Box or Twin Corral Box Canyons.

Elevations Burr Point, 1610 meters; the river bottom, about 1165.

Hike Length and Time Needed Roughly, this hike is only about 6 kms long, top to bottom. While it's not a difficult or dangerous walk, the going is a little slow and time consuming. It'll take the average person about 3 hours to walk down, a little longer to walk back up. In other words, it'll take a full day, to do this hike, round-trip. The author has been up or down the route with a heavy pack on four trips. It took him two and a half hours down, three hours up. The minor cliffs mentioned were not a problem, but inexperienced hikers may want a short rope to get large packs up or down a couple of them.

Water There's normally water in the "water pipe" along the access road(it's well water between a well and a stock tank). There's river water, but purify that. If it's not long after a good rain, you'll have a minor seep and pothole water at Twin Alcoves. If you're day-hiking, plan to take your own. Always have plenty in your car.

Map USGS or BLM map Hanksville(1:100,000), or Fiddler Butte(1:62,500).

Main Attraction Very fine views of a deep river canyon; easy access to the middle part of the Dirty Devil River Gorge; and one of the biggest alcoves around in the *Great Alcove*.

Ideal Time to Hike Spring, fall or even winter warm spells. Summer temps are especially warm at the river bottom.

Hiking Boots Any dry weather boots or shoes.

Author's Experience The author has been up and down this route a total of 6 times, four trips with a large pack. For fotos of the Great Alcove, hike in the mornings.

38   The Great Alcove, seen from along the Burr Point to Dirty Devil River route.

MAP 13, BURR POINT—DIRTY DEVIL R. HIKE

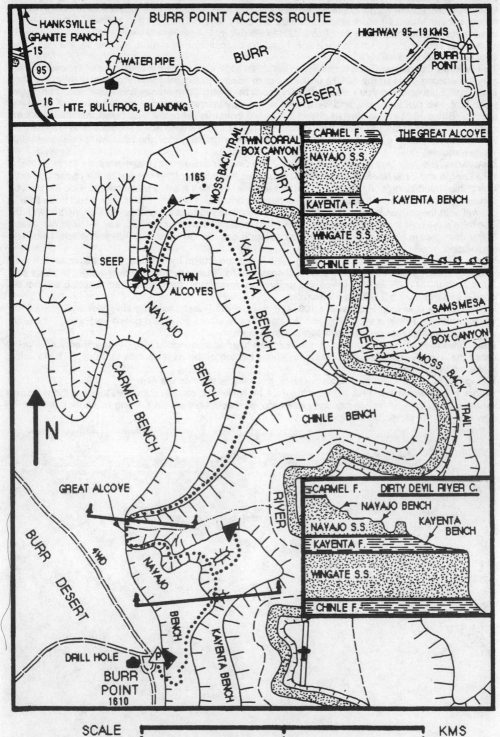

BURR POINT ACCESS ROUTE

HANKSVILLE
GRANITE RANCH
15
95
WATER PIPE
16 HITE, BULLFROG, BLANDING
BURR
DESERT
HIGHWAY 95–19 KMS
BURR POINT
P

THE GREAT ALCOVE
CARMEL F.
NAVAJO S.S.
KAYENTA F. ← KAYENTA BENCH
WINGATE S.S.
CHINLE F.

MOSS BACK TRAIL
TWIN CORRAL BOX CANYON
DIRTY
1165
SEEP
TWIN ALCOVES
NAVAJO BENCH
CARMEL BENCH
KAYENTA BENCH

SAMS MESA
BOX CANYON
MOSS BACK TRAIL
DEVIL
CHINLE BENCH

N

GREAT ALCOVE
BURR DESERT
4WD
NAVAJO BENCH
RIVER
KAYENTA BENCH

DIRTY DEVIL RIVER C.
CARMEL F.
NAVAJO BENCH
NAVAJO S.S.
KAYENTA BENCH
KAYENTA F.
WINGATE S.S.
CHINLE F.

DRILL HOLE
P
BURR POINT
1610

SCALE 0   1   2 KMS

Twin Corral Box Canyon

Location and Access Twin Corral Box Canyon is the large drainage to the south of the Biddlecome-Ekker Ranch. As the name indicates, this canyon is a "box", with no real routes into or out of, except for the canyon mouth where it drains into the Dirty Devil River. The best and simplest way to get into this canyon is to come in from Burr Point. Get to Burr Point by leaving Highway 95 between mile posts 15 and 16, and driving 19 kms to the Point. Read the description of the route on map 13, the Burr Point-Dirty Devil River Hike.

Trail or Route Conditions Once inside Twin Corral, it's easy walking. In the lower end of the canyon, you may walk along parts of the 1950's uranium boom mining track, called here by the author, the *Moss Back Trail*. Further along you'll walk in the dry creek bed, which sometimes has water in it. The author visited the two northern forks and went most of the way up the main canyon, but found no entry-exit points. But a BLM ranger insists there is an old constructed cattle trail down into the box from someplace south of the Ekker Ranch. This author never found it, and AC, the owner of the ranch, isn't about to tell any hiker of its whereabouts. This means a challenge for the hiker who enjoys looking for new routes.

Elevations The Dirty Devil River, 1165 meters; Twin Corral Flats, about 1900 meters.

Hike Length and Time Needed It's about 20 kms from the mouth of the canyon to the upper box end. Doing this round-trip in one day is too much for anyone, so you'll want to make camp inside the canyon someplace, perhaps near the middle. If you get an early start from Burr Point, then you'll have time to get well into the canyon before camping. That would allow you to see the upper box on the second day. The third day could be used to return to Burr Point, or hike to another canyon, say for example, Sams Mesa Box. Some hikers may want to stay a fourth day, to be sure and have enough time for exploration.

Water There's water in various places in the canyon, as shown by the heavy dark lines on the map. That's how the author found it after a wet fall season. You'll have to treat the river water. In years past, there were many cattle in the canyon, but today, very few. If you take water from a spring source, you should be OK drinking it without purification.

Map USGS or BLM map Hanksville(1:100,000), or Robbers Roost Canyon and Fiddler Butte(1:62,500).

Main Attraction This is a very deep and isolated canyon where you'll find peace and quiet. There are many good campsites, and plenty of territory to explore.

Ideal Time to Hike Spring or fall, but not during the high water period in May. Remember, you've got to cross the river. Summers are too hot, and winter fording of the river sounds terrible! Autumn colors make fall the best time.

Hiking Boots Any dry weather boots or shoes, but waders to cross the river.

Author's Experience From his camp on the river, he walked up canyon about two thirds of the way, and returned in 8 hours. Another day on another trip, was spent rim-walking, trying to locate that rumored cow trail into the canyon.

Upper Twin Corral Box Canyon, as seen from the rim.

MAP 14, TWIN CORRAL BOX CANYON

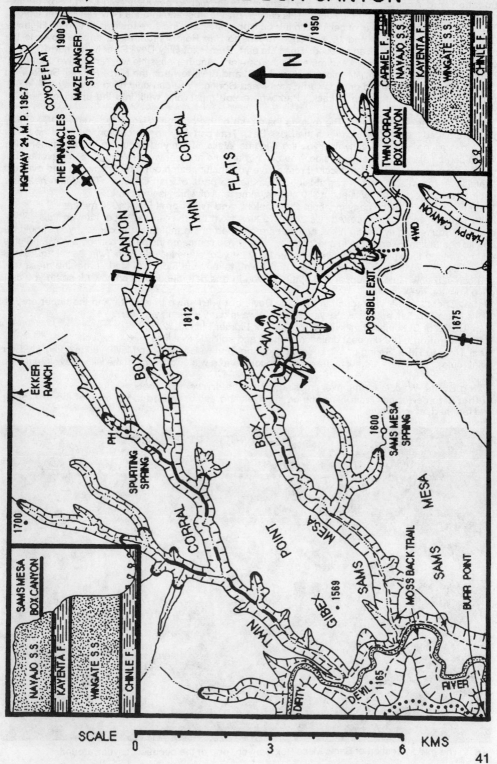

SCALE 0 ‖‖‖‖‖‖ 3 ‖‖‖‖‖‖ 6 KMS

Sams Mesa Box Canyon

Location and Access Sams Mesa Box Canyon is sandwiched between Twin Corral Box on the north, and Happy Canyon on the south. This canyon drains west and into the Dirty Devil River Gorge. There are two possible ways of getting into this canyon. First, and the sure route, is to turn off Highway 95 between mile posts 15 and 16, and drive 19 kms to Burr Point. From there, a route down to the mouth of Sams Mesa Box can be used. Read the part, Burr Point-Dirty Devil River Hike, map 13, for a description of the access road and route into the canyon. Another possible way, is to drive east from Highway 24, from between mile posts 136 and 137, and drive towards the Maze Ranger Station. At Coyote Flat, turn south and drive toward Sams Mesa Spring. You can only drive part way with most vehicles, because of the sandy track. Park where you must, and walk into the upper part of the canyon.

Trail or Route Conditions The route to the mouth of this canyon is explained on map 13. Once you've crossed the river, you can use the Moss Back Trail part way up this canyon, then it's the usual canyon walking, which is easy until you the Wingate Walls. Then you'll come to several minor falls, which can be skirted on the south side. You can get around and above the Wingate and Kayenta, but getting through the Navajo is difficult. From above you might search out a route down in and over the Navajo. In the middle part, it has striking similarities to parts of Zion Canyon. The depth near the geology cross section arrow is about 350 meters, almost all of which is vertical.

Elevations Mouth of the canyon, about 1160 meters; and Twin Corral Flats, 1900 meters.

Hike Length and Time Needed It's about 15 kms from the river to the upper canyon falls. This means if you're a fairly strong hiker, and you are camped at the mouth of the canyon, you should be able to see the entire drainage in one long day. But, if you can camp inside the canyon a ways, it'll give you more time to explorer the canyon the next day. If your plans include both Twin Corral and Sams Mesa Box Canyons on the same trip from Burr Point, take about 5 days of food. From the mesa top, you can see down into the upper end of the canyon in one day, depending on how far south you can drive from the main road.

Water There's water year-round in the Dirty Devil, but you'll have to treat it. And the upper end of Sams Mesa Box has running water year-round. Always carry water in your car.

Map USGS or BLM map Hanksville(1:100,000), or Fiddler Butte(1:62,500).

Main Attraction The deepest drainage around, and solitude in a little known canyon.

Ideal Time to Hike Spring or fall, but not during the high water period in May(if you're using the Burr Point route). Summers are hot in the canyon bottom, and a winter crossing of the Dirty Devil seems too much.

Hiking Boots Waders for the river crossing, otherwise dry weather boots or shoes.

Author's Experience From his camp on the river, the author walked to the base of the exit route, and returned, all in 8 hours.

42   The middle section of Sams Mesa Box Canyon, one of the deepest canyons around.

MAP 15, SAMS MESA BOX CANYON

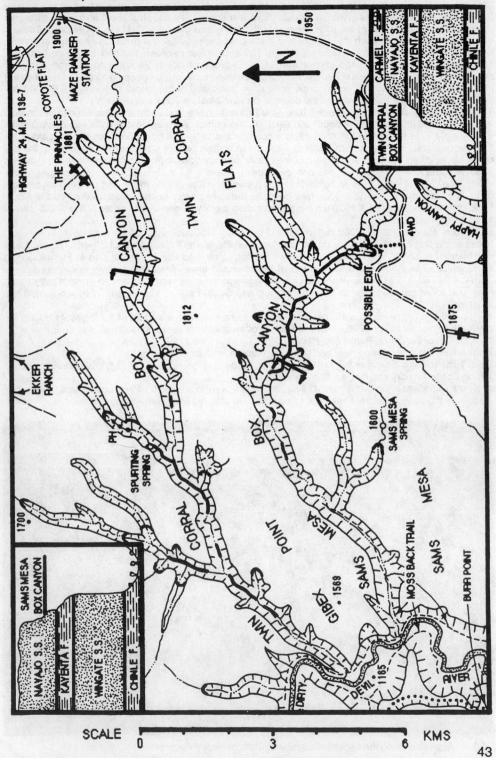

HIGHWAY 24, M.P. 136-7
COYOTE FLAT
1900
1950
MAZE RANGER STATION

THE PINNACLES 1881

N

CANYON

CORRAL

TWIN CORRAL FLATS

CAMEL F.
NAVAJO S.S.
KAYENTA F.
WINGATE S.S.
CHINLE F.
TWIN CORRAL BOX CANYON

HAPPY CANYON

4WD

POSSIBLE EXIT

1675

1812

BOX

EKKER RANCH

PH.
SPURTING SPRING

CANYON (X-H)

CANYON

BOX

1600
SAMS MESA SPRING

MESA

1700

SAMS MESA BOX CANYON
NAVAJO S.S.
KAYENTA F.
WINGATE S.S.
CHINLE F.

CORRAL

POINT

MESA

MESA

SAMS

MESA

SAMS

MOSS BACK TRAIL

BURR POINT

GIBEX 1569

TWIN

DEVIL 1165

DIRTY

RIVER

SCALE 0   3   6 KMS

43

Upper Happy Canyon

Location and Access The upper part of Happy Canyon is located directly south of the Maze Ranger Station. This canyon flows to the west and into the Dirty Devil River, not far north of where Poison Spring Canyon reaches the river. Although there are some very fine, but short narrows just above where Happy Canyon enters the river, the most interesting part of Happy C. is this upper part. There's only one simple way to reach this region, and that's from Highway 24, the main road linking Hanksville with I-70 and Green River. Between mile posts 136 and 137(or between 133 and 134), turn east and southeast, and proceed to the ranger station, a distance of about 74 kms, on a good and well maintained road. Get the latest information from the rangers, before proceeding further. To get to the best entry point, which is in French Spring Fork, drive back west of the ranger station about 5 or 6 kms, and turn south onto a bumpy road to the drill site shown. Most vehicles can make it.

Trail or Route Conditions From the drill hole, you'll have to route-find down over the Navajo Bluffs and into the shallow drainage to the south and west. At the bottom are many cattle trails you can follow to the Wingate Falls below. At this drop-off, is a constructed cattle trail going down on the east side. It's a bit eroded now, but it's easy to follow to the canyon bottom, where you can then walk along the dry creek beds, either up or down canyon, or into other side canyons. For the adventurous sort, there's another route down just east of the one described. There's no trail, just a more challenging route, where at one point you'll have to climb down a log someone has placed there, and go over several low cliffs. You can make a circle or loop hike between these two entry points. Also, at the head of South Fork, are the remnants of a 1950's mining exploration track you can use to enter at the south part of this canyon complex.

Elevations Ranger station, 2000 meters; lower Happy C., 1450; drill site, 1900 meters.

Hike Length and Time Needed Hiking the loop between the two trailheads is about 20 kms. This is an all day hike for anyone. You could also go down the log route, and visit the upper part of French Spring Fork, which is likely the most scenic part of this mapped area. One could easily spend all day, or perhaps two days, just in this upper part. If you had two vehicles available, or can enjoy a rather long hike, you could go down French Spring Fork, and exit South Fork, or vise versa. With two cars, a two day hike.

Water Take your own to be sure, but the author found a seep at the bottom of the log route during the wetter-than-normal fall of 1986. There are surely other seasonal seeps throughout this drainage.

Map USGS or BLM map Hanksville(1:100,000), or Orange Cliffs(1:62,500).

Main Attraction A very deep, wild and unknown canyon, with solitude.

Ideal Time to Hike Spring or fall, but summers aren't too bad, because of the higher altitudes.

Hiking Boots Any dry weather boots or shoes.

Author's Experience On two different hikes, the author went down each of the routes discussed to the bottom of the canyon, and returned the same way. He also did some rim-walking for fotos.

44   A rim foto along the upper French Spring Fork of Happy Canyon.

MAP 16, UPPER HAPPY CANYON

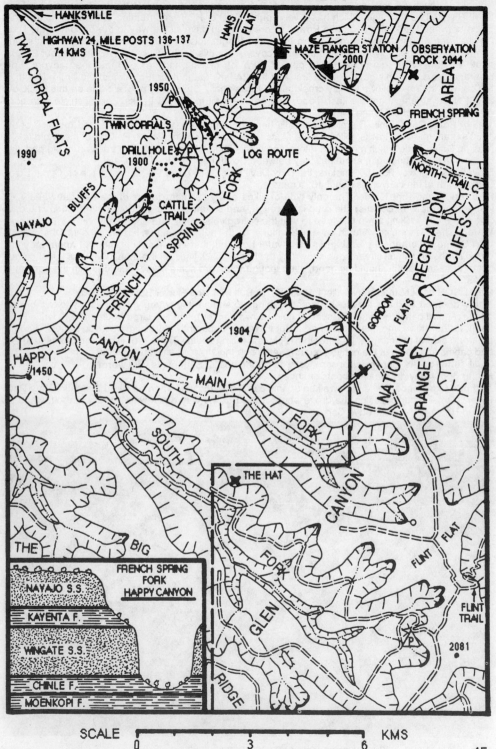

Poison Spring Canyon

Location and Access Poison Spring Canyon is located about halfway between Hanksville and Lake Powell. Highway 95 crosses the upper part of this canyon, which drains to the east and into the Dirty Devil River. This drainage, which has a very rough 4WD or HCV road running to the river, is the only place between Hanksville and Lake Powell where one can drive all the way to the bottom of the Dirty Devil. Even though there's a road along the entire length, this canyon offers side canyon hikes, and some of the few petroglyphs seen in the area covered by this book. To get there, drive about 27 kms south of Hanksville, and right at mile post 17, turn left or east and proceed into the canyon. Low clearance cars can only go about the first 4 of the 24 kms to the river. For almost the entire length of the canyon the road follows the dry creek bed. Occasionally, the county puts a blade on this track, but about twice a year, there's a flash flood, and boulders fill in the old tracks. Any vehicle with good clearance, can make it to the river.

Trail or Route Conditions There are no trails here, but in places, you'll see the faded remains of old 1950's uranium boom tracks, following the Moss Back Member of the Chinle F. One of these old tracks runs up South Fork, which makes an interesting hike. There's even one or two tracks running part way up the canyon to the south, about half way between South Fork and the Dirty Devil.

Elevations Highway 95, 1500 meters; the Dirty Devil River, 1150; and the highest place on Cedar Point, to the south of the canyon, is about 1825 meters.

Hike Length and Time Needed The only type of hikes along this canyon are of the half day variety, or just an hour or two. Because the road is so rough, and so few people get down, even those who drive cars can enjoy walking down this road to visit the petroglyphs, ruins and short canyons.

Water There is running water in several locations, as the author found on his two trips into the canyon. Wall Spring is perhaps the best and safest water hole, but there are also a number of apparent year-round seeps and small streams, as shown by the heavy black lines on the map. Get it as it first comes out of the sand, and it should be good, even though there are some horses and cattle in the canyon at times.

Map USGS or BLM map Hanksville(1:100,000), or Bull Mtn. and Fiddler Butte(1:62,500).

Main Attraction Perhaps the most interesting things to see are the petroglyph panels. The author saw one real good panel(the first PET symbol going down canyon), and two large boulders with writings on them, further down and near South Fork. But there are apparently several more good panels. Look to the north side of the canyon, on smooth rock faces, facing south. There are also some old mine shafts and cabins just south of the canyon mouth. Also one Indian cave, as shown on the map.

Ideal Time to Hike Spring, fall or perhaps winter warm spells. Summer is very warm.

Hiking Boots Any dry weather boots or shoes.

Author's Experience The author walked up this canyon all the way when he hiked the entire Dirty Devil River. On another occasion, he drove about a third of the way down with his VW Rabbit, when he visited Hatch and Fiddler Cove Canyons.

46   Wall Spring, in the middle section of Poison Spring Canyon.

MAP 17, POISON SPRING CANYON

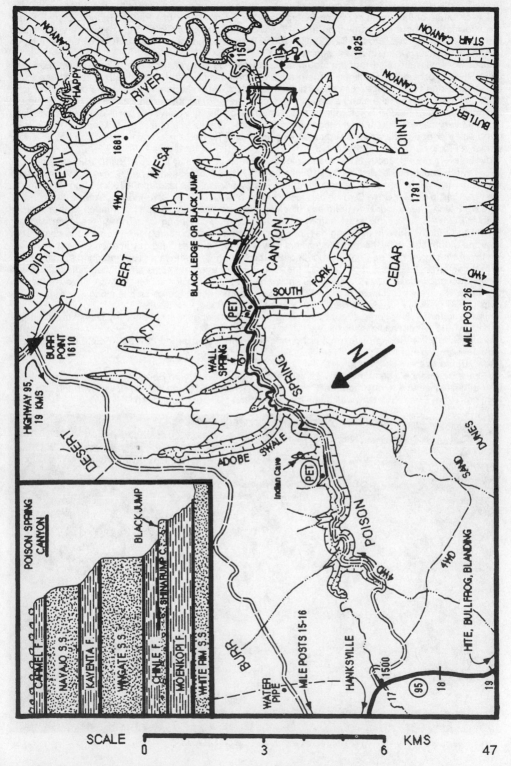

SCALE
0   3   6   KMS

Hatch and Fiddler Cove Canyons

Location and Access These two canyons are located not far north of the Dirty Devil River arm of Lake Powell. Both drainages flow into the Dirty Devil River from the east, and enter the main canyon not far below or south, of the mouth of Poison Spring Canyon. To get there, use Poison Spring Canyon. Read the information about this canyon on map 17. Most people will have to park somewhere in Poison Spring Canyon, and walk to the Dirty Devil. Those fortunate enough to have a HCV, can make it to, or very near the river, where this hike begins.

Trail or Route Conditions From the mouth of Poison Spring Canyon, you simply walk down the Dirty Devil River, crossing it many times. There are a few cattle in the canyon, so you'll be able to use some of their trails and short-cut across some of the meanders, thus shortening the hike. For this river part of the hike, it's best to take along a walking stick of some kind, about a meter and a half long, to probe for possible deep hidden holes. Once at the mouths of the two canyons, you'll have easy walking. Hatch is very deep at first, then it becomes more shallow, with some narrows. Fiddler Cove C. is very deep and moderately narrow right up to the blocking falls. There's a good chance you can box in a deer or two in Fiddler Cove, as did the author.

Elevations Trailhead, about 1150 meters; mouth of Hatch, about 1130; Cedar Point, 1825 meters.

Hike Length and Time Needed It's 9 or 10 kms from the mouth of Poison Spring Canyon to the mouth of Hatch. This will take two to three hours for the average person. It's also about 10 kms from the river to the headwall in Fiddler Cove C. This part alone will take at least 4 hours, round-trip. After walking 7 or 8 kms up Hatch, the author didn't find any blocking falls, so you can go up Hatch much further than in Fiddler Cove. It is possible to walk from a campsite on Poison Spring C., and visit the lower parts of Hatch and Fiddler Cove in one long day, but it's recommended you time your hike so as to camp at or near the mouth of Hatch Canyon. Slow hikers may want as much as a full day in each canyon.

Water About three kms up from the mouth of Poison Spring C., is the last seep and good running water in that canyon. During a wet fall season, the author found a few potholes and limited running water in both Hatch and Fiddler Cove Canyons, as shown by the heavy black lines on the map. If you're there in dry times, it's likely you'll have to rely on river water, so take some Iodine tablets along.

Map USGS or BLM map Hanksville(1:100,000), or Fiddler Butte(1:62,500).

Main Attraction A river gorge about 685 meters deep, the deepest part of the Dirty Devil; and a couple of narrow and entrenched canyons in the White Rim S.S.

Ideal Time to Hike Spring or fall, but not during the high water period of May. Fall is the very best, summers are too hot !

Hiking Boots Wading boots or shoes.

Author's Experience The author drove a third of the way down Poison Spring C., walked the rest of the way and camped at the very mouth of Poison Spring. Second day, he walked down river and into both canyons a ways on a hike that was much too long, about 10 hours, round-trip.

48   Narrows in the White Rim Sandstone of lower Hatch Canyon.

MAP 18, HATCH AND FIDDLER COVE CANYONS

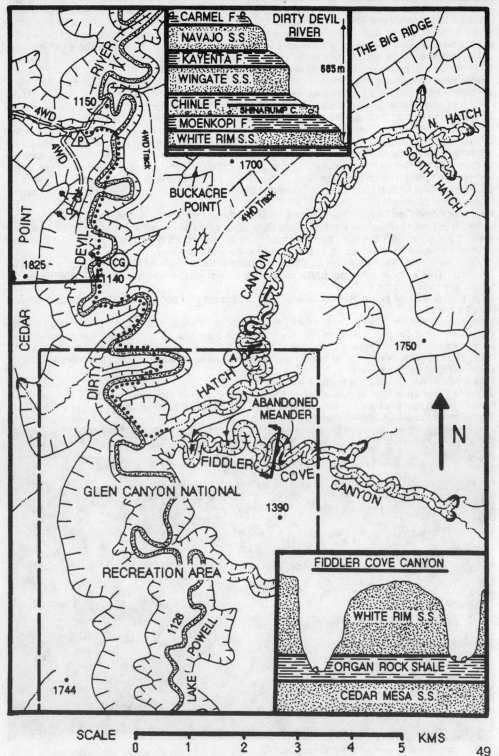

CARMEL F.
NAVAJO S.S.
KAYENTA F.
WINGATE S.S.
CHINLE F.   SHINARUMP C.
MOENKOPI F.
WHITE RIM S.S.

DIRTY DEVIL RIVER

585 m

THE BIG RIDGE

N. HATCH

SOUTH HATCH

RIVER

4WD

4WD

4WD Track

1150

P

BUCKACRE POINT

1700

4WD Track

POINT

DEVIL

CG

1140

1825

CEDAR

1750

DIRTY

CANYON

A

HATCH

ABANDONED MEANDER

FIDDLER   COVE   CANYON

N

GLEN CANYON NATIONAL

1390

RECREATION AREA

1128

LAKE   POWELL

1744

FIDDLER COVE CANYON

WHITE RIM S.S.

ORGAN ROCK SHALE

CEDAR MESA S.S.

SCALE   0   1   2   3   4   5   KMS

Butler, Stair, and Marinus Canyons

Location and Access Access to these hikes is very easy. You simply park on Highway 95, the main road running between Hanksville and Hite and Lake Powell. First, head for a point about 10 or 12 kms up North Wash from Lake Powell. This is about 50 or 55 kms south of Hanksville. For a hike up either Butler or Stair Canyon, park just down canyon from mile post 31. Both canyons come together next to the highway. There's a wide place there, where you can park and camp. To hike Marinus Canyon, park between mile posts 34 and 35, and at the mouth of the canyon. All of these canyons head in Navajo Slickrock country on the west side, and high above, the Dirty Devil River.

Trail or Route Conditions The only kind of trails in these canyons are those of cattle, and they're only in the lower ends. You simply walk up the usually dry creek beds, or along side the small streams. There are some small and large falls in all these canyons, so you'll be required to route-find if you want to get to the canyon heads. Perhaps the best objective of all, is the eastern part of Cedar Mesa, where you'll have a fine view into the Dirty Devil River Canyon, with a drop of about 685 meters. This is the deepest this canyon gets. If going up Stair Canyon, regress from the two blocking falls 300-400 meters, and climb the southeast wall. Then route-find to the top of the Navajo Bench, and walk the bumpy slickrock to the overlook. On the map, it looks easier to get out of Butler Canyon and onto the mesa top, where you can then head east for a canyon view. The author is familiar only with Stair Canyon.

Elevations Cedar Point, 1825 meters; Butler and Stair Canyons Trailhead, 1300; and Marinus Canyon Trailhead, 1220 meters.

Hike Length and Time Needed You can walk up any of these canyons for just an hour or two, or for half a day. If you want to reach an overlook of the Dirty Devil, take a lunch and water and plan for an all day hike. If you go up Stair Canyon, then it's about 13 or 14 kms from the bottom to the overlook. It's not so long a hike, but it's slow and go, as you have to route-find all the way.

Water The author knows only Stair C. There are some potholes and some running water as shown on the map. That water in the upper parts, above some minor falls, will be safe to drink(which is above where any cattle can get to).

Map USGS or BLM maps Hanksville and Hite Crossing(1:100,000), or Fiddler Butte and Browns Rim(1:62,500).

Main Attraction Easy access, canyons with moderately good narrows and falls, and fine views of the Dirty Devil River Gorge. Also from any place on top of the slickrock and outside the canyons, you'll have a splendid view of the Henry Mountains.

Ideal Time to Hike Spring, fall, or maybe even during some winter warm spells. Summers are just too hot to enjoy at these altitudes.

Hiking Boots Any dry weather boots or shoes.

Author's Experience The author hiked up Stair Canyon, located the route out of the canyon to the Navajo Bench, but because of other commitments, didn't have time to go all the way to the overlook. But the route looked OK from that point.

50   A fine scene of the Henry Mountains. From the Kayenta Bench above Stair Canyon.

MAP 19, BUTLER, STAIR, MARINUS CANYONS

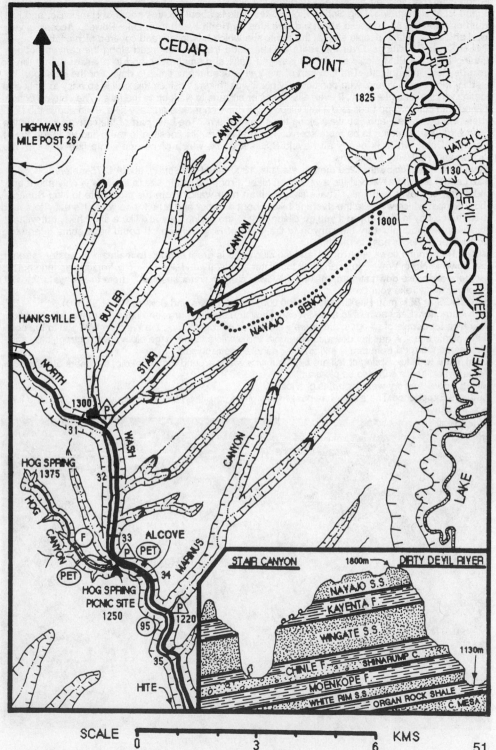

CEDAR POINT

N

DIRTY

HIGHWAY 95
MILE POST 26

HATCH C.

1825

1130

DEVIL

1800

BUTLER

CANYON

CANYON

STAIR

NAVAJO BENCH

HANKSVILLE

RIVER

NORTH

POWELL

1300 P

31

WASH

STAIR

CANYON

LAKE

HOG SPRING
1975

32

HOG

ALCOVE

F

33

CANYON

PET

P

MARINUS

34

PET

HOG SPRING
PICNIC SITE
1250

95

P

1220

CANYON

35

HITE

Geologic cross-section (inset)

STAIR CANYON   1800m   DIRTY DEVIL RIVER

Navajo S.S.

Kayenta F.

Wingate S.S.

Chinle F.   Shinarump C.

1130m

Moenkope F.

White Rim S.S.

Organ Rock Shale

C. Mesa

SCALE
0   3   6   KMS

Hog Canyon

Location and Access Hog Canyon, sometimes known as Hog Spring Canyon, is located along Highway 95, the main road linking Hanksville, with Hite and Lake Powell. Right on the highway is a large parking lot and BLM sign stating, Hog Spring Picnic Site. This is about 55 kms south of Hanksville, and just south of mile post 33. It's also about a dozen kms up North Wash from Lake Powell. Access is very good and easy. Many people stop at the picnic site which has toilets and covered picnic tables.

Trail or Route Conditions Over the years a hiker-made trail has emerged along the canyon bottom, running from the BLM picnic site to the Kayenta Falls and small pool, and to a lesser extent, on up towards Hog Spring itself. The first part of the trail is used many times a day. For the most part it's used by highway travelers, who don't usually qualify as "hikers". Since this trail is so easy to walk and doesn't require a lot of energy, it even allows senior citizens to walk up to the falls. The canyon bottom is lined with cottonwood trees and a few willows. All of which makes an easy hike, even above the falls, where the trail fades, and you walk along the small stream. The best part of the canyon itself, is the lower end, which seems to be more scenic. For real hikers, it's possible to route-find up to the top of Trachyte Point, which is nearly all Navajo S.S. slickrock, which gives one some fine views of the canyon and the Henry Mountains.

Elevations The picnic site, 1250 meters; the falls, 1300; and Hog Spring, about 1375 meters.

Hike Length and Time Needed It's a very short hike. From the picnic site to the falls is only about one and a half or maybe two kms. That's about half an hour walk. From the picnic site to Hog Spring is about 5 kms, which will take the average hiker about an hour and a half, one way. It's easy to spend about half a day in the canyon if you go all the way to the spring. If you'd like a short hike, but without other people, you might try the canyon to the north of Hog Canyon. It could have some interesting narrows, and it too is easy to reach.

Water Hog Spring flows year-round, and the discharge is great enough to maintain a constant stream flow down to North Wash. You can drink the water safely, if you take it directly from the spring source, but there are cattle down stream, making the lower canyon water suspect. There are no water taps at the picnic site. Take your own.

Map USGS or BLM map Hite Crossing(1:100,000), or Mt. Hillers and Browns Rim(1,62,500).

Main Attraction Easy access to a desert canyon with a small, year-round flowing stream. A short and easy hike for people of all ages, and there's a panel of petroglyphs on the Wingate Wall just to the north of the picnic site. A half km down canyon from the picnic site is a large alcove with petroglyphs, and just across the road from that is still another panel of petroglyphs.

Ideal Time to Hike Spring or fall are best, but with water around for a cool dip, summers are possible. Winter warm spells can also be pleasant.

Hiking Boots Any dry weather boots or shoes.

Author's Experience The author has passed this place countless times, but only once did he stop for a look up canyon.

The Kayenta Falls and pool, in the middle part of Hog Canyon.

MAP 20, HOG CANYON

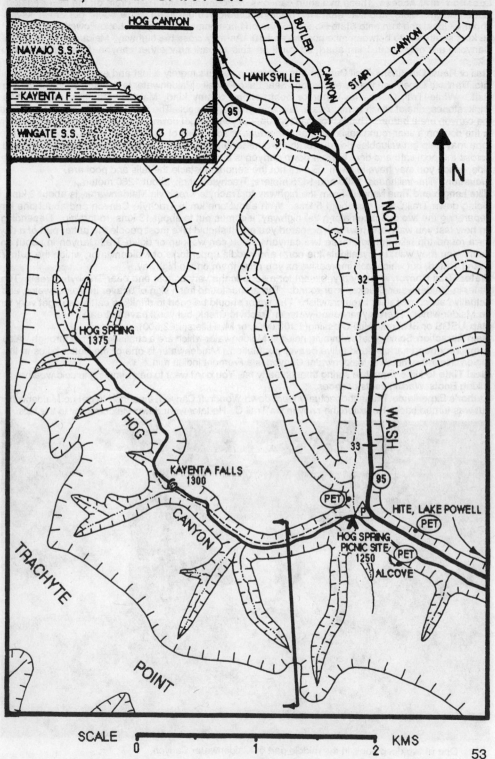

HOG CANYON

NAVAJO S.S.

KAYENTA F.

WINGATE S.S.

BUTLER CANYON

STAIR CANYON

HANKSVILLE

95

31

N

NORTH

32

33

95

WASH

HOG

HOG SPRING
1375

KAYENTA FALLS
1300

CANYON

TRACHYTE

POINT

PET

PET

P

HITE, LAKE POWELL

PET

HOG SPRING
PICNIC SITE
1250

PET

ALCOVE

SCALE

0   1   2

KMS

53

Maidenwater and Trail Canyons

Location and Access These two short canyons, Maidenwater and Trail, drain off the lower eastern slopes of Mt. Hillers, and flow east into Trachyte Creek. To get there, drive south out of Hanksville about 42 kms, and turn onto State Road 276, the one heading to Bullfrog and Lake Powell. Drive about 15 kms south and to between mile posts 9 and 10. As they cross the highway, Maidenwater and Trail Canyons are only about 1 km apart, so you'll be able to park near either canyon, for a circle or loop hike.

Trail or Route Conditions Trail Canyon has nothing to see, it's merely a fast and easy way to get down into Trachyte Creek and the lower canyons near Lake Powell. Maidenwater is the canyon you'll want to visit. While Trail C. has no water or obstructions of any kind, Maidenwater has at least two chokestones, one of which forms a dam, falls and good sized pool. The falls and pool near the middle of the canyon are a barrier. That is, you can't go up, but you can get down. Since there will likely be water in the pool on a year-round basis, take an *inner tube* or some kind of *float device*, and a *short rope*. The rope may help get valuables down over the two meter high falls easy, and the float device will get you across the pool safe and dry. Further down canyon is another chokestone, with a deep pool on the lee side, which you may have to swim. But it's not the serious obstacle the falls and pool are.

Elevations The trailheads, 1400 and 1425 meters; Trachyte Creek, about 1260 meters.

Hike Length and Time Needed From the highway to Trachyte Creek via Maidenwater, is about 6 kms. Going down Trail Canyon is about 5 kms. With about one km in Trachyte Canyon and about one km separating the two drainages along the highway, it comes out to about 13 kms, round-trip. Depending on how fast you walk, and how well prepared you are, it should take most people the better part of a day for a round-trip hike through these two canyons. You can walk up or down Trail Canyon in about an hour. You may want to investigate the north and middle upper forks of Maidenwater, which the author hasn't visited, but which look impressive as you pass them on the highway.

Water Trail Canyon is totally dry, except for a seep in the very bottom end near Trachyte Creek. The water in Maidenwater Creek is year-round. The author found fresh sign of beaver in Maidenwater, and actually saw some rather large crawfish. The water should be good to drink, as cattle can't get very far up Maidenwater. There's year-round water in Trachyte Creek, but you'll have to treat it.

Map USGS or BLM map Hite Crossing(1:100,000), or Mt. Hillers(1:62,500).

Main Attraction Some great swimming holes in Maidenwater which are a challenge to get through. Also some very good narrows and a live beaver population. Maidenwater is one of the better hikes in this region. Near the mouth of Maidenwater Canyon is a Fremont Indian ruin.

Ideal Time to Hike From late spring through early fall. You don't want to be swimming in cold weather.

Hiking Boots Wading boots or shoes.

Author's Experience The author actually went down Woodruff Canyon, then tried to get up Maidenwater but was turned back. He exited the canyon via Trail C. He later went down Maidenwater to the falls.

54   One of two deep pools in the middle part of Maidenwater Canyon.

MAP 21, MAIDENWATER AND TRAIL CANYONS

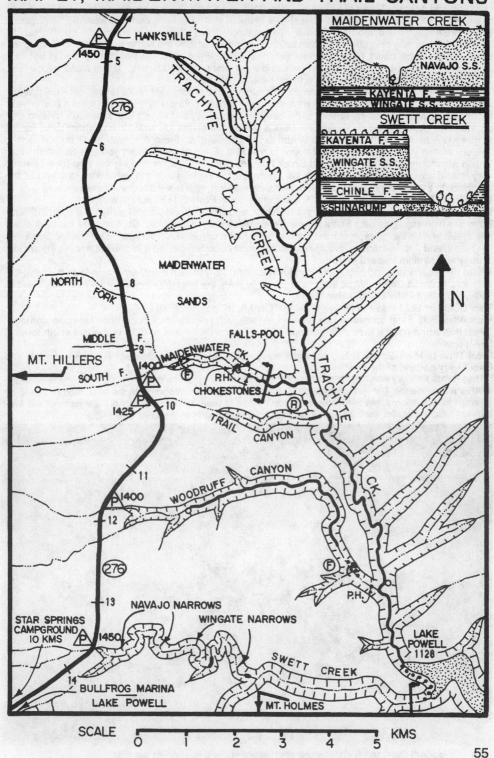

MAIDENWATER CREEK

NAVAJO S.S.

KAYENTA F.
WINGATE S.S.

SWETT CREEK

KAYENTA F.

WINGATE S.S.

CHINLE F.

SHINARUMP C.

HANKSVILLE

1450

5

276

6

7

TRACHYTE CREEK

MAIDENWATER

SANDS

NORTH FORK

MIDDLE F.

MT. HILLERS

SOUTH F.

8

9

1400

FALLS-POOL

MAIDENWATER CK.

P.H.

CHOKESTONES

1425

10

TRAIL CANYON

11

WOODRUFF CANYON

1400

12

276

13

STAR SPRINGS CAMPGROUND 10 KMS

1450

NAVAJO NARROWS

WINGATE NARROWS

14

BULLFROG MARINA LAKE POWELL

SWETT CREEK

MT. HOLMES

TRACHYTE CK.

F.

P.H.

LAKE POWELL 1128

N

SCALE

0 1 2 3 4 5 KMS

Woodruff and Swett Creeks

Location and Access These two canyons, Woodruff and Swett Creeks, are located east of Mt. Hillers and north of Mt. Holmes. They drain the slopes of these two mountains and flow east into the Trachyte Creek drainage, thence into Lake Powell. To get there, drive south out of Hanksville on Highway 95 about 42 kms(to mile post 26). Then turn south on State Road 276, the highway running to Bullfrog and Lake Powell. Drive about 20 kms to near mile post 12, to enter Woodruff Canyon; or, and to between mile posts 13 and 14, to reach the car-park and entry point to Swett Creek. If you make a loop-hike, you'll have about 2 kms of road-walking to get back to your car.

Trail or Route Conditions Woodruff Canyon has running water for most of it's length, so expect a few willows and tall grasses typical of well watered desert canyon bottoms. However, it's not a bushwhack. It's easy walking. Toward the bottom of the canyon, it narrows, and there's one falls you'll have to skirt on the east. Later, a big chokestone makes a deep pool on it's lee side. It was chest deep for the author when he passed it, and he nearly had to swim through it. From Woodruff, you'll enter Trachyte Canyon, where you'll walk along the stream to the lake. Even at high water, you can walk the Chinle Bench around the lake, to enter Swett Creek from the bottom, if you're making the loop hike. There's very little, if any, running water in Swett Ck.; therefore the walking is in the usual dry creek bed all the way back to the highway. Swett Creek is very easy walking, with few if any impediments.

Elevations The trailheads, about 1400-1450 meters; Lake Powell, 1128 at high water.

Hike Length and Time Needed From the highway, and down Woodruff to Trachyte, is about 12 kms. From the highway and down Swett Creek, it's about 16 kms to the lake. So, from one car-park down one creek and up the other, and road-walking back to the car, is about 33 kms. This sounds like a very long walk, and it is; but most hikers in reasonably good condition can do it in one full day, as the walking is easy and straight forward.

Water There's water(and cattle) throughout Woodruff Canyon and on down Trachyte to the lake, but very little in Swett Creek. What there is in Swett, is likely the best drinking water on this hike. Best to take you're own water if you're day-hiking.

Map USGS or BLM map Hanksville(1:100,000), or Mt. Hillers(1:62,500).

Main Attraction Easy access to little known canyons with solitude(except perhaps for some boaters). Swett has some good narrows in the upper end. You might try one or both of the two south forks of Swett Creek.

Ideal Time to Hike Spring or fall, or maybe some winter warm spells. Summer brings small gnats and flies, to say nothing of the heat.

Hiking Boots Any dry weather boots or shoes.

Author's Experience The author spent 9 1/2 hours walking down Woodruff to the lake, then he made an attempt to get out via Maidenwater, but didn't make it past the falls and pool. He got out via Trail Canyon. Next day, he took 4 hours to walk down Swett nearly to the lake, and return.

56   Woodruff Canyon. A chokestone and resultant deep pool on its lee side.

MAP 22, WOODRUFF AND SWETT CREEKS

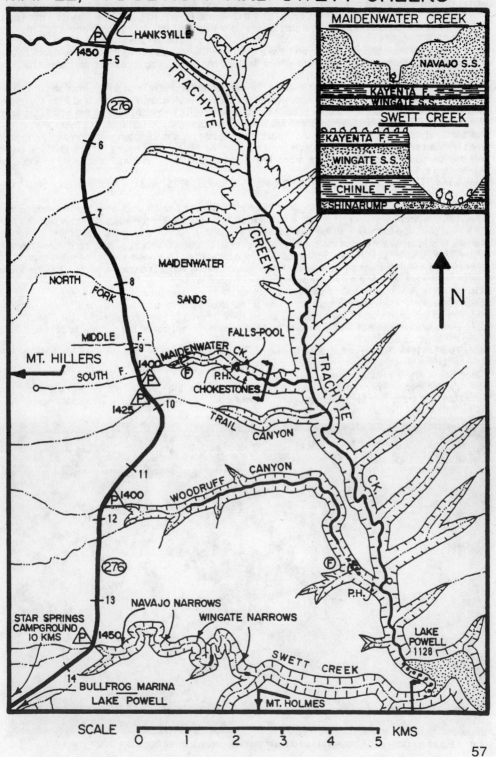

MAIDENWATER CREEK

NAVAJO S.S.

KAYENTA F.

WINGATE S.S.

SWETT CREEK

KAYENTA F.

WINGATE S.S.

CHINLE F.

SHINARUMP C.

HANKSVILLE

1450

5

276

6

7

TRACHYTE

CREEK

MAIDENWATER

SANDS

NORTH

FORK

8

MIDDLE   F.

9

MT. HILLERS

SOUTH   F.

1400 MAIDENWATER CK.

FALLS-POOL

P.H.

CHOKESTONES

1425

10

TRAIL

CANYON

TRACHYTE

11

WOODRUFF   CANYON

CK.

1400

12

276

P.H.

13

NAVAJO NARROWS

WINGATE NARROWS

STAR SPRINGS
CAMPGROUND
10 KMS

1450

SWETT   CREEK

LAKE
POWELL
1128

14

BULLFROG MARINA
LAKE POWELL

MT. HOLMES

N

SCALE

0   1   2   3   4   5   KMS

Fourmile Canyon

Location and Access Fourmile Canyon is but one of dozens of canyons draining into Lake Powell. This particular one heads on the eastern slopes of Mt. Ellsworth, and the south slopes of Mt. Holmes, and flows east to the lake, formerly Glen Canyon of the Colorado River. To get to this canyon, drive south out of Hanksville to State Road 276, which is very near mile post 26. Drive south about 32 kms to a point about 200 meters north of mile post 20. There's a parking spot on the east side of the road where most people will have to park. But if you have a 4WD or HCV, you can drive the steep and rocky track up to the granite ledges on Mt. Ellsworth, where the hike can begin. You could also park about half way up this track, for a closer run at Pass 1725.

Trail or Route Conditions You can begin at the car-park on the highway or at any point along the track running towards Ellsworth. You can walk over Pass 1725; or walk down the creek bed from the upper most car-park. Once you're into the Fourmile Creek drainage, it's a straight walk all the way to the lake. There are a couple of places where there are some short narrows and potholes, but there are no real obstacles. It's easy walking all the way. This canyon is so far off the beaten path, the author doesn't even remember seeing any sign of cattle, and certainly no footprints of hikers. If you like, you could exit the canyon bottom somewhere along the Kayenta Benches, and walk due east to the flats overlooking Lake Powell.

Elevations Highway car-park, about 1650 meters; the pass, 1725; and the lake at high water, 1128 meters.

Hike Length and Time Needed The length of this hike is about 17 or 18 kms, from the highway to the lake. But the distance in kms depends on which route you take around the pass, and how high the lake is. If your plans are to make it to the lake and back in one day, plan on a long day. But there is water at the lake and in the lower part of the canyon, so you might consider camping, and doing it in two days.

Water There's water at Fourmile Spring, but it's not a large flow. This water should be good to drink as is, but it had a slightly swampy taste to it. There's also running water in a couple of places in the lower canyon, and you'll likely find a number of potholes with good water.

Map USGS or BLM map Hite Crossing(1:100,000), or Mt. Hillers and Browns Rim(1:62,500).

Main Attraction Perhaps the best attraction is the total solitude and the lack of any sign of other hikers, with the exception of the area next to the lake, where boaters occasionally visit. You'll also have some unique views of Mts. Ellsworth and Holmes, if you get out of the canyon bottom and walk along the Kayenta Bench.

Ideal Time to Hike Spring or fall, but it is possible to enjoy a hike during a warm spell in winter. Early summer brings heat and small gnats and other insects.

Hiking Boots Any dry weather boots or shoes.

Author's Experience After camping down at the small pond near the Del Monte Mine, the author got an early start and made it to the lake and back, in about 8 1/2 hours, round-trip. It was a late spring day, but he remembers the heat well.

58   Fourmile Canyon. Late spring and early summer brings small frogs like this.

MAP 23, FOURMILE CANYON

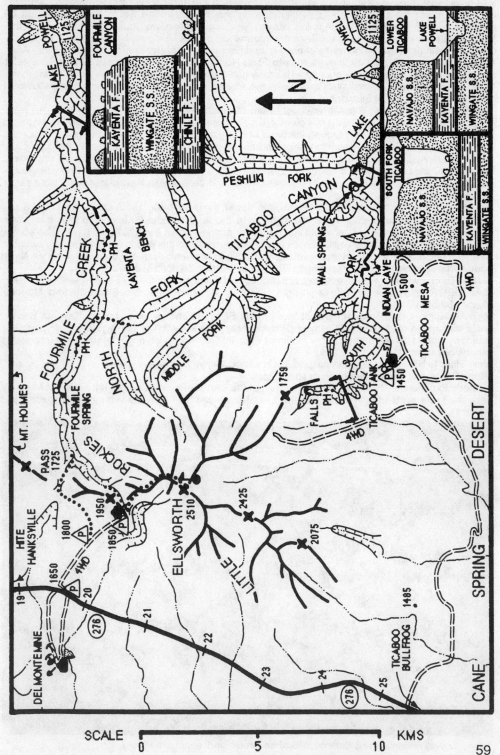

FOURMILE CANYON

LAKE POWELL 1125

KAYENTA F.

WINGATE S.S.

CHINLE F.

LOWER TICABOO

LAKE POWELL

NAVAJO S.S.

KAYENTA F.

WINGATE S.S.

SOUTH FORK TICABOO

NAVAJO S.S.

KAYENTA F.

WINGATE S.S.

N

LAKE POWELL 1125

PESHLIKI FORK

TICABOO CANYON

WALL SPRING

FORK

INDIAN CAVE

TICABOO MESA 1500

4WD

CREEK

KAYENTA BENCH

FOURMILE

NORTH FORK

MIDDLE FORK

SOUTH

1759

FALLS PH

TICABOO TANK

P 1450

DESERT

MT. HOLMES

FOURMILE SPRING

PH

ROCKIES

PASS 1725

1950 P

1850

ELLSWORTH 2510

2425

2075

4WD

HTE HANKSVILLE

1800 P 4WD

1650

20

21

LITTLE

22

TICABOO BULLFROG 1485

SPRING

19

276

23

24

25

276

DEL MONTE MINE

CANE

SCALE

0   5   10

KMS

59

Ticaboo Canyon-North Fork

Location and Access The North Fork of Ticaboo Canyon begins on the eastern slopes of Mt. Ellsworth and flows east, then southeast to Lake Powell. Ticaboo has three forks; the North Fork, which is discussed here; the Middle Fork, also included on this map; and the South Fork, which will be discussed on the next map. To get to this canyon, you could walk down South Fork, then up into the North Fork from very near the lake. Read the information on this hike possibility on map 25, Ticaboo Canyon-South Fork. The other route of entry is to drive south out of Hanksville on Highway 95. After 42 kms and near mile post 26, turn south onto State Road 276. Drive south about 32 kms, to a point about 200 meters north of mile post 20. This hike has the same trailheads or car-parks as for those hiking down Fourmile Canyon. Walk or drive the two kms to the end of the rough road running southeast and to the granite cliffs of Ellsworth.

Trail or Route Conditions You can walk right from the highway and to Pass 1725, or you can walk northeast and down the beginning of Fourmile Creek, from the end of the side road on the slopes of Ellsworth. It's possible to skirt around the base of Ellsworth, but it's rough, and the going slow. It's best to walk down Fourmile Creek to where the canyon isn't so deep, then walk out to the top of the Kayenta Bench. From there walk due south until you reach the head of the North Fork. At one point, the two canyons are less than a km apart. Once inside the North Fork, you can walk unobstructed to the lake. As you walk down canyon, it becomes deeper and deeper, with Navajo Bluffs and walls rising higher and higher.

Elevations Highway car-park, 1650 meters; the upper most car-park, 1850; Lake Powell, 1128.

Hike Length and Time Needed From the highway to the lake is about 20 kms. To hike this entire distance in one day and return, is all but impossible for anyone. Even if you did do it, it would be so long and tiresome, you wouldn't enjoy it. So it's recommended you do this one in two days; one day to the lake, and one day for the return trip. If you have access to two vehicles, then you could enter via North Fork, and exit up South Fork, or vise versa This could perhaps be done in one long day.

Water There's water at Fourmile Spring, at the bottom of the canyon at the Wall Spring, and at the lake.

Map USGS or BLM map Hite Crossing(1:100,000), or Mt. Hillers, Mt. Ellsworth and Mancos Mesa(1:62,500).

Main Attraction Great views of the east face of Mts. Ellsworth and Holmes from the Kayenta Bench, and a wild and wooly Navajo S.S. canyon. With an inner tube and with the lake high(or walking with the lake low), you could get around to the mouth of Peshliki Canyon, which might be the more interesting canyon of the two.

Ideal Time to Hike Spring or fall, and possibly in winter. Summers are very warm.

Hiking Boots Any dry weather boots or shoes.

Author's Experience The author has been down to the lake via Fourmile and South Fork, but has only seen the lower parts of the North Fork. He has also viewed it all from the summits of Ellsworth and Holmes.

60　　　Wall Spring in the lower end of Ticaboo Creek, and near Lake Powell.

MAP 24, TICABOO CANYON-NORTH FORK

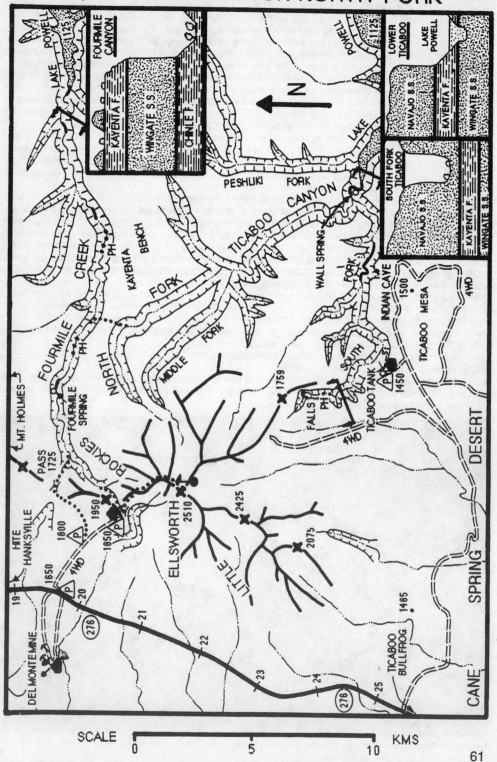

SCALE

0   5   10   KMS

Ticaboo Canyon-South Fork

Location and Access   The South Fork of Ticaboo Canyon is one of the better hikes around. To get there, drive along State Road 276, the paved highway running from Highway 95(the link between Hanksville and Hite) to Bullfrog. At a point southwest of Mt. Ellsworth, and between mile posts 25 and 26, turn east onto a very rough and seldom-if-ever-maintained road.   This road runs east to Ticaboo Mesa, a sandy plateau overlooking Lake Powell.   Drive about 13 kms, to a point just east of a long low hill.   Up to this point, the road is very rough, but any car with reasonable clearance, and with a shovel available, can make it.   It's slow and go all the way.   You may have to stop occasionally to push rocks off the road, or to smooth out some gullies; but the author made it with his VW Rabbit. After the 13 kms, turn left or northwest, and drive down hill maybe 400 meters to the Ticaboo Tank.   This is a storage tank for spring water which is piped from up-hill someplace.   You can take drinking water directly from the storage tank, instead of from the cattle trough.

Trail or Route Conditions Ticaboo Tank is at the very top of an old constructed cattle trail running down into the South Fork. It was probably built during the Depression by the CCC boys.   There are few if any cattle using it today, but it's in fairly good condition.   Some places are washed out or have fallen away, but it's easy to find and follow, right to the canyon bottom.   Once at the bottom, you can walk west or up canyon, and visit some pretty good narrows and a very deep and enclosed canyon.   Going down canyon, you can easily walk to the lake in the dry creek bed.

Elevations Ticaboo Tank, 1450 meters; the lake, 1128 meters at high water.

Hike Length and Time Needed You can walk up canyon 3 to 4 kms to the big headwall and 30 meter falls, or from the tank to the lake, is about 8 or 9 kms. Any person in good physical condition can walk from the trailhead to the lake and back in about half a day, but there are things to see. So to see up canyon, down canyon, side canyons, and the cave, will occupy a full day. You could also camp down near the lake, and take in North Fork and Peshliki Canyon. If the lake is at or near the high water level, you'll need an *inner tube* or some kind of *float device* to make it about 300 meters across the lake to the mouth of Peshliki C. In times of low water, you can walk it.

Water   Very good water in Ticaboo Tank, and running water in the middle and lower end of South Fork, and at the lake. If you're there shortly after a storm, you'll find many potholes up canyon as well.

Map   USGS or BLM map Hite Crossing(1:100,000), or Mt. Ellsworth and Mancos Mesa(1:62,500).

Main Attraction   A deep and narrow canyon, total solitude, and a cave which was used by Fremont Indians.   This cave would allow you to camp without a tent.

Ideal Time to Hike   Spring or fall, or maybe in winter warm spells.

Hiking Boots   Any dry weather boots or shoes.

Author's Experience   The author took more than 2 hours to drive from the highway to the tank, then camped.   Next morning he hiked and took the entire day going up and down canyon, from the canyon headwall to the lake, including a visit to the Indian cave.

Just one of several very narrow side drainages in the South Fork of Ticaboo Creek.

MAP 25, TICABOO CANYON-SOUTH FORK

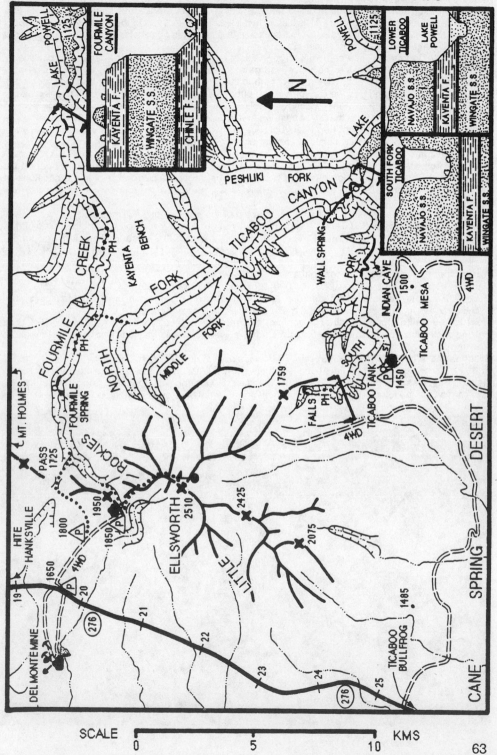

SCALE
0   5   10   KMS

South Caineville Mesa Trail

Location and Access The South Caineville Mesa is located about half way between Capitol Reef National Park and Hanksville. This mesa has an old sheep trail to the top, which in turn offers some fine views of surrounding hills made of the Mancos Shale. To get there, drive along Highway 24 to a point between mile posts 100 and 101, which is just east of Caineville. On the south side of the road you'll see a small hill. Park at a gate just to the east of that hill. This point is less than a km from the old abandoned cement truck near mile post 101.

Trail or Route Conditions You can walk through this gate, as the owners don't care. But don't take vehicles in. Immediately inside the fence and gate, keep to the right to get on the west side of a narrow, but very deep little gully. Then walk south to the river. Cross the Fremont, and look for an old track running towards and into the canyon coming out of the prominent cove in the S. Caineville Mesa. Once inside the drainage, it's easy to find and follow this faded track. When you reach the second major drainage coming in from the left or east, enter it and head southeast. In about 200 meters you'll come to a fork. Take the right hand canyon. As you walk southeast up this short drainage, you'll eventually be able to see and walk along another old track on the right side. As the drainage narrows, the track become more visible. As you arrive on top of the minor mesa(it's the Ferron S.S.), the track fades, but from there on it's a trail only. You'll be able to see the trail, as it zig zags up the slope. At the very top the trail veers west, then east, and finally goes up through a narrow crack in the capstone of the mesa, the Emery S.S. On top the trail totally fades, so you're on your own from there to any vantage point you want.

Elevations The river crossing, about 1375 meters; top of the trail, about 1790 meters.

Hike Length and Time Needed This is a short hike, only about 4 kms from the car-park to the top of the sheep trail. In cooler weather, most hikers can get to the top of the mesa in about 2 hours, so the round-trip could be done in about half a day. But if you're interested in getting to one of several overlooks, it may take you the better part of a day for the round-trip.

Water There's none around, except in the river, so take your own.

Map USGS or BLM map Hanksville(1:100,000), or Factory Butte(1:62,500).

Main Attraction An interesting close-up look at the barren blue-grey hills of the Mancos Shale. Excellent views in any direction from the mesa top. Normally easy access.

Ideal Time to Hike Spring or fall. The depth of the Fremont is normally ankle to knee deep. Pick up a walking stick if the river seems deep or fast. There's a week or two in May you'll not be able to make a crossing.

Hiking Boots Waders for the river crossing, otherwise dry weather boots or shoes.

Author's Experience Short on time because of the short late fall days, the author almost had to run to the top of the mesa, to get fotos before the light ended. Round-trip was about two and a half hours. He didn't have time to look for the old sheep herders cabin somewhere on the south end of the mesa.

The top of the trail to the South Caineville Mesa, as it cuts through the Emery Sandstone member.

MAP 26, SOUTH CAINEVILLE MESA TRAIL

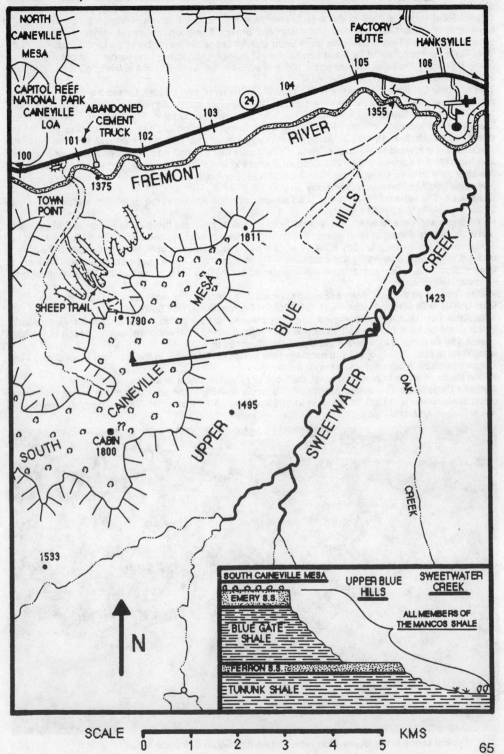

NORTH CAINEVILLE MESA

FACTORY BUTTE

HANKSVILLE

105

106

CAPITOL REEF NATIONAL PARK CAINEVILLE LOA

ABANDONED CEMENT TRUCK

104

103

1355

102

101

100

1375

FREMONT

RIVER

TOWN POINT

1811

MESA

BLUE

HILLS

CREEK

1423

SHEEP TRAIL

1790

CAINEVILLE

UPPER

1495

SWEETWATER

OAK

CABIN 1800

SOUTH

CREEK

1533

N

SOUTH CAINEVILLE MESA	UPPER BLUE HILLS	SWEETWATER CREEK
EMERY S.S.		ALL MEMBERS OF THE MANCOS SHALE
BLUE GATE SHALE		
FERRON S.S.		
TUNUNK SHALE		

SCALE

0 1 2 3 4 5

KMS

65

Sweetwater Creek-Upper Blue Hills

Location and Access The Upper Blue Hills and Sweetwater Creek, are both located about 20 kms west of Hanksville, and to the south of State Road 24. This highway is the main link between Hanksville and Capitol Reef National Park to the west. The thing that makes this entire region so interesting and unique, is the Blue Gate Member of the Mancos Shale. The scenery here is similar to some of the places near Green River. The hills have been eroded in special ways, because of the make-up of the Blue Gate, and because of its place sandwiched in between two sandstone layers. To get there, drive along Highway 24 to between mile posts 105 and 106. On the west side of a low hill, park and look for a very faint road running south to the river.

Trail or Route Conditions From the highway, walk to the river, and make a ford to the south side. The track is clearly visible as it heads up a shallow drainage just south of the river. Follow this track upon the benchland between the Fremont River and the drainage coming from the high point of South Caineville Mesa at 1811 meters. Head out in a southwest direction. At one of many points you can get down into this shallow dry valley. Along the way you may or may not see a faint cow trail veering to the southeast and toward Sweetwater Creek. You can follow the trail into the Sweetwater, or just head southwest to the eastern slopes of the South Caineville Mesa. It's in this whole general area you'll find the blue-grey colored clays of the Blue Gate Shale. Don't make a hike here in wet weather! In just a few steps you'll be carrying a ton of clay on your feet!

Elevations The Fremont River, about 1355 meters; average altitude in the Blue Hills, about 1450; top of South Caineville Mesa, 1811 meters.

Hike Length and Time Needed There is no fixed distance, because there is no fixed destination. You can walk for 6 or 8 kms, or for a dozen, depending on time available. You can make a hike of about half a day, round-trip; or for a full day if you like. One of the BLM rangers in Hanksville once told the author about a sheep trail coming off the east side of South Caineville Mesa, just west of the word "Blue", in Upper Blue Hills. The author never did locate it, so looking for this trail could be a challenge for someone with energy.

Water There's year-round water in Sweetwater and the Fremont, but don't drink it. Take your own.

Map USGS or BLM map Hanksville(1:100,000), or Factory Butte(1:62,500).

Main Attraction Unique scenery in the blue-grey colored Mancos Shale, and wild and desolate solitude. If you could find that old sheep trail on the east side, it would offer excellent views. Much of the area covered by this map is included in the Blue Hills-Mount Ellen WSA.

Ideal Time to Hike Spring or fall, but not during the period of high water in the Fremont River during May. Forget this place in summer, it's a firey inferno.

Hiking Boots Waders to cross the river, then any dry weather boots or shoes.

Author's Experience The author spent nearly 6 hours walking to the east side of the mesa, then came down Sweetwater and back to the river at 1355 meters. This was in November, and with wet clay, it made for heavy duty walking.

Typical scene in the Upper Blue Hills, just east of South Caineville Mesa.

MAP 27, SWEETWATER CK.–U. BLUE HILLS

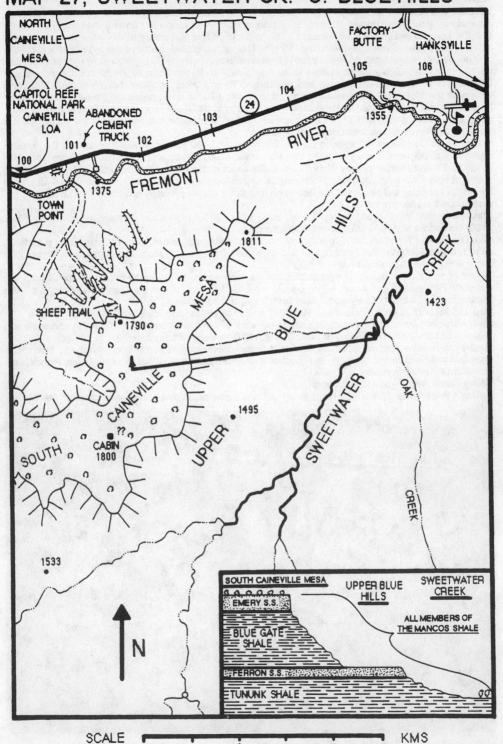

NORTH CAINEVILLE MESA

FACTORY BUTTE

HANKSVILLE

105

106

CAPITOL REEF NATIONAL PARK

CAINEVILLE

LOA

ABANDONED CEMENT TRUCK

24

104

103

1355

102

101

100

1375

FREMONT RIVER

TOWN POINT

1811

HILLS

BLUE

CREEK

1423

SHEEP TRAIL

MESA

1790

CAINEVILLE

1495

SWEETWATER

OAK

??

UPPER

CABIN 1800

SOUTH

CREEK

1533

SOUTH CAINEVILLE MESA | UPPER BLUE HILLS | SWEETWATER CREEK

EMERY S.S.

BLUE GATE SHALE

ALL MEMBERS OF THE MANCOS SHALE

FERRON S.S.

TUNUNK SHALE

N

SCALE 0 1 2 3 4 5 KMS

67

Bull Mountain

Location and Access The hike or climb getting attention here is one of the minor peaks in the Henry Mountains. It's Bull Mountain, located due south of Hanksville, and east and northeast of Ellen Peak and the Lonesome Beaver Campground. This peak is composed totally of the intrusive rocks which make up all of the higher summits in the Henrys. The rock is called diorite porphyry, which is a type of granite. To get to Bull Mtn., drive south out of Hanksville on Highway 95 to just before mile post 10, and turn right or west. Drive about 11 kms to the Fairview Ranch, then turn south toward the mountains. Drive about 10 or 11 kms on a rocky and rough road 'till you're just southwest of the summit area, and very near the high point on the road going on to Sawmill Basin and Lonesome Beaver Campground. Look for a wide place in the road and park. Another way to get there from Hanksville is to turn south at the post office(100 E.), and follow that road south until you reach the Fairview Ranch, then it's the same route to the mountain as previously described.

Trail or Route Conditions There's no trail on this mountain, you just go straight up picking the easiest route(or the toughest if you prefer) to the top. It's a steep climb, and you'll have to work your way around cliffs and steeper places and up gullies, but anyone should be able to handle it. The easiest way is to first walk east to the ridge top, then north along to the summit. It's possible to climb Bull Mtn. from the northeast and from near the Granite Ranch, but that place is privately owned and you'd have to get permission from the owner.

Elevations Bull Mtn., 2800 meters; the car-park, about 2350; high point on the Sawmill Basin Road, 2400; Lonesome Beaver Campground, 2525 meters.

Hike Length and Time Needed From the car-park to the summit, is only about 2 kms, but it's a steep one. It might take you about one or one and a half hours to reach the top, and certainly no longer than half a day for the round-trip hike.

Water There's no water on the mountain, but you could stop at the small ditch just up-hill from the Fairview Ranch and get water which comes from Bull Creek. Or if you continue on towards the campground, you can get very good water from the upper part of Bull Creek.

Map USGS or BLM map Hanksville(1:100,000), or Bull Mountain and Mt. Ellen(1:62,500).

Main Attraction From the summit, one has a fine view of the desert country to the north and east, and an even better view of Mt. Ellen and Sawmill Basin to the west and southwest.

Ideal Time to Hike This one could be climbed from mid or late May and on through about mid November. But each year is different. Even in the dead of winter, you can at least get to the Fairview Ranch, and walk from there if necessary.

Hiking Boots Any rugged hiking boots.

Author's Experience The author has passed this way many times, but hasn't yet climbed to the summit.

Bull Mountain left, and Mt. Ellen Peak on the right.

MAP 28, BULL MOUNTAIN

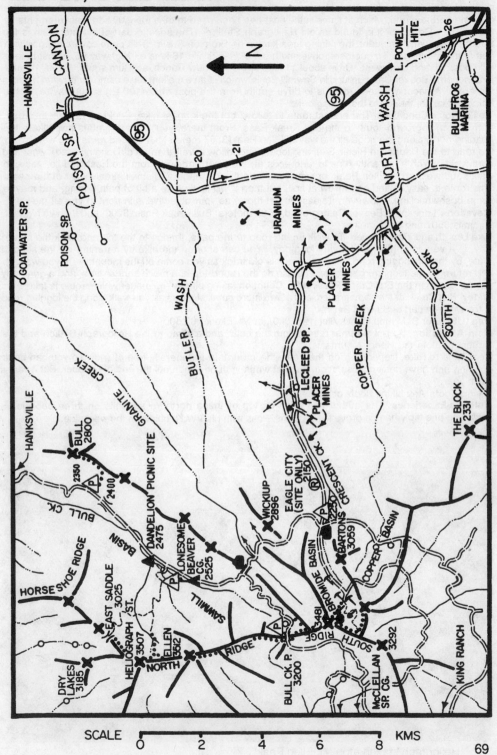

HANKSVILLE

CANYON

HANKSVILLE

17

POISON SP.

GOATWATER SP.

POISON SP.

95

95

20

21

N

L. POWELL
HITE

26

NORTH WASH

BULLFROG MARINA

URANIUM MINES

SOUTH FORK

BUTLER WASH

PLACER MINES

COPPER CREEK

LECLEED SP.

PLACER MINES

2150

THE BLOCK
2331

GRANITE CREEK

BULL CK.

BULL
2800

2350

P 2400

DANDELION PICNIC SITE
2475

LONESOME BEAVER CG.
2525

BASIN

WICKIUP
2896

EAGLE CITY
(SITE ONLY)

2250

BARTONS
3059

CRESCENT CK.

COPPER BASIN

KING RANCH

HANKSVILLE

HORSESHOE RIDGE

EAST SADDLE
3025

HELIOGRAPH
3507

SAWMILL

ST.

ELLEN
3512

NORTH

RIDGE

BROMIDE BASIN

3481

SOUTH RIDGE

McCLELLAN
3292

DRY LAKES
3185

BULL CK. P.
3200

McCLELLAN
SR CG.

SCALE

0   2   4   6   8   KMS

69

Mt. Ellen Peak

Location and Access Mt. Ellen is a huge hulk of a mountain, composed of two distinct parts. There's the northern ridge, which has the highest point in the Henry Mtns., and the pyramid-shaped peak at the extreme northern end, which at times in the past has been used to take triangulation measurements by the USGS. On top of it is found an old Heliograph Station. The second part of the mountain is the South Ridge, which includes the mining area known as Bromide Basin. This page covers the northern half of the mountain. To get there, drive south out of Hanksville 16 kms on Highway 95, to just before mile post 10, and turn west. Drive about 11 kms to the Fairview Ranch, and turn south. Drive 16 kms to Lonesome Beaver Campground in Sawmill Basin which is an excellent base camp for several hikes in the area. A second access route is to drive south from the post office(100 E.) in Hanksville, to the Fairview Ranch, thence to the campground.

Trail or Route Conditions The easiest route to follow, but the longest hike, would be to walk the road from the campground south to the Bull Creek Pass. From there, you'll find a hunters and hikers trail heading north along the ridge all the way to Ellen Peak(3507 meters). A second route is to walk down the road to the Dandelion Picnic Site, and locate and follow a trail(then an old logging road), west and northwest, which apparently runs to, and ends at, the East Saddle. From the East Saddle, you can walk southwest up to Ellen Peak, or simply walk up the drainage and small stream east of the peak. This route is easy to find and follow at first, but then it will likely take a bit of path finding, and maybe some bushwhacking. However, it's easy to get there, as your objective is in front of you all the way.

Elevations Lonesome Beaver Campground, 2525 meters; Bull Creek Pass, 3200; and the two highest summits 3507 and 3512 meters.

Hike Length and Time Needed To walk up the road to the pass, thence to the top and back the same way, is a very long hike, and a very long day. You can shorten the hike by returning via the second route, by the old logging road. You can see this old track as you come off the mountain. If you walk up and return by the logging road route, you can do the round-trip in a much shorter time, and a generally shorter day than the Bull Creek Pass route. Count on taking all day, no matter which route is taken.

Water Bull Creek at the campground, and at two more small streams as you walk along the logging road in the western part of Sawmill Basin.

Map USGS or BLM map Hanksville(1:100,000), or Mt. Ellen(1:62,500).

Main Attraction A cool summer retreat from the heat, and a climb to the Heliograph Station and the highest peak in the Henry Mountains.

Ideal Time to Hike Depending on the year, the mountain is generally free of snow so you can begin climbing and have easy access about the first week in June, and until the end of October. But it varies each year.

Hiking Boots Any hiking boots or shoes.

Author's Experience The author has been on top of these northern summits on three occasions, including one trip when he drove to Bull Creek Pass with his VW Rabbit from the west side.

70   Heliograph station atop Mt. Ellen Peak.

MAP 29, MT. ELLEN PEAK

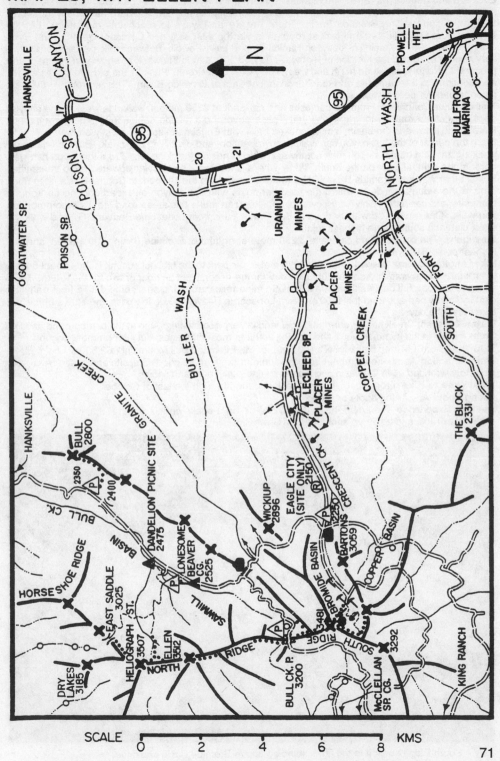

N

HANKSVILLE

CANYON

POISON SP.

95

17

95

20

21

26

L. POWELL
HITE

NORTH WASH

BULLFROG
MARINA

GOATWATER SP.

POISON SP.

BUTLER WASH

GRANITE CREEK

URANIUM MINES

PLACER MINES

SOUTH FORK

COPPER CREEK

LECLEED SP.

PLACER MINES

HANKSVILLE

BULL 2800

2350 P

2400

BULL CK.

BASIN

DANDELION PICNIC SITE 2475

LONESOME BEAVER CG. 2525

WICKIUP 2896

EAGLE CITY (SITE ONLY) R 2150

CRESCENT CK.

THE BLOCK 2331

HORSESHOE RIDGE

EAST SADDLE 3025

SAWMILL ST.

P

SAWMILL

BARTONS P 3059

BROMIDE BASIN

COPPER BASIN

KING RANCH

HELIOGRAPH 3507

ELLEN 3512

NORTH

RIDGE

3481

BULL CK. P 3200

SOUTH RIDGE

P

3292

DRY LAKES 3185

McCLELLAN SR. CG.

SCALE

0   2   4   6   8   KMS

71

Mt. Ellen-South Ridge

Location and Access Mt. Ellen, the highest summit in the Henry's, is a huge mountain mass, with a northern portion and a southern ridge. This page concentrates on the southern half of the mountain, the peaks surrounding Bromide Basin. There are several ways to reach this mountain, but the shortest, least complicated and fastest route in is via the east side and Crescent Creek. First, drive along Highway 95, the main link between Hanksville and Lake Powell. Between mile posts 20 and 21, or very near m.p. 26 and the junction of Highways 95 and 276, turn to the west, as shown on the map, and proceed to North Wash, then north and west along Crescent Creek. Pass by the old site of Eagle City, and continue to the campsite and road junction just east of Bromide Basin. This is probably the best place to park for people with cars.

Trail or Route Conditions From the campsite and car-park at 2250 meters, walk due west up the canyon on a very steep road. Along the way you'll pass several old mining cabins and mining equipment. Finally, you'll arrive in the basin, a mine-pocked bowl with Engelmann spruce, mostly on the south side. From the center of the basin, you can walk in any direction and directly to any peak. But there is an old track zig zagging up the slope to the southwest, which ends on the ridge top. From there you can walk north to the highest point on the South Ridge, where is located a small solar-powered radio transmitter. Still another way into Bromide B., would be to drive south from the car-park to Copper Basin, then north around the mountain side to where the road connects with the canyon and road coming up from the campsite and car-park. Only very powerful vehicles can make this steep road, so it's recommended you walk. One could also walk or drive to Bull Creek Pass from Lonesome Beaver CG., and walk the short distance south to the highest point.

Elevations The car-park and campsite, 2250 meters; bottom of Bromide Basin, about 3000; and the highest peak, 3481 meters.

Hike Length and Time Needed From the 2250 meter car-park to the highest summit is only about 5 kms, but it'll take the average person about half a day for the ascent; just an hour or two for the return. Might as well plan for a full day, as there are lots of old mine relics around to see, some dating from early this century, a few perhaps from the 1890's. From Lonesome Beaver CG. to the pass, then the summit, will take most of a day.

Water Crescent Creek has a year-round flow, and is very good water. Also at the campground and Bull Creek. Early in the summer, you'll find running water in most drainages, but later on most dry up.

Map USGS or BLM map Hanksville(1:100,000), or Mt. Ellen and Bull Mountain(1:62,500).

Main Attraction Another cool retreat from the summer heat, and a good campsite and water. Also, a lot of history wrapped up in the basin and the old mining equipment and cabins.

Ideal Time to Hike From about the first week in June, through the last of October.

Hiking Boots Any hiking boots or shoes.

Author's Experience The author has climbed one or more peaks on this South Ridge on three trips to Crescent Creek, and again on another trip to Sawmill Basin.

South Ridge summit to the right, standing above Bromide Basin and mine.

MAP 30, MT. ELLEN-SOUTH RIDGE

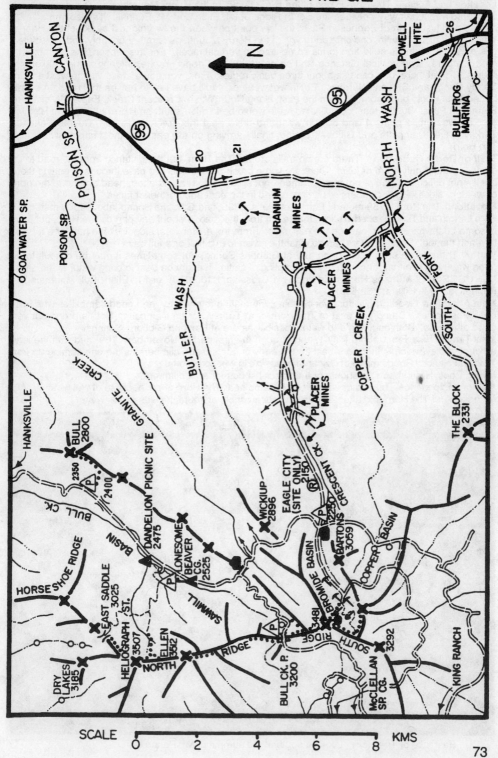

N

HANKSVILLE

POISON SP. CANYON

17

95

95

20

21

L. POWELL / HITE

26

NORTH WASH

BULLFROG MARINA

GOATWATER SP.

POISON SP.

POISON SP.

URANIUM MINES

PLACER MINES

SOUTH FORK

COPPER CREEK

BUTLER WASH

GRANITE CREEK

PLACER MINES

THE BLOCK 2331

HANKSVILLE

BULL 2800

2350

2400

DANDELION PICNIC SITE

BULL CK.

BASIN

LONESOME BEAVER CG. 2525

DANDELION 2475

WICKIUP 2896

EAGLE CITY (SITE ONLY) 2150

CRESCENT CK.

BARTONS 2250

BARTONS 3059

COPPER BASIN

HORSE SHOE RIDGE

EAST SADDLE 3025

HELIOGRAPH ST. 3507

SAWMILL

BROMIDE BASIN

3481

CRESCENT

KING RANCH

DRY LAKES 3185

NORTH ELLEN 3512

RIDGE

SOUTH RIDGE

BULL CK. P. 3200

McCLELLAN SP. CG.

3292

SCALE 0   2   4   6   8   KMS

73

The Horn

Location and Access The Horn is one of the minor peaks of the Henry Mountains. This granite block is located about half way between the South Ridge of Mt. Ellen and Mt. Pennell. It's also immediately next to and just south of Pennellen Pass, the low point between the two highest peaks of the Henrys. While much of the granite, or *diorite porphyry*, of the Henry Mountains is rather crumbly and brecciated, this particular chunk is solid and forms some smooth vertical faces. For this reason, it is of interest to rock climbers. The vertical distance isn't so great, but it is good granite, offering some challenging routes. To get there, one can use about three basic routes. First, you could arrive via the west and the Sandy Ranch and Stevens Narrows. But in wet weather, you'll have hell to pay on that road. A slightly better route would be to come in from the east; along North Wash, Crescent Creek, Eagle City site, and Pennellen Pass. But the least complicated route would be to drive south on Highway 276 from Highway 95. Between mile posts 4 and 5, turn west and drive past the Trachyte Ranch, Coyote Benches, Turkey Haven Campsite and Gibbons Spring, finally arriving on the east and most impressive side of The Horn.

Trail or Route Conditions There are no trails around The Horn, but the distance from the road to the steeper parts is only a km or less. There are some brush and boulders to pass through in getting there, but it's not difficult. If you're not a rock climber, but still want to reach the top, head around to the north or western sides. Rock climbers will be interested in the east and northeast faces.

Elevations The Horn, 2758 meters; Pennellen Pass, 2395; and Gibbons Spring, about 2500 meters.

Hike Length and Time Needed It's less than a km from the road to about any part of The Horn, but there is some bushwhacking, at least on the east side. From the easier west side, it'll take half, or a full hour to reach the top. Rock climbers can do what they wish to in a half or a full day.

Water There is water at Box Spring and at Gibbons Spring, but sometimes it may be difficult to get good water out of either, because of the trampling of cattle. It might be best to bring water to the area.

Map USGS or BLM maps Hanksville and Hite Crossing(1:100,000), or Mt. Ellen, Bull Mountain, Mt. Pennell, and Mt. Hillers(1:62,500).

Main Attraction Good granite for rock climbing, interesting fotography, and good campsites with huge ponderosa pines. Camp just east of The Horn or at Turkey Haven Campsite. Both are dry, but very good otherwise. Both camping and water possibilities are at Box and Gibbons Springs.

Ideal Time to Hike From about May 1, and through the first part of November. The road with the least amount of clay(which is therefore best for the early or late season climbers) is the one coming up from Trachyte Ranch. Roads made of *clay* are *impassible* in wet conditions.

Hiking Boots Hiking boots or shoes, or the special shoes for rock climbers.

Author's Experience The author was forced to camp near The Horn once because of wet weather. After hiking around The Horn and after the sun was out a couple of hours, he was on his way.

East face of The Horn. Looking south at the summit of Mt. Pennell.

74

MAP 31, THE HORN

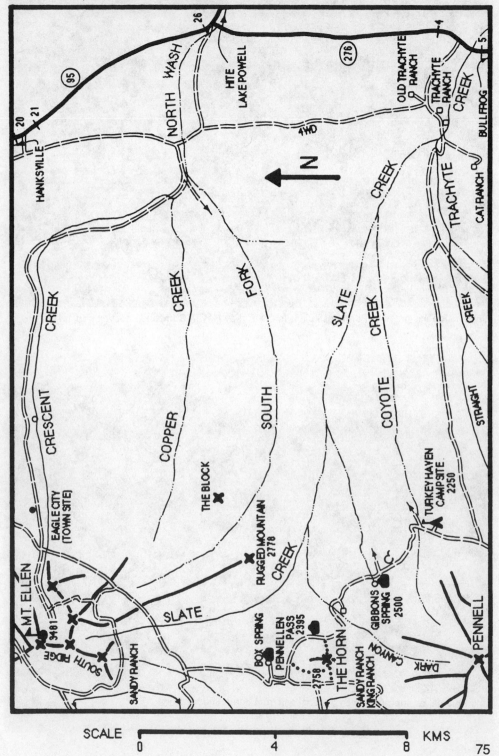

SCALE

0   4   8   KMS

Deep inside this grove of Ponderosa pines is the Turkey Haven Campsite(undeveloped, no water).

Mt. Pennell, as seen from the northeast and from near Gibbons Spring

Part of the old flume which carried water to the Wolverton Mill on the upper part of Straight Creek.

This is the small solar powered radio transmitter atop the highest point on Mt. Ellens' South Ridge.

Mt. Pennell

Location and Access Mt. Pennell is the second highest peak in the Henry Mountains. Despite its relatively high altitude, there are trees all the way to the top. There are several ways to get there; from the west and Sandy Ranch; from the south and the Ticaboo area; and from Star Spring and the Mt. Hillers region. But the best and least complicated way of getting to the normal route of ascent, is to drive along State Road 276, the link between Highway 95 and Bullfrog. Between mile posts 4 and 5, turn west and drive past the Trachyte Ranch, the Coyote Benches and to the east slope of Pennell. At a major road junction, turn south(or north to Turkey Haven Campsite) and proceed to the wooded area on Straight Creek. You can camp on the creek, and begin the hike from there.

Trail or Route Conditions From the campsite where the road crosses Straight Creek, you can either walk back north along the road until the first junction, then road-walk west and up the canyon on it's north side to the peak southwest of the main summit; or you can follow the faint track running west up stream along side the creek to a couple of cabins owned by the Hunts of Hanksville. From there continue west on the same faint track or trail to the Wolverton Mill site(read more about this in another part of this book), then where it's convenient, walk up hill due north to the road mentioned earlier. From there you walk to the end of the road or track on southwest peak, where is located a small solar-powered radio transmitter. From the transmitter, walk northeast along the summit ridge to the top. You'll see enroute, several small adits or exploration mine pits. Easy walking all the way.

Elevations Trachyte Ranch, 1500 meters; campsite on Straight Creek, 2400; and the summit, 3466 meters.

Hike Length and Time Needed From the campsite to the summit, is only about 7 or 8 kms. But the rise is over a 1000 meters, so most people will want about 3 hours to reach the top, another hour or two down. The time it takes will depend more on how much you want to poke around in the Wolverton Mill site ruins or investigate the solar powered radio transmitter, than the actual walk itself. This is a fine hike, but some will hate to see all the cat-tracks and other scarring done by miners who have searched the south slopes of the mountain looking for gold.

Water Straight Creek has a year-round flow, and it's good water.

Map USGS or BLM map Hite Crossing(1:100,000), or Mt. Pennell and Mt. Hillers(1:62,500).

Main Attraction Another cool hideout from the desert heat. You'll have some interesting views from the summit, especially to the southwest and southeast. A chance to explore the old historic Wolverton Mill site.

Ideal Time to Hike Since this is a south slope hike, you can probably make this climb from late May until early November. There are some clay spots along the road not far west of the Trachyte Ranch, but you can generally make the drive to the base of this mountain about any time during the warm season.

Hiking Boots Any hiking boots or shoes.

Author's Experience The author has been to the Wolverton Mill site twice, and once to the top of the mountain.

Mt. Pennell from the south and from the upper part of Bulldog Ridge.

MAP 32, MT. PENNELL

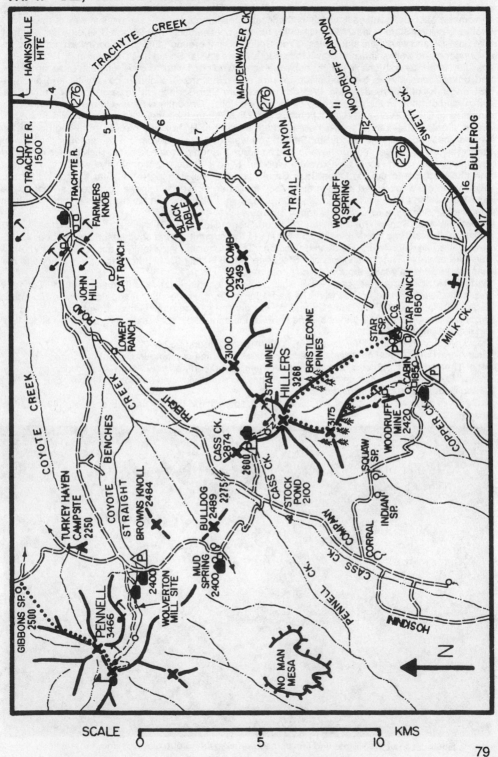

Mt. Hillers

Location and Access Mt. Hillers is the third highest peak in the Henry's, after Ellen and Pennell. One can get to this mountain from the north and the Trachyte Ranch area; from the south and from Ticaboo; or from the east and southeast, which is the least complicated, fastest, and easiest way of approach. First, drive along State Road 276, the highway running between Highway 95 and Bullfrog. Just south of mile post 17, and where the sign states, "Starr Springs Campground", turn to the northwest and drive up a very good and well maintained gravel road about 7 kms to Star Spring and Campground(USGS maps spell the name *Star* with one "r"). For people with cars who don't want to drive long distances on rough and dusty roads, this is the best place to park and climb from. Another possibility, and one not requiring a lot of bad-road-driving, is to drive west from Star Spring, and toward the Woodruff Stone Cabin, and climb from there. See map 34 for more details. Or continue around to the west side of the mountain to Cass Creek, and climb it from the Star Mine Route. See map 36 for more details.

Trail or Route Conditions There is no trail to the summit of Hillers; you merely route-find up one of several route possibilities. From Star Spring, you walk up the ridge from the campground. This is a rugged and steep route. You do have to zig zag around rough places and cliffs. High on this ridge are bristlecone pines. The route up above the Woodruff Mine is steeper, but generally easier. The easiest and shortest hike to the top is via Cass Creek, and the trail running to the Star Mine. That route involves an old wagon road, a moderately good trail, then above the mine, a very steep section to the top. But getting to the trailhead on Cass Creek, requires driving some bad roads. Only those with at least higher clearance cars should attempt this route.

Elevations Star Spring, 1850 meters; Woodruff Stone Cabin, 1850; trailhead on Cass Creek, 2600.

Hike Length and Time Needed From Star Spring to the summit via the southeast ridge is about 7 or 8 kms, but an all day hike for the average person. The Woodruff Mine Route is about 7 kms, and an all day hike as well. The Cass Creek and Star Mine Route is only about 3 kms from the trailhead to the summit, and will only take about half a day, round-trip.

Water Star Spring has very good water which is piped a short distance to the campground. Formerly this water was used by Al Star when he had a large ranch at the site. If you don't like campground noise, you can camp just to the east and down from the campground circle. There's a spring at the Woodruff Stone Cabin, and just above the cabin at the mine site. There's a spring below the Star Mine, but it could dry up at times.

Map USGS or BLM map Hite Crossing(1:100,000), or Mt. Hillers(1:62,500).

Main Attraction Old mining relics, bristlecone pines, and a fine campground and other campsites.

Ideal Time to Hike The southern routes could be climbed perhaps year-round, even during winter dry spells. But for the most part, the climbing season is from mid-May and through mid November.

Hiking Boots Any rugged hiking boots.

Author's Experience The author has been to the top on three occasions, and by each of the routes described.

South Face of Mt. Hillers, and fins of the Glen Canyon Group of sandstone formations.

MAP 33, MT. HILLERS

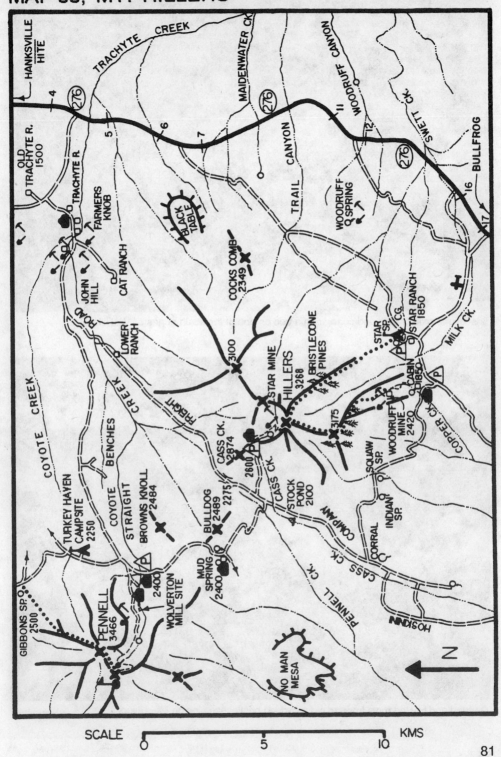

SCALE

0   5   10   KMS

Bristlecone pine branch and cone, from a tree on one of the south ridges of Mt. Hillers.

Gnarled and twisted roots from an old and dead bristlecone pine on Mt. Hillers.

A close-up look at the Star Ranch house, showing the fine rock work done by Franz Weber.

Mid-way up the south slopes of Mt. Hillers are these Chinle Formation fins.

Star Mine Trail

Location and Access The Star Mine on Mt. Hillers was prospected and first claimed by Al Star, the same man who built, owned and operated the Star Ranch next to the Star Spring Campgrounds. This mine and vertical shaft date from the 1890's. In recent years, other prospectors have reestablished the mining claim, and today you will see a windlass used to lower a bucket and to pull up ore samples. Upon the author's visit, the first of June, it was covered with snow, so the depth is unknown. To get to this trail, first look at map 33, Mt. Hillers. That map shows the access routes. Drive State Road 276, which runs between Highway 95 and Bullfrog. Between mile posts 4 and 5, turn west and proceed past the Trachyte Ranch, the Lower Ranch, and to Stanton Pass. About one km south of this pass turn east, and drive a steep road to the pass between Cass Creek Peak and Mt. Hillers. The last 2 kms of this road are rough, but any higher clearance car can make it. Or drive to mile post 17, and turn northwest towards Star Spring, but proceed to the south side of Hillers, past the Woodruff Stone Cabin, Squaw Spring, a corral, a stock pond, and to the trailhead on Cass Creek.

Trail or Route Conditions From the trailhead in the grove of big ponderosa pines, walk up the steep canyon on an old wagon road, which at the moment is very much overgrown and is choked with deadfall. But the going isn't so difficult. After a km or less, you'll see the ruins of two very old and rotted log cabins. Then the route turns more into a trail and steepens. You'll pass another old rotted cabin, then the trail zig zags up the slope, and ends at the mine shaft. From the mine, you can route-find up the steep north face to the summit of Hillers.

Elevations The trailhead, 2600 meters; Star Mine, about 3000, and the summit of Hillers, 3268 meters.

Hike Length and Time Needed It's only about one km from the car-park to the old cabins; perhaps about one and a half kms from the car-park to the mine; and the total distance from the trailhead to the summit of Hillers is about 3 kms. This doesn't sound like much, but it's very steep all the way, and will take you perhaps two hours to reach the mountain summit. If you don't spend too much time at the cabins or the mine, you can do this hike, to the mine and the summit, in about half a day round-trip.

Water There's no water at the trailhead, but on a June 1, the author found a small flow in upper Cass Creek in two different places. You should perhaps carry water with you if you're there in a long dry spell or late in the season. The springs could dry up, as they're not listed on any map. Always carry water in your vehicle.

Map USGS or BLM map Hite Crossing(1:100,000), or Mt. Hillers(1:62,500).

Main Attraction Old cabins and mine dating from about the 1890's. Great campsite, and perhaps the easiest and fastest way to reach Hillers summit.

Ideal Time to Hike Do this hike from about late May until late October.

Hiking Boots Any rugged hiking boots.

Author's Experience The author did this hike to the mine and summit in about half a day, but from the Hoskinini Freight Road. As it turned out, he could have taken his VW Rabbit to the trailhead.

84   On the trail to the Star Mine on Mt. Hillers. Crumbling cabin from perhaps the turn of the century.

MAP 34, STAR MINE TRAIL

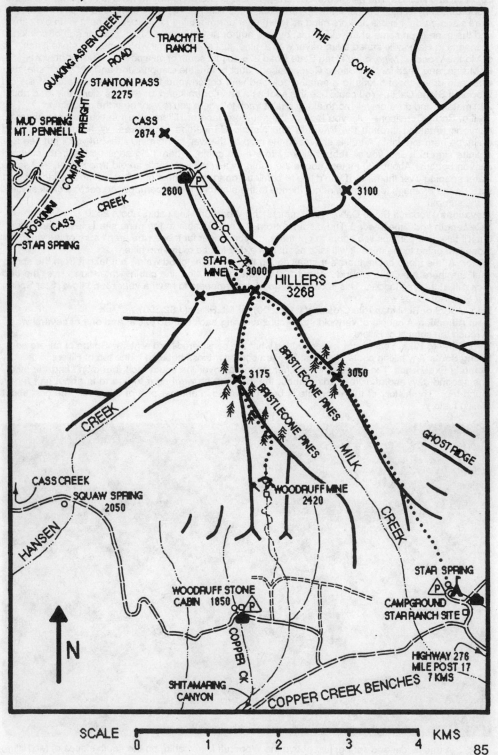

QUAKING ASPEN CREEK

TRACHYTE RANCH

THE COVE

ROAD

STANTON PASS 2275

MUD SPRING
MT. PENNELL

CASS 2874

COMPANY FREIGHT

HOSKINN

CASS CREEK

STAR SPRING

2600

P

3100

STAR MINE

3000

HILLERS 3268

CREEK

3175

BRISTLECONE PINES

3050

BRISTLECONE PINES

MILK

GHOST RIDGE

CASS CREEK

SQUAW SPRING 2050

HANSEN

WOODRUFF MINE 2420

CREEK

STAR SPRING

P

WOODRUFF STONE CABIN 1850

P

COPPER CK

CAMPGROUND
STAR RANCH SITE

HIGHWAY 276
MILE POST 17
7 KMS

SHITAMARING CANYON

COPPER CREEK BENCHES

N

SCALE

0   1   2   3   4   KMS

85

Woodruff Mine Trail

Location and Access The hike featured here is an old and eroded trail to what is supposedly the old Woodruff Mine, located on the southern ramparts of Mt. Hillers. The word *supposed* is used because there's some doubt in this authors mind as to whether or not a mine really exits. There is an old cabin, and the mine is on some of the old maps, but the author never found a shaft, drift, or adit of any kind. Someone in Hanksville stated there never was a mine, just an old hermit who hoped to strike it rich. To get to the Woodruff *Mine,* drive along State Road 276 to just south of mile post l7. Turn northwest at the BLM sign, and head for Star Spring Campground. Just before the campground and old ranch site, turn west and drive about 5 kms to a small creek bed with cottonwood trees and the remains of the old Woodruff Stone Cabin. You could use this spot as a base or trailhead, or regress along the road about 200 meters, and drive or walk north along a faint track to where you're very near the mountain.

Trail or Route Conditions As you look at the southern face of Hillers, you'll see a number of small canyons breaking through the Wingate and Navajo Sandstone buttresses. Walk into the second drainage from the right. A trail is shown on the map all the way to the mine site, but you'll not see any definite sign of it until you're about half way to the old cabin. Then it zig zags up the talus covered canyon bottom. About 100 meters above the cabin, is a small water fall, an old tree ladder, and some water seeping over the falls. If you'd like to continue on to the summit of Hillers, climb this ladder, and walk up the drainage to the main ridge, thence to the summit. This is perhaps the second easiest route to the summit.

Elevations Woodruff Stone Cabin, 1850 meters; the Woodruff Mine cabin, about 2420.

Hike Length and Time Needed The distance from the stone cabin to the mine site is less than 2 kms, but it'll take you perhaps two hours to get there, maybe longer for those who aren't sure of the way. For those just going to the mine, it will take about half a day for the round-trip hike.

Water At the stone cabin there's a small spring that produces good water, but take it from the spring itself, as there are cattle around. About 100 meters above the mine cabin, water flows over the bed rock cliff at the tree ladder. This is definitely good, and appears to have a year-round flow. Star Spring is a good source as well.

Map USGS or BLM map Hite Crossing(1:100,000), or Mt. Hillers(1:62,500).

Main Attraction A couple of very old stone cabins dating back to the 1890's, and one of several ways to reach the summit of Hillers.

Ideal Time to Hike Year-round, except during what are considered hard winters. Spring or fall are best.

Hiking Boots Any hiking boots or shoes. Rugged boots for those heading to the top of Hillers.

Author's Experience The first day the author looked all over the south face, but didn't find the mine. The second day, and after re-reading about the location, he went right to it, and in about half a day, round-trip. The history of this mine site is better covered in another part of this book, the part about mining history.

86   A tree ladder and spring, just above the Woodruff Mine cabin, on the south slopes of Mt. Hillers.

MAP 35, WOODRUFF MINE TRAIL

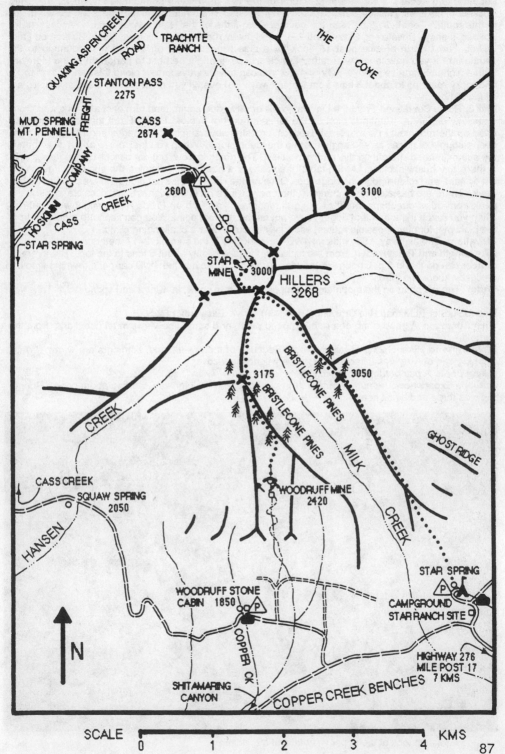

QUAKING ASPEN CREEK

TRACHYTE RANCH

THE COVE

STANTON PASS 2275

FREIGHT ROAD

MUD SPRING MT. PENNELL

CASS 2874 ✕

HOSKINN COMPANY

CASS CREEK

✕ 3100

2600 P

STAR SPRING

STAR MINE 3000

✕

HILLERS 3268

BRISTLECONE PINES

✕ 3050

✕ 3175

BRISTLECONE PINES

CREEK

MILK

GHOST RIDGE

CASS CREEK

SQUAW SPRING 2050

WOODRUFF MINE 2420

CREEK

HANSEN

STAR SPRING

P

CAMPGROUND STAR RANCH SITE

WOODRUFF STONE CABIN 1850

P

COPPER CK

SHITAMARING CANYON

COPPER CREEK BENCHES

HIGHWAY 276 MILE POST 17 7 KMS

N

Mt. Holmes

Location and Access Featured here is one of the two mountains sometimes known as the Little Rockies. This is Mt. Holmes, which rises to 2417 meters. The other half of the duo is Mt. Ellsworth, just to the south. Together, they form the southern two-fifths of the Henry Mountains. Access to Mt. Holmes is easy. Drive along State Road 276, the highway running from Highway 95 to Bullfrog on Lake Powell. Just north of mile post 16, look for a side road running off toward the mountain to the southeast. If you have a car with rather low clearance, it might be best to park right at the highway. With a higher clearance car or a HCV or 4WD, you can drive a ways further along this sandy, then rough and rocky road, up to about 3 kms from the highway. But even if you must park at the highway, it's not a long climb.

Trail or Route Conditions From the highway, walk or drive due south, then turn east at a fork, and cross a shallow drainage. Continue east on the roughest part of this old track. From the end of the road, head up the mountain in a southeast direction, crossing several minor drainages enroute. You'll pass over a couple of ridges as you angle east up the steep slope. When you feel you're about due north of the summit, head straight up this northern valley. The going is slow, but not difficult or dangerous. Nor is there any bushwhacking. At the top of the valley is a headwall, indicating the summit. Veer to the left or east, and route-find to the ridge top. Once on the ridge, walk west along the crest to the highest peak. There are basically three summits; the one you'll be on is the highest. It's possible to climb this peak from other directions, but it's a rugged mountain. A climb up Freds Ridge might work out, but when you reach the top of that ridge, you're not on the highest point. You can scan the mountain from the highway, for other possible routes, especially if you're after a challenging climb.

Elevations The highway, 1550 meters; 4WD car-park, 1775; the summit, 2417 meters.

Hike Length and Time Needed From the highway, the hike is only about 5 kms to the top. The average climber can do this in 5 or 6 hours, round-trip. If you can make it to the 4WD car-park, then the time can be cut by about one third.

Water There's none on the mountain, except perhaps from snow, in winter and spring only. Take your own water.

Map USGS or BLM map Hite Crossing(1:100,000), or Mt. Ellsworth(1:62,500).

Main Attraction A good climb of a rather rugged peak, and some fine views in all directions from the summit.

Ideal Time to Hike Spring or fall are best. Because of the low altitude, summers are warm. Winter climbing can be very easy, because of the very light snow cover.

Hiking Boots A pair of rugged climbing boots.

Author's Experience The author ran up this mountain from the highway, starting about noon. Round-trip was three and a half hours.

A telefoto look at the upper west face of Mt. Holmes.

MAP 36, MT. HOLMES

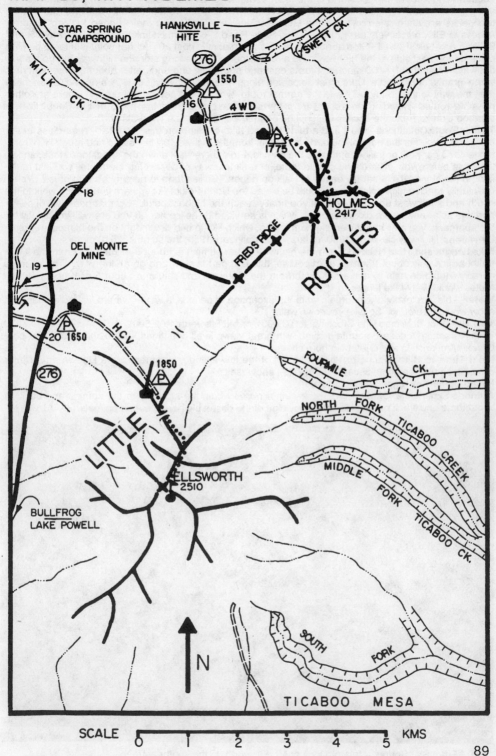

STAR SPRING
CAMPGROUND

HANKSVILLE
HITE

SWETT CK.

15

276

1550

MILK CK.

17

16

4 WD

1775

18

HOLMES
2417

ROCKIES

DEL MONTE
MINE

FREDS RIDGE

19

20 1850

HCV

FOURMILE CK.

276

1850

NORTH FORK TICABOO CREEK

MIDDLE FORK TICABOO CK.

LITTLE

ELLSWORTH
2510

BULLFROG
LAKE POWELL

SOUTH FORK

N

TICABOO MESA

SCALE 0 1 2 3 4 5 KMS

Mt. Ellsworth

Location and Access Mt. Ellsworth is the most southerly of all the peaks in the Henry Mountains. It, along with Mt. Holmes, lies to the east of State Road 276, and just west of Lake Powell and Hite. These two peaks are often referred to as the Little Rockies, a reflection on their rugged looking features. Access to Ellsworth is very easy. Drive along State Road 276, the main link between Highway 95, and Bullfrog and Lake Powell. Stop about 200 meters north of mile post 20. At that point is a large parking place on the east side of the highway, and a road running north along side the highway but up a steep dugway. After about a 100 meters, it turns east and southeast and ends after about 2 kms, right next to the granite of Ellsworth. Cars must be parked along side the highway, but HCV's or 4WD's can make it all the way to the granite. This is the normal route, which most people will prefer. There are other possible routes, including an ascent from the southeast, and from the head of the South Fork of Ticaboo Creek. Read the access description on map 25, if that route interests you.

Trail or Route Conditions You'll find a fairly rugged hike or climb on this mountain, regardless of the route you take. For the normal route, drive or walk from the highway up this steep and rough HCV road to the 4WD car-park or trailhead, next to the granite. From there walk down the sandstone slope, and up the ridge before you. There's no simple route, or a simple way of describing the route. You just route-find up the slope. It's generally easier to walk up ridges. Gullies tend to be choked with brush. You'll eventually reach a high point, which could be called the North Peak. From there you'll ridge-walk to the south and southwest up and down 'till you finally reach the highest point. On that peak, you'll see a portable solar-powered radio transmitter, which is serviced by helicopter. If you are walking quietly on the approach, you may see desert big horn sheep, which like to bed down right on the highest peaks.

Elevations Highway car-park, 1650 meters; 4WD trailhead, 1850; the summit, 2510 meters.

Hike Length and Time Needed From the highway to the summit is about 5 or 6 kms. From the 4WD trailhead it's only about 2 kms, but of course, this last part is slow and go all the way. The average person should be able to make the climb(from the highway) and return in about 5 or 6 hours. Other routes would likely take longer.

Water This is a totally dry mountain, with the exception of periods in winter, where limited amounts of snow would be around. So take your own water.

Map USGS or BLM map Hite Crossing(1:100,000), or Mt. Ellsworth(1:62,500).

Main Attraction A desert mountain climb with great views in all directions, including towards Ticaboo Creek. A chance to see desert big horn sheep.

Ideal Time to Hike Spring or fall. Because of the low altitude, summers are a little warm. Winter climbing should be easy, because of the light snowpack.

Hiking Boots Any rugged hiking boots.

Author's Experience On a June 21, the author hurried from the highway to the summit and back, in about three and a half hours. He saw many sign of the desert big horns, but no animals.

90   From Star Spring, a telefoto look at Mt. Ellsworth, to the southeast.

MAP 37, MT. ELLSWORTH

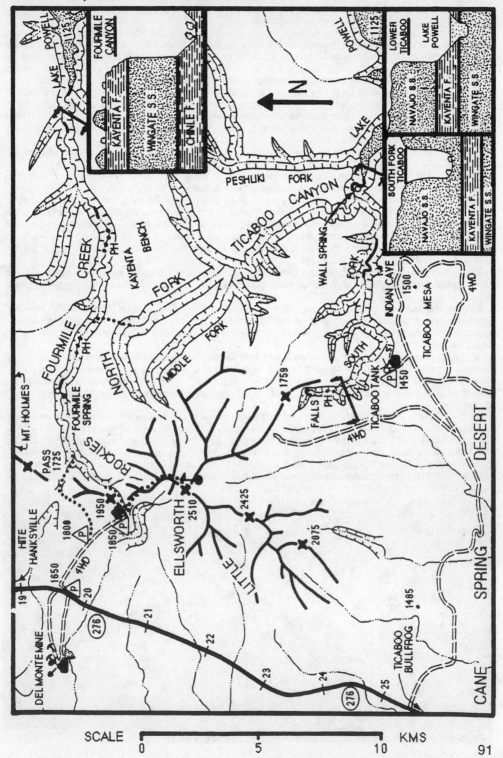

SCALE

0   5   10   KMS

History of the Henry Mountains Region

Archeological Studies—Native Americans

Little or nothing was done in the way of archeological research in the Henry Mountains region until rather late in our own history. Interest in the area south of Hanksville was first aroused after the geological mapping expeditions of Charles B. Hunt in the 1930's. Hunt was studying the geology of the area along Bull Creek, west of the Fairview Ranch, when he noted some archeological remains in the gravels of the creek bed. This revelation prompted further studies, starting about 30 years later.

An exploratory expedition by Julian Steward in 1932 for the U. of Utah, was the first time a trained archeologist had a look at the area. He took a wagon from the eastern slopes of the Henry Mountains, down North Wash to the Colorado, then launched a boat and sailed down to Lee's Ferry. It was he who first suggested that the Henry Mountains were on the northern periphery of the Mesa Verde and Kayenta Anasazi Cultures to the south.

Alice P. Hunt, wife of Charles B., undertook field studies in 1966 along Bull Creek, west of the Fairview Ranch. The Hunt survey recorded 221 archeological sites, but the study was never published.

In 1976, Claudia Berry of the U. of Utah coordinated a study with Jesse D. Jennings, of the sites previously studied by the Hunt survey. A second project followed in 1977, to finish the data.

Here are some of the results of the studies made along Bull Creek. By using the radio carbon dating procedure, it was found there has been continuous habitation in the area for the last 8000 years(from about 6000 BC). In the beginning, the culture which we now call the Archaic Culture, was that of a hunter-gathering type. It later progressed to the stage we call the Fremont Culture. The Fremonts adopted the use of corn, from the Anasazi to the south, but they still continued to use the hunter-gathering system to supplement the diet.

As weather patterns changed, and the climate became drier, the Fremonts were forced back into the hunter-gathering life style. That was their state of existence when the early European explorers found them.

Besides the use of corn, the Fremont Indians incorporated into their culture the use of the bow and arrow, ceramics or pottery, and architecture, borrowed from the south and the Mesa Verde and Kayenta Anasazi cultures. The Fremont Culture lasted for about 650 years, from about 750 A.D. to about 1400 A.D.

The archeologists found this evidence along Bull Creek. The Fremonts had and used circular pit dwellings, rectangular surface structures, and clay-rimmed or flagstone paved fire pits. They used pottery, strikingly similar to the Kayenta Anasazi to the south. They always made homes near the source of water, in this case Bull Creek. Most of the dwellings were found to be of the single family farmer type.

For the modern day hiker or traveler, there isn't much to see in this region in the way of cliff dwellings, petroglyphs or pictographs. It seems most of the really interesting archeology sites are now lying below the waters of Lake Powell. However, there are some pretty good petroglyphs(writings pecked into the rock surface) and pictographs(figures painted onto the surface of the rock) in the middle and lower portions of Poison Spring Canyon and at or near the mouth of Robber Roost Canyon. There are only a few other widely scattered sites throughout the region. See the hiking section in this book for the locations of these sites in the two mentioned canyons.

Petroglyphs, as seen in the middle parts of Poison Spring Canyon.

Poison Spring Canyon Petroglyphs, showing desert big horn sheep.

Small alcove and minor Fremont Indian ruins, in the middle part of No Mans Canyon.

Bone and flint chips in the Fremont Indian ruins in No Mans Canyon.

Cowboy Cave

The following information comes from the University of Utah Anthropological Papers, #104, 1980.

Cowboy Caves, officially designated Cowboy Cave and Walters Cave, were brought to the attention of the U. of Utah Archeological Survey in the spring of 1973 by Edward McTaggart of the Price, Utah, BLM office. Inspection of the site was followed by a test cut. The site proved to contain a rather thick deposit of cultural debris. Moreover, the test cut revealed that the cultural deposit sealed a thick stratum of "chopped" vegetation identifiable as herbivore dung. There was dung from bison, mammoth or elephant, deer, elk, big horn sheep, ground sloth, an extinct horse, and camel.

The importance of a site where association of man with extinct megafauna led to its selection as the object of study for the annual field school for training in archeological field procedures and techniques of the University of Utah Dept. of Anthropology. The 1975 summer session was held there. The school was directed by Jesse D. Jennings. Most of the work was done on Cowboy Cave, leaving Walters Cave to be studied later. More than half the dung remains in Cowboy Cave, making later studies possible.

Excavation was conducted under permit by the BLM. The sites have been nominated for the National Register of Historic Places.

Cowboy Cave is located in a short tributary canyon of Spur Fork, which is a part of the Horseshoe Canyon system. The location is northwest of the Maze Ranger Station. See the route description to Cowboy Cave in the hiking section of this book.

The two caves face southeast, allowing the winter sun to penetrate. They lie in the bottom-most layers of the Navajo Sandstone, just where the Kayenta Formation comes into contact. Just in front of the cave site is a minor seep, which presumably has some kind of moisture in it the year-round. The water comes from the contact zone of the Navajo and Kayenta. Just down stream are several large potholes which usually contain water. The setting seems dry today, but a few thousand years ago, it was much wetter.

The altitude is about 1750 meters. The biggest of the two caves is Cowboy, measuring 12 x 33 meters. Walters Cave is smaller, about 11 x 15 meters. The height of the entrance of each cave is about 5 meters.

The stratigraphy of the site seemed bewilderingly complex when the first exploratory trench was sunk alongside the west wall at the front. After an initial period when the situation defied explanation, understanding finally dawned. What became very clear was that the cave's history divided itself into five episodes, periods, layers or units. Each unit consists of a sterile sand layer, which is beneath a second layer of prehistoric data of one kind or another.

The material found in Unit I has already been mentioned, the dung from bison, mammoth, sloth, camel, etc,. Layer or Unit I is at the bottom and is the oldest; while Unit V is at the top and is the youngest. See the idealized cross section of Cowboy Cave to see the different Units and carbon dating, listed in years "Before Present". The oldest layer of Unit I is about 13,000 years old. Another way of saying it, is that it dates back to about 11,000 BC.

All the layers of Units II through V, have human cultural deposits. Unit II had flecks of charcoal and scattered artifacts. Just above that was a layer of leaves from the gambel oak. This dated 8900 B.P. Above the leaves, and still in Unit II, lumps of charcoal and a few fire zones were found.

Unit III consisted of the debris generated by a long-term occupancy of the cave. Large extensive hearth surfaces were distributed between the ashy debris and the walls. The occupancy of Unit III lasted about 800 to 900 years. Important finds in this layer were the clay figurines, dating back to about 6700 and 6400 years B.P., or from about 4700 to 4400 years B.C.

Between Units III and IV, was a very thick layer of sand, indicating a long period when nobody occupied the cave. The layer between Units accumulates because of wind blowing it in, and from the sand slowly peeling off the roof.

Unit IV had artifacts from wall to wall, with the usual charcoal and fire debris. In this layer were found split stick figurines, one of the most important finds in the cave. In all, 22 of these figurines were found, almost all of which were in Unit IV. Also found in Unit IV was one animal skin bag, dating back to about 3300 years B.P., or from about 1300 BC.

Unit V has all or many of the artifacts seen in the III and IV, but generally in greater numbers. One of the best finds in this layer was a leather sack filled with shelled corn. Carbon dating set the age as about 2000 years B.P., or from about the time of Christ.

Inside Cowboy Cave are some cowboy glyphs, one of which is that of Lorin Wilson, dating from 1893. Presumably because of this inscription, the cave got it's name.

COWBOY CAVE--IDEALIZED CROSS SECTION

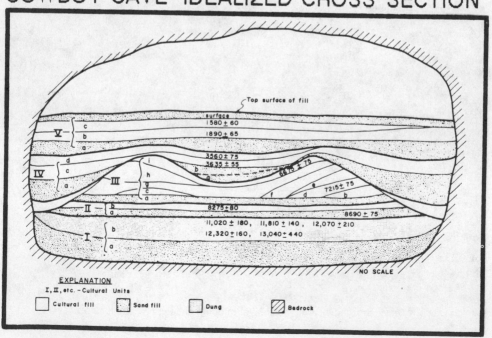

Walters Cave on the left, Cowboy Cave to the right.

Inside Cowboy Cave, showing the one meter layer of dung, dating back about 13,000 years.

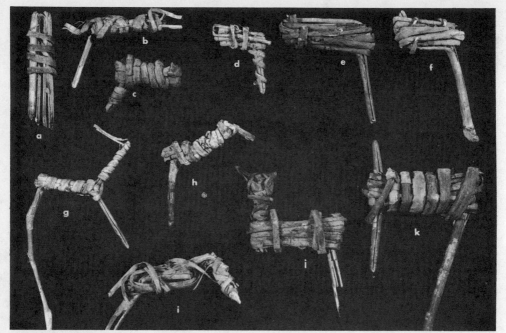

Split stick figurines found in Cowboy Cave.

Settlements in the Fremont River Valley

In the early to mid 1880's, Mormon settlers under the guidance of the LDS church, began making settlements along the lower Fremont River. The settlers for the most part came from earlier founded communities in the San Pete and Sevier Valleys to the north. In 1882 and 1883, the foundations of Caineville, Blue Valley(later known as Giles), and Graves Valley(later known as Hanksville) were laid. Here's a short history of each, in addition to four other small communities, Notom, Aldrich, Mesa and Clifton.

Notom

This small settlement was known at various times as Pleasant Valley, Notom, and also as Pleasant Dale. It's located on Pleasant Creek about 7 or 8 kms upstream or southwest of where the creek empties into the Fremont River.

The first settler to what was then known as Pleasant Dale, was Jorgen C. Smith. He arrived early in 1886. He was of German descent, but migrated from Denmark. He was an influential man who was well educated. He spoke 5 languages, and had attended medical school for a time before arriving in America.

Jorgen C. Smith was one of the very first men to have settled at Richfield in the Sevier Valley. Because he knew something about drugs, he opened a drug store there. When he moved to Pleasant Dale, he took his supply of drugs with him. Because of the isolation of the region, and because of his medical background, he assumed the role of doctor, and was called on many times.

Since this community began about 4 years after the beginning of Caineville, it soon had a post office. Jorgen C. Smith was the first postmaster, and it was he who first suggested the name, Notom, which was first applied to the post office.

Soon after settlement, an LDS branch was organized, with Jorgen Jorgensen as the leader. In 1888, Jorgen C. Smith was made the presiding elder. Not long after that, the branch was discontinued, as many people who had lived at Pleasant Creek moved down stream to Aldrich.

Since most people were attending church and school in Aldrich after about 1890, and since several families had moved there, Notom slowly faded, and by about 1900, only one ranch was left occupied.

Today little or nothing remains of the original settlement, which is now called Notom on all maps. One of the earliest ranches was settled by Enoch Larsen, then was passed on to Will Bowns, Henry Robison and now to the Durfey family.

SETTLEMENTS—FREMONT RIVER VALLEY

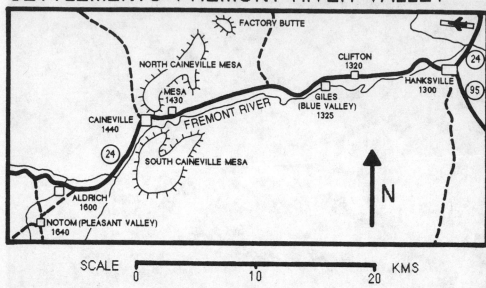

FACTORY BUTTE

NORTH CAINEVILLE MESA

CLIFTON
1320

HANKSVILLE
1300

MESA
1430

FREMONT RIVER

GILES
(BLUE VALLEY)
1325

CAINEVILLE
1440

24

95

SOUTH CAINEVILLE MESA

24

N

ALDRICH
1600

NOTOM (PLEASANT VALLEY)
1640

SCALE 0 10 20 KMS

NOTOM AND ALDRICH

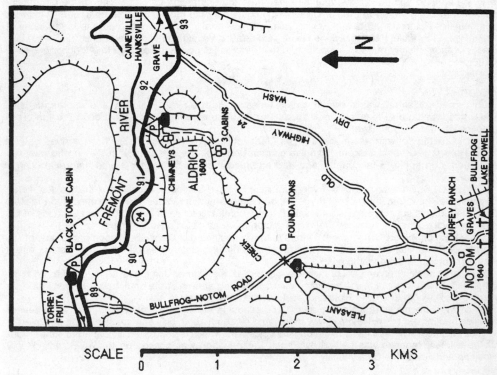

CAINEVILLE
HANKSVILLE

GRAVE

93

92

N

FREMONT RIVER

91

3 CABINS

24

DRY

WASH

HIGHWAY

CHIMNEYS

ALDRICH
1600

24

OLD

DURFEY RANCH

BULLFROG
LAKE POWELL

BLACK STONE CABIN

90

FOUNDATIONS

CREEK

BULLFROG—NOTOM ROAD

89

TORREY
FRUITA

PLEASANT

NOTOM
1640

GRAVES

SCALE 0 1 2 3 KMS

CAINEVILLE AND THE BEHUNIN CABIN

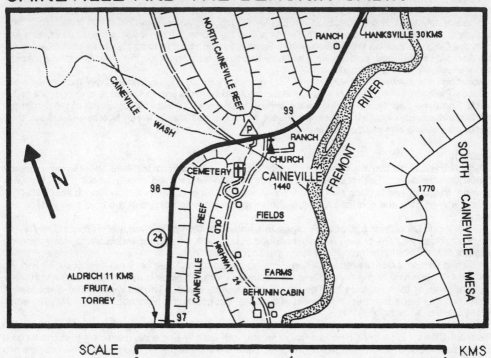

SCALE ████████████████ KMS
0   1   2

Lonely grave, just south of Notom.

To get to Notom, drive along Highway 24. Between mile post 92 and 93, or between m.p. 88 and 89, turn south and drive 7 or 8 kms to the junction of the road, where the Durfey Ranch is located today.

Immediately west of the corrals at the Durfey Ranch, are some remains of old foundations and orchards. Before snooping around, it's best to asked the Durfeys first. If you drive south about a km from the Durfey Ranch on the Bullfrog-Notom Road, you can observe two solo grave sites. One is on the west side of the road, enclosed in a white pickett fence on a small hill; the other is on the east side and immediately next to the road.

About half way between Highway 24 and Notom, and where the good gravel and well maintained road crosses Pleasant Creek, are several foundations of old homes; one to the east, one or more to the west. Someone said there's another grave site somewhere on the little hill just south of the campsite, but this author didn't locate it. Since these sites are about half way between Notom and Aldrich, they could have been a part of either community.

Aldrich

Aldrich was a small farming community located mostly along the Fremont River about where Pleasant Creek joins the river. The first settler was Mosiah Behunin, who moved there in about 1882. Probably no more than a dozen families ever lived there at one time. It became known as Aldrich about 1890. A school was erected and operated for a few short years, accommodating children from both Aldrich and Notom.

In 1892, an LDS branch was officially organized, under the Caineville Ward, with Richard Crowther as the presiding elder. The branch was discontinued about 1900, when people decided to move away on account of the limited farm ground available and flooding problems.

You can visit several sites today. Along Highway 24, about half way between mile posts 89 and 90, and on the north side of the river, is a stone cabin built with the black lava cobblestones, which were brought down by the river from the Thousand Lake Mountain area. The walls still stand, but it has no roof. You can wade the river easily most of the time, but not during high water time in May, or when heavy rains blanket the area.

About half way between mile posts 91 and 92, you can park just off the highway on either side of the Pleasant Creek. Pleasant Creek is small, and you can usually find a narrow place to cross without getting your feet wet. Less than half a km up the creek from the highway, and on the west side, are two cobblestone fireplace chimneys.

If you walk up stream further, about one km from the highway and on the west side of Pleasant Creek, you will find a very well preserved homestead. Located there are three cabins, one of which looks to be

Three old cabins along lower Pleasant Creek, which were part of Aldrich.

Black Stone Cabin, on the north side of the Fremont River, at Aldrich.

From near Caineville. South Caineville Mesa, left, and Henry Mountains beyond.

101

one of the first built in the area. The other two were built later, and look as though they may have been occupied   as late as maybe World War II.   There's also a chicken coop and derrick in an old corral. This is one of the better preserved sites in the entire Fremont River Valley.

Along Highway 24, between mile posts 92 and 93, and right where the old Highway 24 veers southwest toward Notom, is another grave site on the north side of the road. The grave is that of the baby John Richard Crowther, who died December 21, 1891.

Caineville

Caineville was once a thriving community along the lower Fremont River, about half way between Hanksville and the upper valley towns of Torrey, Loa and Bicknell.

Sources differ slightly as to the exact date of the first settlement in Caineville. It was either in the fall of 1881 or 1882, that Elijah Cutler Behunin first arrived. Behunin built a cabin for the winter, and was joined in the spring by his brother Mosiah, and a few more families. In March, a group of Mormon elders arrived and made surveys for locations of canals and ditches in the area of both Caineville and Blue Valley. That party consisted of William Stringham, Yergen Jergensen, Chauncey Cook, David King, Walter E. Hanks and the Behunin brothers.

The settlement grew rapidly. For the first 10 years or so, there was no town as such, as all families lived on their farms. Up until 1892, Caineville was organized into an LDS branch only, it being a part of the Blue Valley Ward(located about half way between Caineville and Hanksville). But in 1892, things changed. Walter Hanks, who at that time was living at the Floral Ranch on the upper part of Pleasant Creek, was called to be the bishop of Caineville. On December 13, 1892, he was made bishop, with George P. Pectol and George B. Rust as his counselors.

Some time after Hanks moved in, George Carrell(could it be Wm. T. Carrell?) sold his farm for the townsite, and it was marked off in lots. A town meeting place was built, but soon after a larger building was erected, for use as both a school and a church. This one still stands. The first store was a branch of the Fremont Mercantile from up valley, and was run by a Joseph Anderson. A post office was opened as early as the late 1880's.

The first tragedy occurred in the community in the winter of 1892-93. Diphtheria struck, and 7 children in all were lost. There were no doctors; people just made do without.

In the first years of settlement the farms in Caineville produced such crops as fruits of various kinds, melons, cane, alfalfa, grains, and most vegetables. Farm products which were sold for cash or barter, were sorghum, dried fruits, corn, melons, and winter apples. Most of these products went to the higher and colder upper valley towns, where most of them couldn't be grown.

A small sorghum mill was constructed, and apparently did rather well for the life of the community. Everyone grew cane, as everyone needed something sweet in their diet.

One interesting scheme they tried, but failed with, was the growing and production of silk. They planted mulberry trees in about 1900, and soon afterwards raised silkworms. It was tried in other southern Utah towns, but failed everywhere it was tried. Some silk was produced, but it was unprofitable.

In the short history of Caineville, there were two devastating floods. The first occurred on September 22, 1897. It raised hell all along the Fremont River, and was the beginning of all later erosional problems and the cause of the deep sided bank cuts now seen along the river today. Before that flood the width of the Fremont was narrow, with grasses and willows everywhere. There were no deep cut banks along the river at all. A number of simple bridges spanned it from Caineville to Hanksville. BLM people in Hanksville say that was the beginning of the down-cutting in Buck, Pasture and Beaver Canyons as well.

In the years following this big flood, there was minor flooding every two or three years, washing out dams. Homes along the river had to be moved back and away from the flood bank, some more than once. But this they lived with.

The second big flood came down the Fremont in 1909. This one washed out all the diversion dams and bridges between Caineville and Hanksville, with the exception of the one at Hanksville. After this second flood, church officials advised the people to move. Most everyone left in 1910, just abandoning their farms and homes. After a few years, other men in the area who owned cattle, bought some of the land for next to nothing, or bought it from the county for the taxes.

To get to Caineville, which today has several scattered ranches, drive along Highway 24, about halfway between Torrey and Hanksville. Just west of mile post 99 is the former town center. Just to the south, and easily seen from the highway, is the church-school building built in the 1890's. It's very near a ranch house, but you can visit the building, as it seems to be a public place.

From the church, drive south on a good county road(which is the old and original Highway 24), for about one and a half kms. Where you see an old and abandoned farm house with corrals and some

102

Behunin Cabin and memorial plaque, just south of Caineville.

Caineville Cemetery, with South Caineville Mesa in the background.

very old sheds and log cabin on the left, stop and park. Just to the west and across the canal, and half hidden by brush and willows, is the original Behunin Cabin. Inside the fenced off area is a monument erected by the Daughters of the Utah Pioneers(#193) in 1953. It states, *"Caineville was settled in 1881 by Elijah Cutler Behunin, followed by Chauncey Cook, George P. Pectol, George S. Rust, Wm. T. Carrell and others. This log cabin was built by Mr. Behunin in the autumn of 1881 and occupied by his family of nine. Mrs. Behunin was the only white woman here the first winter. Nearby cemetery site was given by Mr. Carrell. He was the first citizen to be buried therein. Altogether there are about 35 graves. The only bishop of Caineville was Walter Hanks."*

You can drive to the cemetery, but maybe the easiest way to get there is to park in the gravel pit just off the highway, and walk south across Caineville Wash. It's only about 200 meters or less from the highway. The oldest grave is that of Wm. T. Carrell, Sept. 18, 1819--April 5, 1892. There are several others dating from the 1890's.

There are other old sites around, but there are still several occupied farms in the area, so permission is needed before any exploring can be done.

Mesa or Elephant

Little is known of this very small community, probably because it was so near to Caineville, that is was included as part of Caineville by every historian who has written on the subject. Only Charles B. Hunts has made a distinction.

In 1887 O. N. Dalton and James Huntsman, later joined by J. W. Dalton, founded the village of Mesa, also known as Elephant, about 5 kms east of Caineville, and in a few years 10 families were living there.

But they didn't stay long, for the great flood of 1897, did more damage to Mesa than to other communities in the valley. Mesa was practically abandoned by 1898. The author hasn't seen, but there are undoubtedly some kind of remains of Mesa, in the area just north of the large cove in the South Caineville Mesa, and along the Fremont River.

Giles or Blue Valley

Another ghost town along the Fremont River was first known as Blue Valley, then Giles. It was located about half way between Caineville to the west, and Hanksville to the east. It was first settled in the spring of 1883, about the same time as was Hanksville and Caineville. The name Blue Valley was given because of the blue-grey colored clays of the nearby hills. These clays are actually the Blue Gate Member of the Mancos Shale Formation. It's the same formation as in the Upper and Lower Blue Hills.

Old church-school in Caineville still standing, after nearly 100 years.

Hyrum Burgess was one of the very first men to enter and help settle the valley. Other names of settlers in the first years were Giles, Meyhew, Shirts, Wilson, White and Hunt.

Blue Valley was divided in two by the Fremont River; part was to the north, part was to the south. The south side of the river had more room for settlement. Because the river was so narrow at that time, there was one simple bridge connecting the two parts.

Altogether, the area farmed was about 3000 acres, which supported about 200 people in the peak population year of 1900. It must have looked impressive, with canals and ditches, and alfalfa, corn and cane fields. They also grew fruits, vegetables, melons and artichokes. In the fall of the year, they would make barrels of sauerkraut out of cabbage, for use throughout the winter months.

They had a blacksmith by the name of William Shirts. And N. J. Nielson was a stone mason and adobe expert, who helped to build most of the homes in town and the church-school. You'll see his work in the ruins. The town helped build and Henry Lords ran the first sawmill in Sawmill Basin on the north slope of Mt. Ellen in the Henry Mountains. There was never really a store of any kind in town, but on occasion people did sell some goods out of their homes on a temporary basis. They did have a post office for a few short years.

As in all Mormon communities, the church was the social club and the government. At first, the community(which was 100% Mormon) was organized as a branch of a ward in the upper valley. In 1885, a full sized ward was formed, which also included Graves Valley(later known as Hanksville) and Caineville. The first bishop was Henry Giles, the man who had been acting as branch presiding elder. He died on November 11, 1892. His grave is in the Giles cemetery. In 1895, the name of the community was officially changed to Giles, after it's leading citizen.

The same fate struck Giles as happened to Caineville, and to a lesser extent Hanksville. On September 22, 1897, a huge flood came down the Fremont River, washing out diversion dams and the bridge spanning the river. But the town bounced back and did fine until the second big flood. That came in the fall of 1909. This one again washed out diversion dams and after that it appeared impracticable if not impossible to repair the damage. They simply couldn't get water to the fields. So they gave up. The ward was officially disorganized in April, 1910, and the members counciled to leave. Some went to the Uinta Basin, while others went to Hanksville.

In 1913, money was invested by several families to remake the canals and diversion dams, but without success. A few years later one man attempted farming by pumping water out of the river, but that proved too costly. Someone also drilled a well, for irrigation purposes, but that failed. By 1919 the town was totally deserted.

Giles today is an interesting place to visit. Right at mile post 109, is a stone house beside the road. It

Typical scene along the Fremont River near what was formerly Mesa or Elephant.

is obviously well constructed, and is known as "the road house." It was originally the Abbot Cabin, and was a way station for travelers. Just east of mile post 112, on the south side of the road in a grove of cottonwood trees, is another well built stone home(this home could easily be part of the community of Clifton). On the north side of the river, there are a number of other ruins, mostly just foundations, and remains of corrals.

On the south side of the river are more ruins, mostly foundations. Most of these are found northeast of the tip of Steamboat Point(locally it's called Battleship Rock). To get there, you can park about anywhere on the highway, but the author stopped just west of mile post 109, and waded the river from there. Most of the foundations you'll see are well built, and made of stone. Remember, the town was supported by a stone or adobe mason. You'll also find lots of corrals, piles of manure, and broken bottles. By searching around, you may find a lot more than did the author.

One of the more interesting places to visit is the cemetery, also on the south side of the river. The BLM has fenced it off to preserve it. The author counted 16 graves, all in small family plots. The family names are Hunt, Robison, Giles, Bjorneson, Abbot and Pierce. They all date from the end of last century or early in the 1900's.

Clifton or Kitchentown

Another community which has all but been forgotten is Clifton, sometimes known as Kitchentown. About 1889 Clifton was founded by Bert Avery just east of Blue Valley, later known as Giles. According to Charles B. Hunt, by the early 1890's the settlements of Clifton and Giles together had about 20 families.

Clifton was part of the Giles Ward of the LDS church. In April, 1910, as a result of the big flood of 1909, the ward was disorganized, and the families were advised to leave. Many families went to Hanksville, others were relocated to the upper Fremont River Valley communities of Loa, Torrey and Bicknell.

Hunt says Clifton was located just east of Giles. This author doesn't know exactly where that might be, but guesses it's in the area of the stone home near mile post 112 on Highway 24.

Graves Valley or Hanksville

Of all the communities along the lower part of the Fremont River, Hanksville is the only one surviving today. It was originally known as Graves Valley, named after a John Graves, who apparently was a member of one of John W. Powell river expeditions of 1869 or 1872.

According to the history of the region by the Daughters of the Utah Pioneers, the man who first settled

Looking north from the South Caineville Mesa, with the location of the old settlement of Mesa and the Fremont River in the valley below.

GILES OR BLUE VALLEY AND CLIFTON

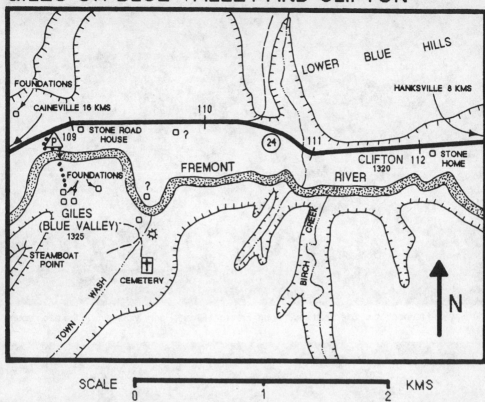

LOWER BLUE HILLS

FOUNDATIONS

CAINEVILLE 16 KMS

HANKSVILLE 8 KMS

110

P 109

STONE ROAD HOUSE

?

24

111

CLIFTON 1320 112

STONE HOME

FREMONT

RIVER

FOUNDATIONS

?

GILES (BLUE VALLEY) 1325

STEAMBOAT POINT

CEMETERY

BIRCH CREEK

TOWN WASH

N

SCALE 0   1   2 KMS

The Road House at Giles, at mile post 109, on Highway 24.

Chimney and foundation at Giles, just south of the Fremont River. Henry Mountains in the background.

Giles Cemetery, with the 16 or so graves, all dating back to the turn of the century.

Graves Valley was Ebenezer Hanks. This man was from Iron County, and was talked into making the new community by A.K. Thurber of the Sevier Valley.

On March 10, 1882, Hanks along with a small group consisting of Charlie Goald, Samuel Goald and family, E. H. McDougall and family, and Joe Sylvester, left Parowan. They arrived in Graves Valley in April, 1882. Settlers who soon followed had names like Brown, Gibbons, Rust, Mecham, Ekker, Turner, Robison, Hunt, Noyes, and others. Many of these names are familiar around Hanksville today.

Ebenezer Hanks was a colorful character and a fine leader. One reason he made the move to this lonely outpost was because he had two wives. If you go to the cemetery today, you'll see his gravestone. Inscribed on it are the names of Hanks and both of his wives.

Hanks was injured in a accident while building a barn, and died later, partly as a result of those injures. That was in 1884, only two years after arriving. In 1895, the community was renamed Hanksville, after its founding leader.

One of the first things to be done after arriving was to build a diversion dam, canals, and ditches, so that water could be used to irrigate fields and grow crops. The first diversion dam was at the same site where a later and better dam was built. A man named Peter Brown led the construction of this diversion dam, which for the most part has remained in place since that first construction. Since it was built on what appears to be a rock outcropping, it was never damaged to the extent as were upstream dams, which were destroyed by the floods of 1897 and 1909.

The first homes or shelters in town were made of logs, but later many homes were made of stone. The men who built these were M. P. Nielson, the man who did most of the work in Blue Valley or Giles, and according to Barbara Ekker, a man named Franz Weber. Weber is credited with building the historic chapel in Hanksville, which still stands today, after nearly 100 years. Apparently he is the fellow who built the stone house at the Star Ranch(locally it's spelled Starr, but the USGS uses "Star" on its maps), on the eastern slopes of Mt. Hillers(located next to the Star Spring Campground). He also built the stone structure at the Granite Ranch.

Somehow and some way, Hanksville became the regional center, although it never grew to more that about 200 residents for many years. Sheepmen and cattle ranchers, in the desert and the mountains, used Hanksville as a supply depot, as well as miners, oil men, and even outlaws.

One of the early settlers to Hanksville was Charley Gibbons. He bought a small store from the Anderson brothers, and set up a business consisting of livery stable, a store and a hotel. Charley Gibbons also bought the ranch on the Cottrell Benches, and later moved it down to its present site, which is the Fairview Ranch. One of the young men he hired out as a ranch hand was Robert LeRoy Parker, of Circleville, Utah. This 18 year old lad later became known as Butch Cassidy. There are many stories of the close relationship between Gibbons and Cassidy. Word has it, Charley and Butch kept in touch, even after Butch went to South America.

Well preserved stone house east of Giles, at a place called Clifton or Kitchentown.

109

Recalling early times, in Hanksville.

The old Hanksville Church, built by Franz Weber, nearly 100 years ago.

For many years Hanksville was a branch of the Blue Valley Ward, then after disorganization of Giles, it came under the ward in Torrey. The first presiding elder of course was Eb Hanks. It wasn't until 1935, that Hanksville was organized into a full ward of the LDS church, with Glen Johnson as the first bishop. This tells something about how small the community really was throughout all those years.

There's very little left of the old Hanksville in the town today. The only real old structure is the nearly 100 year old church, which stands empty and silent. There's a new church and an elementary school(junior and senior high school students are bussed to Bicknell daily), a BLM office(information office as well) and housing complex, the reconstructed Wolverton Mill, two garages, two restaurants, a burger stand, five gas stations(all with convenient foods), a motel, a curio and rock shop, another rock shop, a small medical center, and a tourist information office, which seems to be open only periodically and in the tourist season. In the past, cattle ranching has been the main source of income for many residents, but today it's mostly from the government(BLM) and tourists, who must stop and fill up on fuel on their way to Hite or Bullfrog on Lake Powell.

In recent years, and with the building of Lake Powell and marinas, and the increase of tourism, Hanksville has grown. In 1980, there were 227 registered voters, and over 400 residents.

The other small communities of Hite and Eagle City, are discussed in another part of this book.

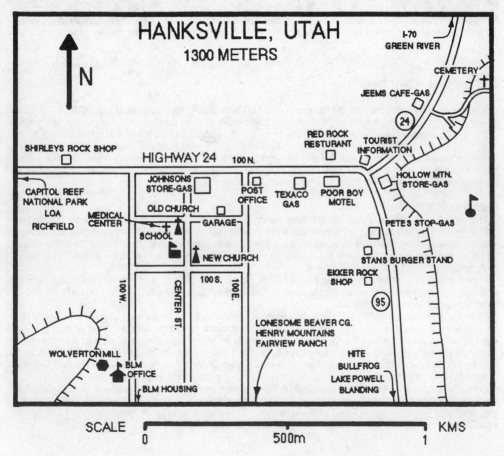

Grave of Ebenezer Hanks, founder of Hanksville. The names of his two wives are also mentioned.

History of Ranches

Scattered throughout the Henry Mountains and Robbers Roost area of southeastern Utah are about 15 very isolated, remote, and lonely outposts of civilization. These are(or were) the ranches of the one of the most desolate and rugged areas in all America. Each has a history and each has a story to tell. Not much is written about some of the men and women who struggled to make a living in the wilderness, but in other cases, the most colorful history and some of the tallest tales every told, ring out from the foundations and ruins of several of the once occupied homesteads. Some of the history is factual and documented, some is merely hearsay and rumor.

Fairview Ranch

The Fairview Ranch was perhaps the first ranch to be settled in the country, and very possibly the one with the longest continuous habitation since it was first established. The original ranch site was located about 3 kms due south and up hill from the present ranch house. Some time later the sloping bench where it was founded were known as the Cottrell Benches. The first cabin at the ranch was at quite a high altitude, around 1800 meters.

The man who first settled there was named R. E. Tomlinson. He had a young wife named Lida Ellen, and three young boys. No exact date has been found when Tomlinson first moved in, but it must have been sometime in the late 1880's.

Pearl Baker in her book, *The Wild Bunch at Robbers Roost,* tells an interesting story about Tomlinson and his wife. Sometime after the family had been at the ranch two or three years, and when they had a herd of colts(about 30 head), he took them to Colorado to sell in the mining areas. He went by way of Green River and Grand Junction. From Grand Junction, he wrote back to Lida Ellen that he was on his way to Montrose, but that was the last anyone ever heard of him. After sometime, and when Lida had decided he had met foul play and would never return, she moved to Hanksville.

One source used by the author, stated that Tomlinson had taken Jack Cottrell with him to Colorado, as a partner. Cottrell had returned alone, and had claimed thieves had overtaken them on the return trip, and that Tomlinson was killed in the gunfight. There were persistent rumors around the country that Cottrell himself had killed Tomlinson, for his wife and the ranch.

RANCHES—HENRY MTNS. & ROBBERS ROOST

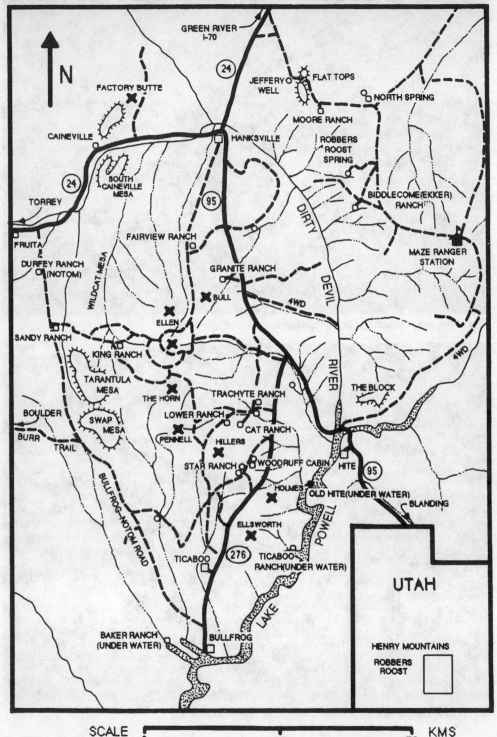

SCALE

0   25   50

KMS

One of the oldest structures at the Fairview Ranch, a chicken coop.

An original stone structure built by Franz Weber, at Granite Ranch.

In the meantime, Jack Cottrell, who was the foreman for J.B. Buhr at the Granite Ranch, had begun to take notice and was courting Lida. As soon as it was settled beyond doubt that Tomlinson had met some kind of foul play, she had him declared legally dead, and she and Cottrell were married.

The third owner of Fairview was Charley Gibbons. No one seems to have a date on his arrival at the ranch, but perhaps it was in the 1890's. Gibbons is the one who moved the ranch down from the Cottrell Benches to the present site, just east of Bull Creek and on the Sawmill Basin Road(this road runs directly from Hanksville to Mt. Ellen). It was Charley Gibbons who caught the wild stallion Wildfire, which was a focal point in one of Zane Grey's western novels. Another book written about the area by Zane Grey was *Robbers Roost*, but it has few if any historic facts about this Henry Mountains Region.

Guy Robison, present owner of the Fairview, states that the original cabin at the upper ranch site, was actually a saloon at Eagle City. It was taken down, and reassembled on the Cottrell Benches and lived in. Later, when Gibbons moved down hill, it was again moved, and at the lower ranch it was used as a chicken coop. In about 1924, it burned down, apparently along with the ranch house. The older of the two homes presently at the Fairview, dates from 1924.

The next owner after Gibbons, seems to have been a Vern Pace. Today Guy Robison and wife live in one house, and their daughter and son-in-law live in the older home.

The easiest way to reach the Fairview, is to drive south out of Hanksville on Highway 95 toward Bullfrog and Hite. Just before mile post 10, turn west and drive about 11 kms. You can also drive south out of Hanksville on 100 E. street. Continue south about 20 kms to the ranch, which is at the junction of the two roads mentioned.

About 2 kms north and down hill from the Fairview is another ranch, called the Grass Ranch. The present owner is Ralph Pace. Little is known of the history of this ranch.

Granite Ranch

A ranch with one of the longest and most colorful histories in the entire region is the Granite Ranch. The ranch was first settled by a J. B. Buhr. According to one source it was in 1889, or in the early 1890's if we believe another writer. Buhr was a tailor from Denver, who suffered from asthma for years. Finally he gave up the city life, for life in the open air, hoping it would help his aliment.

He brought with him a band of horses, but it's not known where he first located. It was either at or near the Roost Spring in the Robbers Roost Country, or at Granite. It seems his main ranch headquarters was at Granite, but with much activity going on in the Roost area.

Buhr's first foreman was a man from the Sevier Valley named Joe Bernard. While working the Roost range with Joe Sylvester, he took time to build troughs at the Roost Spring for the first time. These two men also built a small cabin near the Roost Spring. Sometime in the mid 1890's, Bernard quit, because he was too far away from home. This was shortly after Jack Cottrell had married Lida Ellen Tomlinson. Cottrell became the new foreman. Cottrell worked for Buhr two or three years, part of the time living in the little cabin at Roost Spring.

The little cabin is in between Silvertip and Robbers Roost Spring. Bernard and Joe Sylvester built it and Cottrell moved his family there for a time. Only the chimney of that little cabin stands today.

When Cottrell quit, the third foreman for Buhr was a man named Jack Moore. No one knows for sure, but there seems to have been some bad blood between Cottrell and Moore. Pearl Baker devotes an entire chapter to Jack Moore in her book, *The Wild Bunch at Robbers Roost*.

Moore was originally from Texas, but in the late 1880's made his way to Colorado. From there he came to Utah and the mining camps in the Henry Mountains. He spent his first winter at Eagle City, gambling the time away. He was a cow hand who had been Involved with many of the big cattle drives to such places as Dodge City.

Jack told many stories of his escapades in Texas, one of his favorites went like this; "Tell you, boys, they sure did like me in Texas. A bunch of ranchers followed me clean across the state to try to get me back--and they'd had done it, too, if Minnie(his favorite horse)hadn't been faster than anything they rode!"(Baker)

This story of course helps explain how it really was during the wild days in the west when it was standard practice for cowboys to moonlight on the side and take a few cows for themselves, especially if they were working for a big and rich cattle company. It was mostly during Jack Moore's reign at the Granite while he worked for the 3B outfit(as the ranch was called in those days), that Robbers Roost became a part-time home for Butch Cassidy and other members of the Wild Bunch. In fact he was so hospitable to members of the gang, some people considered him a part of it. For much of the time during which the Wild Bunch and other outlaws used the Robbers Roost as a sanctuary, Jack Moore was foreman for J. B. Buhr at the Granite Ranch.

Moore divided his time between the main ranch which was headquartered at Granite at the foot of Bull Mountain, and the small Cottrell Cabin at the Roost Spring. But he didn't like the Cottrell Cabin area because there wasn't much horse feed around. So, according to Pearl Baker, he "moved camp to

Dugout in Buhr Pass, at the head of the Roost Draw." At that place, he built a shelter; half dugout, half shed. It's been said this dugout was under the same tree where the young Bob Parker(Butch Cassidy) once camped. Pearl Biddlecome Baker says the Dugout is located just to the east of the Roost Spring, and north of a corral known as the Ekker Corral. This author found some minor ruins in that area, which may or may not be those of the Dugout.

For several years a young Mormon boy by the name of Neil "Charlie" Hanks(son of Ebenezer Hanks) worked for Moore. It's said that Hanks was the only paid hand Moore ever hired. The rest of his help came from members of the Wild Bunch, who were always hanging around between bank jobs or train holdups. Moore would house and feed them, and the outlaws would help out with the chores, until they were ready to move on.

Many years later Neil Hanks told stories about times at the Dugout and other places. It seems he had trouble determining the difference between the good guys and the bad. Moore was always getting Hanks out of bed in the night to cook for a new bunch of boys. Once Hanks asked Jack about the difference between the two groups, the good and the bad, and Moore told him, "Well, I'll tell you, Kid, outlaws are just fellows, some of them good and some of them no-good. But there's one thing about them, they are usually better looking than in-laws, and a hell of a sight easier to live with"(Baker).

After Jack Moore had settled into his new job, he sent for his wife Nora, who had been living in Colorado. She spent all her time at Granite. Because of her educated background, she nursed Buhr whose asthma wasn't getting any better. She was a great help around the ranch, adding a woman's touch to the place.

An incident happened involving Jack Moore, which helped to bring about the end of the 3B outfit and Buhr's time at the Granite. Jack and another cowboy were rounding up cattle one day on the northern part of the range on the San Rafael Desert. They came upon an unbranded calf following a cow with the Hebe Wilson brand. It was common practice for less-than-honest cowpokes to separate these cattle and put their own brand on the calves. Moore was about half way through this operation, when Ben Gibbons and Jack Cottrell rode up. When Cottrell saw this, he couldn't have be happier. They made tracks for Hanksville, swore out a complaint, and had Moore arrested.

Buhr and Pete Jensen put up $500 each for Moore's bail bond. Jack was to stand trial in Castle Dale, but never did. Instead Jack met Jensen in the San Rafael and returned his $500, then made his way back to the Granite, skirting Hanksville on the way. But some boys saw him and ran for Sheriff Stoddard. The sheriff and Jack Cottrell headed south. At Granite, Moore and another hand named Aikens, were rounding up horses, presumably to take out of the country. That's when Stoddard and Cottrell rode up.

There were several shots fired, but no one shot to kill. Finally Moore got away by circling around and going down a draw. He headed for the Roost, with the two-man posse in hot pursuit. Moore made it to Beaver Box Canyon just ahead of the Sheriff, but in the chase, had lost his gun, which had been under his belt. At the Dirty Devil River, he hid behind rocks, and used a stick to fake a gun. The Sheriff was unaware of Moore's firearm predicament. When night came, Moore got away.

Moore found his way back to the Roost, where with the help of Silver Tip, Blue John and Indian Ed Newcomb, rounded up what little remained of the 3B outfit, and headed for Green River. They sold the cattle quickly, and made tracks for Wyoming, and new territory.

Near Baggs, Wyoming, the four helped themselves to a herd of cattle belonging to a man named Spicer. The was the biggest mistake Jack Moore ever made, and his last. Spicer took after them, and when he drew too close, Moore tried to scare him off. But in the process, he exposed himself on a hill, and according to Neil Hanks' story over thirty years later, Spicer "shot from a mile away, and drilled Jack dead center with a 30-30 slug."

"The boys saw that Jack was hit, and Ed and Silver Tip went on with the horses, while Blue John went back to Jack. He took him to Mid Nichol's saloon, and Mid found them a place to stay. Jack lingered along a few days, but he was shot right through the middle, and couldn't make it. Mid paid his funeral expenses, sent a bill to Mrs. Jack Moore at Hanksville, and she sent him a check for it"(Baker).

Meanwhile back at the ranch, Buhr and Mrs. Moore, who knew each other pretty well by that time, decided to try it together. They hired a crew to round up the remaining herd, and left the country. This was in the year 1899. Later, rumors came back saying they had both been killed at a railway crossing in Texas.

Later that winter, with the gunfight at Silvertip Spring between Sheriff Tyler's posse of Moab and Indian Ed, Blue John and Silver Tip, the era of the Wild Bunch at Robbers Roost came to an end.

After J.B. Buhr left the country, Charley Gibbons took over the Granite. Sometime after that, Elze Marshall ran it, then various members of the Ekker family owned it. Still later, Bill Adams bought it, and it's still in his family. Today, one of his adopted sons, John Casner lives there, while working at the BLM office in Hanksville.

Today, little is left of the original Granite homestead. There is one rock cellar up against the hillside, which was built by Franz Weber(the stone mason who built the old church in Hanksville and the abandoned ranch house at Star Spring). To get there, drive south out of Hanksville on Highway 95. Very near mile posts 13 or 15, turn west and drive about 7 kms to the ranch. There's a gate at the entrence to this private land, so if you'd like to see the place, contact John Casner at the BLM office, for a possible appointment.

Trachyte Ranch

In all the books and literature the author has found on the history of this region, there is surprisingly little said about the Trachyte Ranch. However, there is a lot said about the area surrounding the ranch site.

Cass Hite was on the Colorado River in 1883, and the normal route from there to Hanksville and the Henry Mountains was by way of Trachyte Creek. In the Glen Canyon Gold Rush during the 1880's, there was a pony express mail route from Hanksville to Trachyte, then down Trachyte Creek to Hite. That pony express contract was owned by J. G. Ekker of Hanksville. His sons, Cornelius, John and Andrew, did the riding from Green River to Hite and to the gold diggings in the Henry Mountains. It's been stated it took two full days of riding by horseback from Hanksville to Hite, with an overnight stop at Trachyte. So there must have been some kind of outpost or ranch at Trachyte in the late 1880's or at least by the early 1990's The post office was first opened in Hite in 1889.

But according to Charles B. Hunts professional paper on the *Geology and Geography of the Henry Mountains*, the Trachyte Ranch was first settled by Irvin Robison, about the time uranium was first discovered in the area about 1913. So there seems to be a gap in the history of the Trachyte Ranch. This author has to believe there was something there before 1913. In the year 1929, when E. T. Wolverton was injured on Mt. Pennell while dragging logs off the mountain, the Trachyte was owned by two men, Brinkeroff and Smith.

In Hunts professional paper, he includes a rather good map of the area, as it was in the late 1930's and early 1940's. On that map, he places the old Hoskinini Company Freight Road as by-passing the Trachyte Ranch area. He has it running up North Wash to the South Fork, then south across the upper benches to the Lower Ranch, then south to Stanton Pass. That road was built in the late 1890's. This might indicate there was nothing at Trachyte at that time.

Regardless of when it was first settled, there were two locations for the ranch. The first and original house and ranch were on the Trachyte Bench, just north of the main road into the region. When driving into the area, glance to the north, and you'll see a number of old junk cars surrounding an old log cabin. This is apparently the original ranch house. On that bench are the faded remains of ditches and canals.

The original cabin on the bench, at the old Trachyte Ranch.

The diversion dam along Trachyte Creek, built to take water to the Trachyte Ranch.

The Trachyte Ranch, showing the old cellar, the outhouse and Mt. Hillers in the background.

Sometime later, in the 1930's and 40's, two men apparently co-owned the ranch. They were Anton Bastian and George Wolgamot. It was they who constructed the house and barns at the lower ranch site, just below the upper bench. Also during this same period, a sawmill was built on the upper bench, just above the lower ranch house, and on the lip of the hill. The remains of it can still be seen on the left, just before you descend the dugway off the upper bench. There are still a few old and decayed logs at the site. At the lower ranch are some corrals, an old chicken coop, a cellar, an outhouse, and the foundation of the house. Garth Noyes of the Cat Ranch remembers it was in 1982 or '83 when someone set fire to this old and abandoned house. It burned totally to the ground.

If you drive to the west and down to Trachyte Creek, you'll see several old cars and a building or two in the cottonwoods. These have nothing to do with the Trachyte Ranch. Instead they were part of the uranium mining camps in the area. As you drive across Trachyte Creek, then upon the next bench, you can look down into the creek bed to the north, and see the diversion dam and the beginnings of the canal which took water to the Trachyte Ranch. Presently the land is owned by a Pat Brian.

To get there, drive south out of Hanksville on Highway 95. Then turn south onto State Road 276 at the Bullfrog Junction. Drive south toward Bullfrog about 7 kms to between mile posts 4 and 5, and turn west 'till you see the old junk cars on your right. The road to Trachyte Ranch is good for all cars in about any kind of weather.

Sanford or Cat Ranch

The present day Cat Ranch is located on the northern slopes of Mt. Hillers just to the southwest and up hill from the Trachyte Ranch. This ranch was began back in 1892, by Gene Sanford and another man named Benson. On Hunts old map of the area dating from the 1930's and 40's, it's listed as the Sanford Ranch.

The second owner was apparently Ben Gibbons. It was when the Gibbons were living at the place the ranch got its present name, the Cat Ranch. It seems Mrs. Gibbons liked cats, and she had a bunch. When the family finally gave up on making a living in this wilderness, they left the cats behind when the family moved(the ranch was never totally abandoned, as it was always used by cowboys herding cattle, so someone was there much of the time to keep the cats company). In the summer time, flys would gather by the millions, and the cats multiplied as well, so local cowboys often called the place the Fly and Cat Ranch. Later the "fly" was removed, leaving the ranch with the present name.

At a later date, ownership was passed on to the King family, and was used as both a cattle and sheep ranch. This is the same King family who owned the King Ranch on the west side of the range.

Today, the ranch is owned by a group of individuals(a Mr. Black from San Juan County, a Dr. Lowe from Ogden, and Garth Noyes. The people actually living at the ranch today(1987) are Garth Noyes, his wife Connie, one son and two daughters. Connie is a school teacher at Ticaboo School, while Garth is the Justice of the Peace in Ticaboo.

Presently the Noyes family is trying to expand the cattle herd. They have leased land near Hanksville to grow alfalfa, which they haul up to their home. They grow a nice garden, despite the altitude of about 1825 meters. The house they live in is old, but has been remodeled many times. They have a motor powered generator, but no TV. The place has a number of stock yards, and fruit trees, including pears, peaches, apples and plums. Years ago a ditch was made to divert water from the upper part of Benson Creek, to the Cat Ranch. That small stream is used both for drinking water and for irrigating the garden, pasture, and fruit trees. In all, it's a rather pleasant place to live. Garth has stated to this author that he doesn't mind visits from history buffs.

To get there, drive along State Road 276, the main link between Highway 95 and Bullfrog. Between mile posts 4 and 5, turn west onto a good gravel road. This leads you to, and past, the upper and lower Trachyte Ranch sites, and along Trachyte Creek. Between Farmers Knob and John Hill, is a junction. Take the right fork to reach Mt. Pennell, the Wolverton Mill site and the Lower Ranch; or turn left and drive up hill to the Cat Ranch. There are places with clay, so it can be slick in wet weather, but the road is well used and maintained. The ranch is 9 or 10 kms from the highway. Any car can make it to the ranch, but some may want to remove large stones from the stream bed before crossing Trachyte Creek.

Lower Ranch

Not much is known about the Lower Ranch, which is located due north of Mt. Hillers, and about a km and a half northwest of the Cat Ranch. According to Hunt, it was started by a man named Voight in 1892, at about the same time as the old Sanford(Cat) Ranch was settled, and about the time Eagle City was being abandoned. One person the author talked to thought there was a man named Crockett who later ran the homestead for a time, but that hasn't been confirmed.

The Lower Ranch today is owned by one of the Kings. For many years the King family, which had four boys, have run cattle and sheep in the Henry Mountains area during the winter months, then they'd have a big roundup, and take them over the mountain and desert to the Boulder Mountains,

119

where they grazed for the summer. In the fall another big cattle drive took place with the cattle going back to the Henrys. This is one of the last big cattle drives in the west today.

At the site of the Lower Ranch today, are some rather new and well built corrals, and the foundation of the old and original ranch house. There are also three large locust trees and some old corrals.

To get there, drive along State Road 276, the link between Highway 95 and Bullfrog. Between mile posts 4 and 5, turn west onto a good gravel road. It runs past the Trachyte Ranch, over Trachyte Creek twice(follow the signs and the best road towards Coyote Benches and Quaking Aspen Spring), and about half way from where you cross Trachyte Creek for the second time and the dugway leading to the Coyote Benches, turn to the southwest, where the signs state, "Quaking Aspen Spring". You'll cross the middle part of Straight Creek, then drive about half a km to where you see the corrals on the left. The old homestead site is just up hill from the corral.

Star Ranch

The Star Ranch is the site of the present Star Spring Campground. This very good spring is on the southeast side of Mt. Hillers.

The Star Ranch was settled by Al Star(sometimes you'll see Star spelled with two r's--Starr, but the USGS spells it "Star" on their maps), in the 1880's, but the exact year is unknown. He made his headquarters at the spring for his ranching operations. He raised horses, mules, and cattle, to sell to the miners. Remember, there was a minor gold rush in Glen Canyon of the Colorado during the 1880's, and on the south end of Mt. Ellen from about 1889 to 1892. Star also had a mine high on the northwest slopes of Mt. Hillers, but nothing ever came of that, but a lot of hard work(more information about his mine is found in the hiking section under the Star Mine Trail, and under the history of mining).

Just as Star was getting organized and doing well, the gold played out in both Glen Canyon and in Bromide Basin. He had just hired Franz Weber from Hanksville to build a fine stone house and cellar. The cellar was completed, but the house was not quite finished, when real trouble came. His herds of cattle and horses began to die, both from loco weed and a drought. Star had to abandon everything.

Today you will see the very well constructed ranch house beneath some cottonwood trees just before you arrive at the campground. It's been fenced off now by the BLM to protect the historic site. Just behind the house is the cellar which is in very good condition and very well built. Just below the campground and picnic areas, are other ruins or foundations, but the author doesn't know their history. If you poke around the area, you may find other relics dating from the last century.

A look at the Cat Ranch, with Mt. Pennell in the background.

The Star Spring Campground is one of the nicest campsites around, and a real cool retreat from the heat in summer, when compared to the areas around Bullfrog, Hite and Lake Powell. The BLM has piped water from the spring itself, down to the campground. There are several toilets and about a dozen campsites, nestled in a grove of very large gamble oak trees. Since it's an improved campground, you must pay a small fee for camping. For the "poor" traveler, you can camp for free just down hill from the campground, and next to the road leading to the Woodruff Spring area.

To reach the Star Ranch and campground, drive along State Road 276 which runs on south to Bullfrog. Just south of mile post 17, turn northwest onto a very good gravel road heading directly toward Mt. Hillers. Drive about 7 kms to the old ranch site.

Woodruff Cabin and Ranch Site

Charles B. Hunt doesn't list this ranch on his very good map of the Henry Mountains, which shows the country the way it was in the 1930's and '40's. But there are the tumbled down ruins of several cabins in the area around Woodruff Spring. Surely, these cabins were used mostly by miners who were looking for uranium in the Salt Wash Formation throughout the years, but someone told the author, a man named Woodruff built the first cabin there back in the 1880's or '90's, and must have owned some kind of livestock.

This is the same old hermit who built a stone cabin on upper Copper Creek on the south side of Mt. Hillers, and who built another stone cabin high on the south face of Hillers, where it's said he had a mine(look in the hiking section under Woodruff Mine Trail, for information on how to get to these two locations). Someone also laid a rumor on the author that this old hermit was eventually committed to an institution by a sister.

At Woodruff Spring today, are three old houses or cabins, a couple of junk cars, a fine pasture, three struggling peach trees, some grape vines, and a number of fine campsites. There are also cattle in the area, probably on a year-round basis, so take the water directly from the spring if you're going to be drinking it.

To get there, drive along State Road 276 toward Bullfrog. Just south of mile post 17, turn northwest and head for the Star Ranch and campground. Just after passing the old abandoned Star Ranch house, turn north onto the good road running to the northeast. About 5 kms along this road turn southeast and downhill, and onto a rougher and less used road. The spring and old cabins are in a grove of trees, about one and a half kms from the main access road(see the map, South Henry Mountains Mining Area, for a look at the access route).

The remains of the unfinished Star Ranch house, built by Franz Weber.

121

Ticaboo Ranch

Quoting from Cramptons *U. of Utah Anthropological Paper #72,* "At the point where Ticaboo Creek emerges from a narrow canyon about one and a half kms from the Colorado River, Cass Hite established a home--usually called Ticaboo Ranch--where he lived much of the time that he was in Glen Canyon after 1883. There in an open area of about 3 acres(about 1.2 hectares) alongside Ticaboo Creek where he built a cabin, the chimney of which is still standing(1959, and before Lake Powell reached the area). The foundations of the cabin on the outside measured about 6 by 10 meters and may have consisted of more than one room". He goes on to say there were many other objects of various kinds lying about.

The cabin was near the canyon wall just to the west, and the area was fenced. There was a corral in one place, and nearby a fenced-off vineyard. "A few of the vines, though they had not been irrigated in years, still clung to life. When Julius Stone visited Cass Hite at Ticaboo Ranch, October 23, 1909, his host treated him to grapes and melons fresh off the vine, and was given a sackful of raisins to take along."

Crampton also noted, right next to the corral and vineyard, was a large boulder which had rolled down the slope. It was covered with petroglyphs.

Hite always had good water at the cabin, but just down stream, Ticaboo Creek sank into the sands of the gravel bar. Up stream about a km was a fine stream where it flowed over bed rock and a low waterfall. If you're a boater and in this lower Ticaboo Canyon area, you can walk up stream, and come out at the trail described in the hiking section under Ticaboo Creek--South Fork.

"In 1914 Cass Hite died at his ranch at Ticaboo and is buried there. The grave is marked by a rectangular enclosure composed of boards nailed to four posts. Another grave along side that of Hite, and with a similar enclosure, is reported to be the resting place of one Frank Dehlin".

The water of Lake Powell covered these ruins and historic site sometime in the mid 1960's.

Baker Ranch

The best sources of information for this historic site, now lying below the waters of Lake Powell, come from a number of papers and studies done by many people and various universities. Some of the research of the human history part was done by C. Gregory Crampton, and is documented in the *Anthropological Papers of the University of Utah.* These studies were done because of the building of Lake Powell. They of course concentrated their studies on that part of the land which is below the high water mark of Lake Powell, or 1128 meters elevation. Much of what is known of the Baker Ranch comes from *Cramptons Anthropological Paper #61.*

An old car and cabin at Woodruff Spring.

122

The remains of the Woodruff Stone Cabin at the southern base of Mt. Hillers.

Chimney and foundations of the Ticaboo Ranch, now under water. (Crampton foto)

"Within the Lake Powell Reservoir area there were a few areas put under cultivation in historic times. Baker Ranch on the right side of Halls Creek, 10 kms from Halls Crossing of the Colorado, was one of the largest of these. At one time approximately 100 acres(40 hectares) of pasture, alfalfa and corn were irrigated from waters diverted from the creek--this was before 1936 when Eugene Baker, after whom the place is named, patented 800 acres(about 320 hectares) of land in the vicinity."

"The first(white) settler on lower Halls Creek, is believed to have been Charles Hall who maintained a small farm 3 kms above Baker Ranch while operating the ferry at Halls Crossing, 1881-1884. Thomas William Smith(living in Green River, Utah, in 1962 and son of Thomas Smith who made the original location at Baker Ranch), stated that he remembers the old Hall place, which consisted of a log cabin 5 by 5 meters. He said that Charles Hall would climb over the slickrock slopes of the Waterpocket Fold to a point about 150 meters above the creek bed where he could see the ferry crossing 13 kms away. Smith thought there may have been some way for parties on the opposite side who wished to cross the river, to signal the ferryman. The site of Halls Ranch, which was referred to by name as late as 1922(by other writers), has not been located by this author"(Crampton).

Crampton continues, "The second settler in lower Halls Creek, is believed to have been Thomas Smith who located the Baker Ranch site around 1900. According to Barbara Ekker, it was in 1907 or 1908, that the Thomas Smith family moved there. Smith was a polygamist, with two wives, Eliza and Sarah. In August 1907, all three filed claims on 800 acres of land on lower Halls Creek, under the Desert Land Act of 1877. This must have been just the place Smith and his two wives were looking for; a quiet and isolated placed to live, and away from the law which frowned on a man having two wives.

In the course of time, Smith and family constructed several buildings including two log cabins and one stone structure. After several years of hardship, this property was transferred to Eugene Baker about 1917. A public land survey of the vicinity was made in 1923. The survey notes reflect the improvements on the ranch, which then consisted of about 3 miles(5 kms) of fencing, one three-room frame house, a one-room log cabin, a one-room rock store-house and a large corral and stockyard. Twenty acres(8 hectares) of land, including fruit trees and alfalfa, were under cultivation at the time".

Crampton visited with a number of people and got first hand accounts from several individuals. One was "Carlyle Baker, son of Eugene Baker, living at Teasdale, Utah, in 1960, stated that he spent a number of his younger years at the ranch. During the spring of the year, when storms broke over the Waterpocket Fold, enough water came down Halls Creek before June to irrigate up to 100 acres(40 hectares) of land on both sides of the stream. However, farming was only an adjunct to grazing and the uncertainties of the water supply, the hot climate of the summer months, and the sandy soil led to its abandonment by about 1940. The Bakers later sold the property to other interests who still use the

Baker Ranch, along the lower Halls Creek, now under water. (Parker Hamilton foto)

ranch as a grazing headquarters(1962)".

Baker Ranch is now under the waters of Lake Power, it being one of the last archeological sites to be covered. If in the next few years, the lake waters recede only a few meters, it might be possible to see parts of this lost landmark, if they aren't covered by too much silt and mud.

Sandy Ranch

The history of the Sandy Ranch is closely tied to Notom and the Durfey Ranch. Sometime around the turn of the century, Enoch Larsen consolidated a large ranch at Notom when everybody left the area, but later sold it to Will Bowns, who with Sidney Curtis and Charlie Hunt, then started the Sandy Ranches. This is reported to be about 1900, but this author believes someone must have started a ranch in the same general vicinity a few years before.

Later, and no one seems to know for sure when, the Sandy Ranch(or ranches), was purchased by members of the King family, who also owned the King Ranch to the east. In recent years all property in the area of Sandy and Oak Creek, and the King Ranch have been purchased by an oil man from Tulsa, Oklahoma, named Oliphant.

The ranch headquarters is now on the hill or bench between Oak and Sandy Creek, just back a ways from the Bullfrog-Notom Road. Steve Dalton is the foreman. Along the bottom lands to the northeast of the ranch headquarters are two newly constructed homes or bunk houses for hired help.

To get to the Sandy Ranch, drive along Highway 24, the main road running from Capitol Reef National Park to Hanksville. Between mile posts 88 and 89, turn south onto the Bullfrog-Notom Road and drive towards Bullfrog on a very good and well maintained road. After about 20 kms you'll come to Oak Creek. Continue upon the bench to reach the ranch headquarters, or turn east to reach the bunk houses and corrals. If you'd like to see the ranch, first contact Steve Dalton at Tele. 801-425-3282 for an appointment.

King Ranch

The King Ranch is located on the west side, and at the foot of, Mt. Ellen. It's also just south of a prominent landmark called Steele Butte.

There are conflicting reports by whom, and in what year, the King Ranch was first settled. One report says it was Howard Tipples; another source says it was two men named Baker and Coleman, who first used the land. The approximate date seems to be just after 1900. Sometime later the King family of four brothers; Emery, Leland, Edmond, and Lawrence, came into the country with sheep and cattle. They acquired the ranch which bears their name, and owned it for many years. They also owned at one

The Sandy Ranch, with Mt. Ellen beyond.

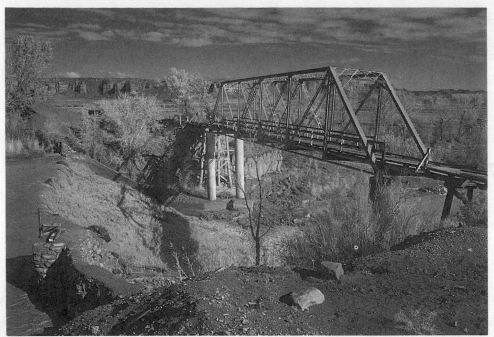

Just west of Hanksville is this old bridge(with one support missing) and diversion dam across the Fremont River. Water taken out of the river here is used by all Hanksville farmers and ranchers.

A close-up view of some of the old ranching equipment used at the Moore Ranch.

Ticaboo Tank(only the cattle watering trough is shown), on the lip of Ticaboo Canyons' South Fork. Mt. Ellsworth in the background.

The Ticaboo Trail, running down from the Ticaboo Tank to the bottom of the South Fork of Ticaboo Canyon.

time or another the Sandy Ranches, the Lower, and the Sanford or Cat Ranch.

In recent years, Oklahoma oil man Oliphant, has bought the King Ranch, along with the Sandy Ranches below, and both areas are administered and worked together.

The author has seen the King Ranch, and there are a lot more new buildings than old, so it's not all that interesting to visit. But if you are interested call the ranch foreman Steve Dalton, at Tele. 801-425-3282, for an appointment. You'll be able to visit the place alone, but they simply want to know who is around.

Get to the King Ranch by driving along Highway 24, the main road linking Capitol Reef National Park with Hanksville. Between mile posts 88 and 89, turn south and drive along the Bullfrog-Notom Road for about 20 kms. At the junction just before you cross Oak Creek, turn east and drive about 20 more kms on a good and well used road to the ranch. If you're there in wet weather, don't even try to drive the last 20 kms. The road passes through several of the clay beds of the Mancos Shale Formation, and when the road is wet, it's impossible to drive it, even for a 4WD!

Durfey Ranch(Notom)

The history of Notom is really the early history of the Durfey Ranch, or vise versa. The first settler to Notom was Jorgen C. Smith, in 1886. Others followed, and a small community developed, but by about 1890, it began to lose population, and by 1900 there was only one ranch family left. Apparently that was the family of Enoch Larsen. He evidently consolidated all the land previously owned by those who left for greener pastures. Later, the ranch passed on to Will Bowns, then Henry Robison, and finally to the Durfey family, who own the ranch today(1987).

The ranch is right at the junction of the old Highway 24(which went from Hanksville to Fruita in Capitol Reef National Park), and the present Bullfrog-Notom Road, which runs south along the Waterpocket Fold to Bullfrog. You'll see hay stacks, corrals, a trailer home, an old wooden house, and just west of the corrals, you'll see some old foundations and the remains of old orchards. If you can find anyone home, they can surely tell you of more old ruins.

Get to the Durfey Ranch, by driving to a point between mile posts 88 and 89, or to between mile posts 92 and 93, and turn south. From either of these roads, it's about 7 or 8 kms to the junction, where the ranch is found. See the map of *Notom and Aldrich,* in the section on Settlements in the Fremont River Valley, which shows the route clearly.

North Spring and the Moore Ranch

According to Pearl Biddlecome Baker, Andy Moore bought or obtained the grazing rights to the area around the North Spring in about 1920. In about 1929 or 1930, he then moved a cabin, which was built

A moderately old house at the King Ranch. Mt. Ellen and Steele Butte in the background.

by one of the Tomlinson boys, from Twin Springs to the present site at North Spring. Also in 1929 or 1930, an oil company drilled a well on Texas Hill, in search for oil. All that came up was water. Later a man named Franz bought the rights, then sold it to Andy Moore in 1939. Today, the Moore Ranch is at Texas Hill, and is operated by Chad Moore and Mike Keiner.

At the old ranch site at North Springs are two old shacks, and a corral. If appearance tells anything, it's likely water was the problem at that site. The two shacks are on top of the mesa, and only about one km or less from the fork in the main road nearby. From the shacks, you still have to walk nearly another km to the north, then drop down into North Wash and walk back up canyon 300 meters or so, to reach the actual North Spring. The water seeps out from under a dry falls and doesn't have much discharge. At one time they tired piping it, but stomping cattle likely put an end to that.

At the Moore Ranch today, sometimes called Texas Well, is an old log cabin, a new double-wide trailer home, a new Quanset hut type storage barn, a good well and pumps, and the corrals for the cattle.

To get there, use the same road as if you were heading to the Robbers Roost Country or to the Maze District of Canyonlands National Park. Drive along Highway 24, the main road linking Hanksville, with I-70 and Green River. Between mile posts 136 and 137 (or between 133 and 134), turn east and southeast. Drive past Jeffrey Well, through the Flat Tops, and just as you reach the top of the long dugway and begin to turn east, you'll then see to the right, the Moore Ranch on the flats of Texas Hill.

To reach the old North Spring Ranch site, continue east about another 15 kms, until you reach a major junction. Turn northeast to reach the trail down into Horseshoe Canyon; or turn south to the Maze Ranger Station. But instead, make a sharp turn to the left or north, and drive about a km to the two shacks and corral on a seldom used road. To reach the North Spring itself, it's probably best to park your vehicle at the corral, and walk. Head north along a faint road or cattle trail. This old road heads down into North Spring Wash. When you reach the bottom, turn south and walk up the dry creek bed to the headwall or falls, where a minor spring is located. There are several other minor seeps in the area and in the shallow drainages.

Robbers Roost or Cottrell Cabin

This wasn't really a ranch as such, just a lonely outpost. But it is a part of the history of the Robbers Roost Country. The Roost or Cottrell Cabin, was built about 1890, or in a year or two after that, by the foreman of the 3B outfit, Joe Bernard. The 3B outfit was owned by J. B. Buhr, who also owned the Granite Ranch. The boys had a lot of cattle in the area, and needed some kind of shelter to store things and for sleeping.

After Bernard quit, the job went to Jack Cottrell. He had just married the widow of R. E. Tomlinson and inherited Tomlinson's Ranch and three sons. Soon after the marriage, Cottrell moved his new family to

Notom, or the Durfey Ranch, with the Waterpocket Fold in the background.

ROOST & SILVERTIP SP. & COTTRELL CABIN

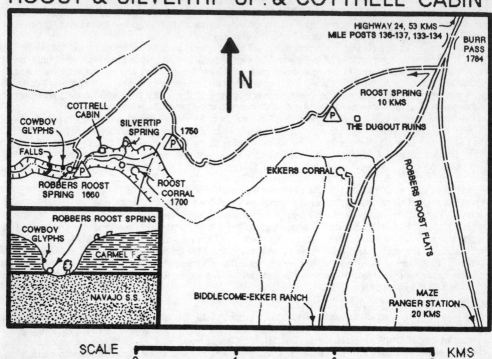

HIGHWAY 24, 53 KMS
MILE POSTS 136-137, 133-134

BURR PASS 1784

ROOST SPRING 10 KMS

THE DUGOUT RUINS

N

COTTRELL CABIN

COWBOY GLYPHS

SILVERTIP SPRING

1750

P

FALLS

P

ROBBERS ROOST SPRING 1660

ROOST CORRAL 1700

EKKERS CORRAL

ROBBERS ROOST FLATS

ROBBERS ROOST SPRING

COWBOY GLYPHS

CARMEL F.

NAVAJO S.S.

BIDDLECOME-EKKER RANCH

MAZE RANGER STATION 20 KMS

SCALE
0   1   2   3   KMS

The Henry Mountains, with the Moore Ranch on Texas Hill.

the cabin, which is located in the upper and shallow end of the South Fork of Robbers Roost Canyon, between Silvertip and Roost Spring. Cottrell was the foreman for only two or three years, so the family didn't stay long in the cabin, perhaps moving out in the mid 1890's.

There are two interesting stories or events which took place in the immediate area of the Robbers Roost Spring which should be told. The first of these is the history behind the naming of one of the long low hills just south of the Roost and Silvertip Springs. The hill is called Dead Man's Hill(Deadman Hill on USGS maps).

This story is told by Pearl Baker in her book, *The Wild Bunch at Robbers Roost*. Apparently the story is true, but there is no name given for the young man who died there. So here it is, whether it be fact or folklore.

Before the Wild Bunch rode the hills of the Roost Country, there was another man who found sanctuary in this red rock canyon country. He was Cap Brown. Cap was a horse thief who roamed these parts even before Hanksville and other Fremont River Valley towns were even settled. He made his living by stealing horses in western Utah, and herded them to the Colorado mining towns to sell, passing through the Henry Mountains and Robbers Roost Country on the way.

Baker believes he is the one who first built the Twin Corrals, and the one who first grazed horses in the high pastures of the Roost Country, such as Robbers Roost and Twin Corral Flats. At one time he also had a small shack somewhere up Bull Valley, about the time Hanksville was first settled.

Cap sometimes did his own stealing, but more often, transported horses which were first stolen by young men such as Mike Cassidy, one of those who worked at the Marshall Ranch near Circleville when Robert LeRoy Parker worked there.

On one of these trips from somewhere in western Utah, and while he was heading across the Burr Desert to the Angel Trail with three young cowboys and a herd of stolen horses, he caught sight of a cloud of dust behind him. Sensing trouble, he hurried the boys on, and got the horses across the Dirty Devil and started them up the eastern half of the Angel Trail. One boy went on, leading the horses, and Cap and the remaining two, laid plans for an ambush. Evidently it was not a posse who was chasing them, but several angry ranchers instead.

Cap gave strict instructions to the boys not to shoot to kill, but just to shoot close enough in front of their pursuers to hopefully scare them away. This they did, and as the ranchers were turning tails and heading back out of the canyon, one turned and noticed one of the boys had left himself open on the slickrock. He took a wild shot, and hit the boy in the leg, not knowing for sure if he had hit the target or not.

It was getting dark, but Cap decided to move on anyway, not knowing if the ranchers would return or not. So the three groped their way in the dark up the slickrock Angel Trail. The boy who was hit, had a

North Spring cabins, the original location of the Moore Ranch.

wound on the outside of the thigh, so he was able to ride some, but he was also able to walk and lead his horse part way.

By the time they got to a camp site in a shallow draw, located not far south of Roost Spring, it was getting light. Cap attended to the boys wound, which was worse than anyone had thought. He became weaker throughout the day, because of shock and loss of blood. That night the boy died, and was buried somewhere near the hill, which ever since has been called "Dead Man's Hill." Pearl doesn't give any dates in this story, but it sounds as if it was just a year or two before Bob Parker(Butch Cassidy) left home, which was in June of 1884.

Another interesting story to come out of the Roost Country is the episode called, *The Gun Battle at Robbers Roost*. Pearl Biddlecome Baker also describes this one in her book, *The Wild Bunch at Robbers Roost*. The characters in this story were Silver Tip, Blue John, and Indian Ed Newcomb, along with Sheriff Tyler of Moab, and his posse.

In about February of 1899, Silver Tip, Blue John and Indian Ed, returned from the Spicer, Wyoming area, with horses they had stolen at about the time Jack Moore was shot dead. They drove them into Colorado, where they were sold. Upon returning to Utah, they picked up a few more horses belonging to someone else, while passing through Monticello and Moab.

One man whose horses were stolen, was Andrew Tangren, of Moab. He filed a complaint, and later joined Sheriff Tyler, as they tracked the horse thieves towards the Roost Country.

As Baker tells it, the three landed at the little Cottrell Cabin in February, 1899, intending to stay there. But the place smelled bad because of rat infestation, so they rode east, up the shallow canyon about half a km or so, then north into a little side canyon holding what has over the years become known as Silvertip Spring. There are several small alcoves in this short drainage, which could make a nice campsite.

So they camped there, next to the little sweet water seep, with their hobbled horses up on the canyon rim, grazing. Meanwhile, the sheriff had tracked them down and was closing in. However, they decided to lay low until morning. At the crack of dawn, Indian Ed got up, put his boots on, and headed down canyon just a bit, to a point where he could climb out of the draw and up on the Carmel Bluff on the east side of the drainage to get the horses. About half way up, the posse opened fire. One shot glanced off the slickrock, and struck Ed in the leg. He immediately hit the dirt, and crawled back into the shelter.

A view of Robbers Roost Spring looking east, and up the shallow beginnings of South Fork of Roost Canyon. The Cottrell Cabin chimney is less than half a km away, to the east.

Close-up of Roost Spring, showing the planks Joe Biddlecome put in just after arriving in 1909.

The short drainage holding small alcoves or caves, and Silvertip Spring(lower right and just out of sight). This is the scene of the Robbers Roost gunfight, which took place in February, 1899.

133

By that time everybody got involved and depending on whose story you hear, there was up to a 100 shots fired from both sides.

The posse was about 100 meters south and at the bottom of the drainage below Silvertip Spring, and didn't have good cover. The three badmen were worried of being trapped in the 10 meter-deep canyon, but luck was on their side this time. None of them were killers, but they did shoot as close to the posse as possible, without hurting anyone. It wasn't long before the posse decided it was too hot for them and fled. The Moab newspaper, *Times-Independent(March 3, 1899)*, reported the posse had run out of ammo, and withdrew reluctantly.

After the gun battle, the three decided to split up and get out the of the horse stealing business. It was reported that Silver Tip, whose real name was Jim Wall, took what stolen horses the group had left and headed south. Later he was caught in a small cabin 60 kms north of Lee's Ferry by a posse, one member of which was Jack Cottrell. He was never convicted of horse stealing, but was put in jail for resisting arrest. Later in time he broke out, and headed for Wyoming, never to be seen again.

Blue John, whose real name was John Griffith(he had one blue, and one brown eye-thus his name), headed east, down the North Trail, across the Colorado at Spanish Bottom, and later turned up in Glen Canyon at Hite. In the fall of 1899, he was reported to have put out in a small boat at Hite, heading for Lee's Ferry. He was never seen again.

Indian Ed Newcomb, was a half blood, and perhaps from Oklahoma. Since he had a minor bullet wound in his leg, he found a sheep camp run by Charl Hanks(another son of Eb Hanks, Hanksville's founding father). He tagged along with this sheep camp for about two weeks, nervously helping out with the chores, until the leg got better. He was thought to have returned to Oklahoma, and straightened his life out.

Sometime between the mid 1890's and 1909, when Joe Biddlecome brought his family to the Roost Spring, the Cottrell Cabin burned to the ground. One story says someone tried to smoke out a rat hiding in the cabin, but succeeded too well. When Joe Biddlecome(who was the father of Pearl Biddlecome Baker), got there, all that was left standing was the chimney. And that's exactly how it is today, just a chimney standing alone.

To get to the Roost Cabin ruins, drive along Highway 24, the road connecting Hanksville, and I-70 and Green River. Between mile posts 36 and 37(or between 33 and 34), turn east and southeast, and proceed towards the Maze Ranger Station. Drive about 40 kms to a major junction, where the road to Horseshoe Canyon heads off to the northeast. Instead, turn south and drive another 13 or so kms to the high point on the road called Burr Pass.

Ahead of you at that point is Roost Flats. The road splits there; the main road heads due south to the Maze Ranger Station, another heads southwest to the Biddlecome-Ekker Ranch, and a third heads due west. Take the less used of the three roads, the one heading west. Drive about 10 kms to the end of this road, which will be the Roost Spring. People driving cars should always have a shovel handy, to

134   Close-up view of the chimney of the old Cottrell Cabin, just above the Roost Spring.

help smooth the way over mini-gullies. Park at the spring and walk east up the draw on an old wagon road. After only about 300 meters or so, look to the left or north, and you'll see the chimney about 25 meters off the road. See the map "Roost and Silvertip Spring" to see the location.

For people with nice cars, instead of driving the 10 kms from the main road and Burr Pass to Roost Spring, drive only about 8 kms, and park on the mesa rim overlooking the the shallow head of Roost Canyon. From there, you can walk down along an old and very sandy track to the area of the Springs, the Roost Corral and the Cottrell Cabin.

Biddlecome or Ekker Ranch

This ranch is sometimes referred to as the Robbers Roost Ranch, but that's far from a proper term. It came into being long after the Wild Bunch rode the Roost Country.

Joe Biddlecome and his family first began this ranch in the fall of 1915, six long years after arriving in the Roost area for the first time.

Joe Biddlecome was raised in Ferron, Utah, in the Castle Valley, southwest of Price. When he was old enough, he wandered eastern Utah working at various ranches, working for calves, and gradually accumulated a small herd of cattle by the time he married Millie Scharf, in 1904.

Millie was raised in the Utah Bottom along the lower Dolores River, just inside the Utah state line. This is downstream from Dolores, Colorado, and up-stream about 16 kms from the Colorado River.

In the first years after 1904, the Biddlecome's wandered about with their small herd of cattle. They were first in Colorado, then went to the San Rafael Swell country and Ferron Mountain. In the fall of 1908, he landed in the Harris Bottoms, on the lower San Rafael River. He built a cabin, and stayed the winter. Pearl, the oldest of their two daughters, was about two years old then.

The next spring, after Joe had talked to a man named Ern Wild, who had run cattle on the Roost Range for some time, went to the Roost to have a look around. Ern had told Joe he was leaving the Roost, and was heading back home(apparently to Castle Valley). That left the Roost open to the first settler who wanted it. From the cabin on Harris Bottom, Joe took a pack horse and a weeks supply of food and headed south to have a look for himself.

He came back, and Millie asked, "what's it like". Joe said, "Open swales and sand hills at the Roost, sloping up into a high cedar ridge. Beyond is an open high valley, different, richer, with grassy swales running up into the cedar and pinyon ridges. Goes up into the sage in some places. Deep canyons break away on all sides, but they have good feed, too, and will be fine for holding weaners or to gather a trail bunch into"(From Pearl Biddlecome Baker's book, *Robbers Roost Recollections*).

So the family moved to the Roost Country for the first time, arriving in June, 1909, at the Robbers Roost Spring and the Cottrell Cabin ruins. After spending some time at the Roost Spring, they moved to Bluejohn Spring. But Millie hated that place the moment she saw it. She couldn't see very far in any

The Roost Corral, lying just to the east of both the Roost and Silvertip Springs.

direction and felt boxed in. Later that summer, they left most of their belongings at Bluejohn, and moved camp to the east, to the Spur Country(north of the Maze Ranger Station).

The first winter, Joe took Millie and baby Pearl to Hanksville for the winter, as a new baby was expected in February(Hazel was born in Hanksville in February, 1910). Joe spent the winter in the Roost settling the herd into a new land.

For the next several years, Millie, Pearl and Hazel spent the summers at the Roost, and winters in Hanksville. Joe was out on the range most of the time, even in winter.

Life was rough at the Roost. Most of the time, especially in summer, the family slept under the stars, only using a tent in a base camp situation or in winter. Cooking was always done on an open fire. In the warmer months, Millie and the young girls, riding behind the saddle, helped out as much as possible with the cattle. Pearl remembers it was in the summer of 1915, that her father bought two small horses for the two girls, who were then ages 7 and 5. That was the last time the girls "rode behind."

As time went on, and as Millie got tired of living among the Mormons in Hanksville, and as the little girls began to grow, thoughts turned to making a home. Joe had thought Bluejohn would make a fine home, but Millie was opposed to that.

One day as Joe was riding along in the vicinity of what was later called Crow Seep, he noticed the ground was wet, because of a small seep or spring. He also noticed the fine open view in all directions, and especially toward the west, with the Henry Mountains piercing the sky and the Dirty Devil River Gorge lying in between. As he got closer to the seep, he ran onto a small black pony, which he chased and roped. Later, he brought Millie back to have a look. She loved the place the moment she saw it.

Pearl states, "Because the little wild horse was jet black, we called him Crow, and the spring became Crow Seep. We moved right in and started developing this for a permanent location." At first, they camped to the south of the seep. Joe used a slip scraper to dig the sand away from the seep, to expose the bedrock, which made collecting water easier. Finally they had a small pond and a barrel set deep in the sand and rocks, to collect water for home use.

Later it was found most trails to the seep came in from south and west, and with the camp to the south, the cattle were always spooked. So early that fall, they moved camp over a little low hump to the north of the seep, and that became permanent. Joe stretched out a tent to live in, built a rough shed for his saddles, and made his blacksmith shop under a cedar tree.

It must have been about the time camp was moved to Crow Seep, that Millie wanted something better. Pearl states, "the fall of 1915, Mama was most reluctant to return to Hanksville. She kept saying she wouldn't and when the first snows of the season drove over the tent, her husband Joe began to pay attention. Cutting cedar posts as fast as he could, he hauled them in and started putting up a cabin. Although there wasn't a cedar post long enough to reach the length of any wall of the 14' x 16'(4 x 5

The long, low rise is called Deadman Hill, with Mt. Ellen off in the distance.

ROBBERS ROOST COUNTRY

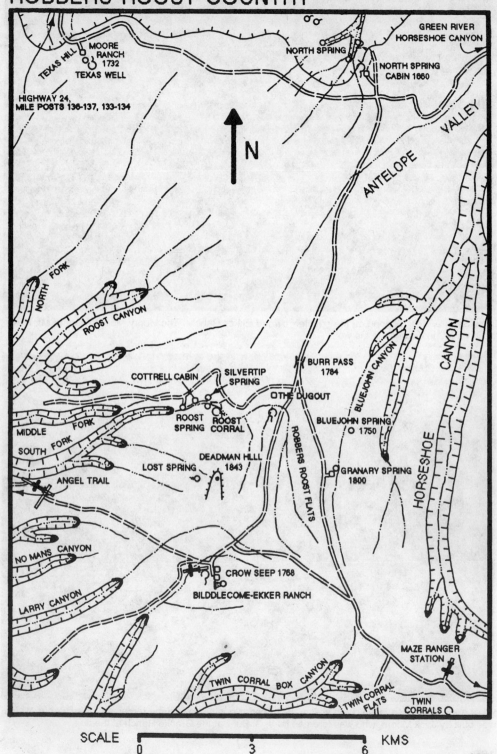

TEXAS HILL
MOORE RANCH 1732
TEXAS WELL

HIGHWAY 24,
MILE POSTS 138-137, 133-134

NORTH SPRING

GREEN RIVER
HORSESHOE CANYON

NORTH SPRING CABIN 1660

N

ANTELOPE VALLEY

NORTH FORK

ROOST CANYON

BURR PASS 1784

BLUEJOHN CANYON

HORSESHOE CANYON

COTTRELL CABIN

SILVERTIP SPRING

O THE DUGOUT

MIDDLE FORK
SOUTH FORK

ROOST SPRING
ROOST CORRAL

BLUEJOHN SPRING
O 1750

LOST SPRING

DEADMAN HILL 1843

GRANARY SPRING 1800

ANGEL TRAIL

ROBBERS ROOST FLATS

NO MANS CANYON

LARRY CANYON

CROW SEEP 1768

BILDDLECOME-EKKER RANCH

MAZE RANGER STATION

TWIN CORRAL BOX CANYON

TWIN CORRAL FLATS

TWIN CORRALS O

SCALE

0   3   6   KMS

137

Crow Seep and stock pond, at the privately owned Ekker Ranch. The Henry Mountains and Mt. Ellen are seen in the distance to the west.

What appears to be a fallen down wall made of cedar posts, may be the remains of the Dugout, which was built by Jack Moore, who was foreman for J. B. Buhr at the Granite Ranch at the time.

Angel Cove and the Angel Cove Spring. Above and to the west on the skyline, can be seen the beginnings of the Angel Trail atop the Navajo Slickrock.

The Flint Trail, as it zig zags down from the Roost Highlands to the Maze District of Canyonlands N. P.

The old Biddlecome Ranch, with original cedar log house on the left.

The cedar log cabin built by Joe Bilddlecome, in 1915. Today, it's part of the Ekker Ranch.

A small stock pond has been built at Bluejohn Spring.

Henry Mountains(Mt. Ellen), the Pinnacles, and Coyote Flat. Just southeast of the Biddlecome-Ekker Ranch.

One of the better springs around is the Granary Spring, located just east of Robbers Roost Flats.

The chimney is all that remains of the old Cottrell Cabin, located between Roost and Silvertip Springs.

Immediately below Roost Spring are found these Cowboy Glyphs. This one shows the markings of Pearl Biddlecome(Baker) when see was a young girl living at her fathers ranch.

French Spring, just a few kms east of the Maze Ranger Station. Joe Biddlecome first developed it.

meters) cabin, he laid up four strong walls, put down a pine-board floor, and topped it all with a shingle roof. He nailed the last shingle on and moved us in the first day of November in a blizzard." This was the beginning of the Biddlecome Ranch.

From the beginning in 1909, Joe Biddlecome began to make improvements on the range. The biggest problem was water. There is no running water in the Roost Country, except for very small streams in the canyon bottoms, and in the Dirty Devil River. In areas where most of the cattle graze, there is no live water. The cattle must drink water from springs, most of which are in the canyon bottoms, from natural potholes in the sandstone creek beds, or from stock ponds made on the mesa tops and along shallow drainages.

Joe Bernard, while he was foreman for Buhr, first built wooden troughs at the Roost Spring in the early 1890's, but they were replaced by Joe Biddlecome. That was in 1909, and those planks are still in place and doing well today. Another of the very first projects to come along was the making of Twin Corral Pond.

Joe was apparently paranoid about cattle falling into some of the pothole type tanks seen throughout the range. These are made by flood waters whirling over the ledges, and gouging deep cisterns with straight sides into the solid rock, usually the Navajo S.S. While they were full, the cattle drank easily, but as the water lowered through evaporation, a cow could fall in, trying to reach the water. Then she would swim around and around, until she drown. Joe fixed many of these, by either filling them in part way with trees or rocks, or by blasting ramps into the sides of others. Either of these modification would allow cows to get out if they fell in.

One important range improvement Joe Biddlecome is credited with doing, was the development of French Spring. It's located about 4 kms southeast of the Maze Ranger Station, and just east and downhill from the main road. It's still used today, but the improvements are falling apart.

In later years, especially during the depression, and with the aid of the CCC boys, other springs were improved, with pipes taking water to storage tanks, for example. The boys also made trails down into some of the canyons, so cattle could get up or down easily. Later owners of the ranch also made trails, improved springs and made corrals.

Corrals are an important feature of the range. On the Roost Range, two types of corrals were constructed. The brush corral was made by cutting trees(cedar or pinyon), then dragging them together to form a circle. The inner branches were cut, leaving a mass of tangled limbs to form the enclosure.

Then there was the stockade type. These were made by cutting posts, and driving them into the ground standing upright, and held together by wire. Joe built the brush type corrals at Hans Flat, the Gordons and on the Spur. The stockade type he built were at the Roost Spring(up-canyon to the east) and at Crow Seep.

Years went by and the range gradually began to be a ranch. Over the years Joe had many bouts with quinsy, a problem having to do with tonsils. In the winter of 1927-8, he was sick much of the time. He finally went to Salt Lake City and had his tonsils removed. On the way back home, he stopped at his sisters place in Castle Gate for a rest. It was there on the morning of June 16, 1928, he died from complications of his tonsillectomy.

It took about a year to settle the estate; dividing the cattle, re-branding, etc. It was decided that Pearl, with her husband Mel Marsing, would buy the others out, and live and work at the ranch. That took place in July of 1929. Two months later Mel died of blood poisoning, which resulted from being hit on the thigh with a knot of a rope, by a horse he was leading. That left Pearl alone with two small boys and a big ranch.

Pearl ran the ranch through the worst years of the depression, then married again, and sold out to her sister Hazel, who had married Arthur Ekker of Hanksville. Hazel and Arthur ran the ranch for many years, raising four children. In 1969, Hazel died of emphysema.

Arthur remarried about a year later, to a childhood friend of the Biddlecome's, Lela Wilcox Anderson. When Arthur died in 1978, their youngest son AC, took over the ranch after a professional rodeo career. He still runs it, along with doing a little dude wrangling on the side. He has a small company called Outlaw Trails, which specializes in taking city folk into some of the canyons of the Maze, the Colorado River, the Robbers Roost Country and to other places in America.

For history buffs who might like to visit the ranch, contact someone in Hanksville about getting in touch with AC for an appointment.

144

The Life and Legend of Butch Cassidy

While the hike into Robbers Roost Canyon is one of the best included in this book, the actual hiking into canyons themselves make up only part of the fascination surrounding this part of the Colorado Plateau. In was in this region and mostly in the 1890's, that a loosely organized band of outlaws, later to become known as "The Wild Bunch", sought refuge in between escapades with the law. For those who have read about, or those who might later become involved with the history of the area, familiar names such as: Gunplay Maxwell, Matt Warner, Joe Walker, Tom Dilly, Flat Nose George and the Curry Boys, Silvertip, Blue John, Indian Ed Newcomb, Tom, Billy and Fred McCarty, Elzy Lay, Harry Longabaugh(the Sundance Kid), and Butch Cassidy, will become household names.

Of all these bandits, the name that stands out above the rest is that of Butch Cassidy. Those who knew the gang, or members of it, seem to agree that he was the leader. Most who have written about the Wild Bunch over the years, attribute most of the imaginative planning of bank and train holdups to Butch Cassidy, although some believe Butch's best friend, Elzy Lay was the mastermind behind many of the stickups.

Butch Cassidy grew up not far to the west of the Robbers Roost Country, and was one of the lucky ones who did not die a violent death. Because the law chased him across two continents, and because there is some confusion as to when he died and under what name, he has become a legend and bigger than life. Because of all the stories and legends, the author has chosen to tell a short history of his life, and has attempted to place the names and the places together. This then is a summery of the life of Butch Cassidy.

For those interested in delving further into the life of Butch Cassidy and others, here are some of the sources the author has used to compile this history. Perhaps the man most responsible for making Butch bigger than life was Charles Kelly, who wrote and published a book, *Outlaw Trail,* in 1938. Other books of the time include Matt Warner's, *Last of the Bandit Riders;* John Rolfe Burroughs, *Where the Old West Stayed Young,* and in recent years, Pearl Biddlecome Baker's two books, which concentrate on this Robbers Roost area, *The Wild Bunch at Robbers Roost,* and *Robbers Roost Recollections.*

But perhaps the best source and the one most used by this author, is the last book published about Butch Cassidy. This is the book entitled, *In Search of Butch Cassidy,* by Larry Pointer. This book includes portions of the unpublished manuscript written by William T. Phillips in 1934, called, *The Bandit Invincible, the Story of Butch Cassidy.* Larry Pointer seems to have the proof that William T. Phillips of Spokane, Washington, who died in 1937, was Butch Cassidy. This book goes into greater detail of Butch's life in South America and in the USA after he returned, and changed his name to Phillips. This book is well documented, and has likely taken more time to research and write than any other book on Cassidy. It appears Mr. Pointer has his man.

In the Phillips manuscript, it's evident that Butch, or Phillips, changed the names of some of the players, and changed the names and locations of some of the stickups on purpose, so as to protect those who may have been alive at that time. It's also very likely that the details had faded in his mind, as he wrote the manuscript 35 to 40 years after the events happened. However, Pointer believed it's authentic, because he has checked into the history of certain places in Wyoming and Colorado, and only someone who had been there around the turn of the century could have written it. More on the Phillips manuscript later In this chapter. *The Bandit Invincible,* is now in print, and published by Jim Dullenty.

Another equally good source is the book *Butch Cassidy, My Brother,* by Lula Betenson(written by Dora Flack). It gives a close look at both Butch and his family. Lula Parker Betenson, was 18 years younger than Butch, and born only a short time before Butch left home for good in 1884. She has memories of the time in 1925, when Butch returned home to Circleville. This book concentrates more on Butch's home life before leaving in 1884, and on the events surrounding his home visit in 1925.

The story of Butch Cassidy begins in Beaver, Utah, on Friday, April 13, 1866. That's when Robert Maximillian and Ann Parker had a son, who they named Robert LeRoy Parker. Other writers and authors have often used the name George LeRoy, but this is in error. Years later the family moved to Circleville, Utah and bought a farm 3 kms southwest of town. It was a small two-roomed log cabin, in a cove of the Sevier River. This became the family home for many years, until they moved to town. It is still owned by the family today, and is farmed by the sons and grandsons of Lula Betenson.

Butch Cassidy's childhood home still stands about 3 kms southwest of Circleville, on Highway 89, between mile posts 156 and 157. From the highway, look to the fields to the west, and in a grove of poplar trees stands the home, along with several old cabins, barns and a corral. To the west of the home are three or four tall Lombardy poplars. These were brought from Beaver, and Bob(as his brothers and sisters called him), and his mother, planted them when he was a boy.

In recent years, while Lula's son Mark was living in Circleville, but farming the land around the old family home, things around the farm began to disappear to souvenir hunters. Saddles, branding irons, wagon wheels, floor planks, nails and even bricks from the fireplace were stolen. Finally it was decided to open the place up to the public, which brought thousands of people from all over the USA and other

The boyhood home of Robert LeRoy Parker or Butch Cassidy, along the highway south of Circleville.

The backside of the Parker Ranch home south of Circleville, Utah.

WILD BUNCH COUNTRY--USA

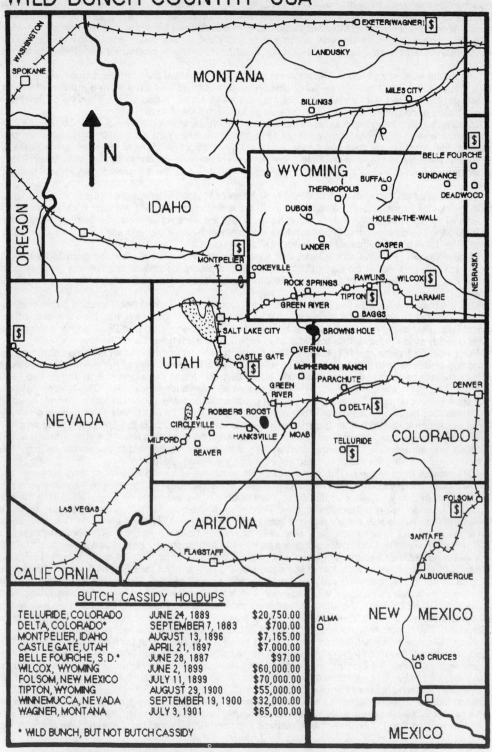

BUTCH CASSIDY HOLDUPS

TELLURIDE, COLORADO	JUNE 24, 1889	$20,750.00
DELTA, COLORADO*	SEPTEMBER 7, 1883	$700.00
MONTPELIER, IDAHO	AUGUST 13, 1896	$7,165.00
CASTLE GATE, UTAH	APRIL 21, 1897	$7,000.00
BELLE FOURCHE, S.D.*	JUNE 28, 1887	$97.00
WILCOX, WYOMING	JUNE 2, 1899	$60,000.00
FOLSOM, NEW MEXICO	JULY 11, 1899	$70,000.00
TIPTON, WYOMING	AUGUST 29, 1900	$55,000.00
WINNEMUCCA, NEVADA	SEPTEMBER 19, 1900	$32,000.00
WAGNER, MONTANA	JULY 3, 1901	$65,000.00

* WILD BUNCH, BUT NOT BUTCH CASSIDY

ADOPTED FROM "IN SEARCH OF BUTCH CASSIDY", BY LARRY POINTER, AND OTHERS

countries to the ranch. But then in June, 1973, the ranch was broken into one night. Taken were a number of priceless items, as the place had been a kind of museum, but without a full time watchman. Finally Mark Betenson closed the place to the public and took down the signs. Today, anyone can stop and view the ranch from the highway, which is only about 150 meters away. If you'd like to see the old ranch house, best to stop in Circleville(a very small town) and ask around for permission to take a closer look.

One has to wonder how a good Mormon boy, one who was raised on a farm and close to the earth, ever got on the road he took. It certainly didn't happen overnight and there were a number of events which got him started, then it was a step by step process until he landed in jail. Then he couldn't turn back, although on several occasions he took steps to turn his life around.

For most families living in the small towns of central Utah, life was a continuous struggle, and for the Parkers, it was no different. In the winter of 1879-1880, the first winter in Circle Valley, the family lost most of their cattle in the severe weather, which set them back financially to the point it took years to recover. Because of this, and because there were six children in the family at that time, Maximillian, Bob's father, farmed and took odd jobs, one of which was in Frisco, the old mining town west of Milford, Utah.

At about this same time, young Bob at the tender age of 13, took employment at the farm of Pat Ryan at Hay Springs, near Milford. While there he had his first encounter with the law. It seems he had ridden all the way into town to buy a pair of trousers, but the store was closed. So he decided to get in and take the pants he needed, but left an IOU, complete with name and address. But the storekeeper didn't like doing business that way and swore out a complaint.

Meanwhile, Ann Parker, Bob's mother, took a summer job at the Marshall Ranch, about 20 kms south of Circleville. This was in the early 1880's. She did dairy work for several summers to bring in extra money for the family. Bob, or LeRoy, as his father called him, also worked at the Marshall Ranch off and on.

This is where Bob took his first real step along the Outlaw Trail. During Bob's second summer at the Marshall Ranch, a cowpoke by the name of Mike Cassidy, drifted into town, and took any odd job he could find. Part of the time he worked at the Marshall Ranch, where he met Bob Parker. During this time Cassidy made friends with a couple of local scoundrels, named Fred and Charley.

Before continuing the story of Robert LeRoy Parker, one must understand a few things about cattle, ranching and rustling in those days. In the years shortly after the coming of the railroad(completed in 1869), the west was all but empty and totally public domain. It was there to be taken and settled. The railroad brought in big cattle herds, as well as the small time rancher or settler. There were conflicts between the two groups. The little man or small rancher had to really scratch to make ends meet, so on occasion they might grab a stray cow or two, especially if it didn't have a brand. This picking off strays from large herds of the "Cattle Barons" was called mavericking. And the little man, who was the underdog, usually didn't mind at all. But at times it would be difficult to draw the line between actual rustling and mavericking. For some, mavericking later turned into honest-to-goodness rustling. For others, it led to taking the next step, and before long they were fugitives.

This seems to be the way Bob got started. He was always for the little man, the underdog, and throughout his life(according to everyone who has written about him), he tried to help the poor and oppressed, in their struggle with the big-monied people. This seems to be one reason why he was caught but once; everyone seems to have liked Bob, and would keep their mouths shut as to his whereabouts. This is also a likely reason Robert LeRoy Parker was able to live with his own conscience all those years. It's been written many times that he never robbed a poor man, only banks and trains.

Bob had known Mike Cassidy for perhaps a year. Mike had taught him how to use a gun, and they got on well together. He apparently got on well with Fred and Charley too. As it turned out, Fred and Charley must have picked up a few of someone else's cattle, and put their brands on them. When the rightful owner found the cows, Fred and Charley produced a bill of sale. They had apparently paid Bob some money to have him sign the bill, to make it look like Bob had owned the stolen cattle, then sold them to Fred and Charley. These two fellows were older and a little wiser than Bob, and Bob was young and naive. A warrant was issued for Bob, but by that time, he was out of the country and heading for Colorado. This happened in June of 1884, when Bob or LeRoy Parker was just 18 years old.

About two months before Bob's departure, his newest little sister was born on April 5, 1884. She, Lula, was barely two months old when Bob left home. She didn't see him again for 41 years. In Lula's book, *Butch Cassidy, My Brother,* she recalls the stories her mother had told the family down through the years of that tearful June morning when Bob left home. Bob, or Butch, told the same version of the same story when he returned home to Circleville in 1925.

According to Lula Betenson, the first stop Bob made was in the mining town of Telluride, Colorado. She seems to think he went straight there, and minded his own business on the way. But Pearl Baker had him helping Cap Brown and others, perhaps Fred and Charley, or Mike Cassidy, take some stolen horses from western Utah through Rabbit Valley, the Lower Fremont River Valley and to the Roost Country. From there it appears he went on to Telluride with some of the stolen horses. Such are the stories surrounding this famous character. Many parts of his life just cannot be verified.

There are some historians who think Bob Parker also worked for Charley Gibbons before Bob ended up getting in trouble in Circleville in 1884. Charley Gibbons is the guy who owned the store and hotel in Hanksville. It's been said Bob was a cow hand on the ranch of Charley Gibbons, but no one seems to know for sure.

Telluride, Colorado, at that time was a boom town. The mines were producing and there was lots of work. Bob had no trouble finding a job hauling ore down from the mountain on mules. In those days Bob sent money home often(according to Lula, whose father had told about Bob's days in Telluride years later).

Bob had taken two horses to Telluride, Babe the riding horse, and a colt named Cornish. Since he couldn't use two horses, he had kept the colt at a ranch down river from Telluride. He visited the colt often at first, but later the visits were less frequent. When the colt was about three years old, Bob got him out of the herd to break him, but perhaps the rancher had forgotten, or just wanted the horse. The rancher swore out a warrant, and had Bob arrested. Bob's friends in Telluride, immediately sent a wire to Bob's father in Circleville, who dropped everything, and headed for Colorado.

Bob had been jailed in Montrose, about 75 kms north of Telluride. When Maximillian arrived, he found Bob sitting in a jail cell reading a magazine, with the door wide open. Bob was surprised to say the least to see his father, and his father was just as surprised to see the jail door open. Later at the trial, Bob was found innocent, because of character witnesses, and was released.

Several years later, and because of the depressed situation in Circleville, Maximillian Parker and son Arthur and his oldest daughter, went to Telluride to open a livery stable. But the altitude was too much for Bob's father, and he went back to Circleville. Bob's brother and sister stayed and worked. But during a July 4th celebration, Arthur fell from a horse during a race, and was injured. He died later, and was buried, before word got back to his family. His tomb stone can still be seen today in Telluride. Bob was not in Telluride at that time.

After the incident with the horse and trial, Bob drifted into Wyoming, looking for more excitement. He worked at odd jobs, and apparently made friends with some of the fellows who later became members of the Wild Bunch. According to Lula and Dora Flack, the eleventh Parker baby was born January 6, 1889. When Bob got word, he sent a hundred dollars, and suggested the baby be named Nina Grace. Lula didn't know of any money being sent home after that. She seems to think, all the money Bob ever sent was honest money, and that when he started making money illegally, he stopped sending.

After a stint in Wyoming, Bob returned to Telluride in the spring of 1889, where he met Matt Warner

The grave stone of the parents of Robert LeRoy Parker or Butch Cassidy, in the Circleville, Utah cemetery.

who was doing some horse racing. Matt Warner was from Levan, Utah, and his real name was Willard Erastus Christiansen. Bob joined Matt in the horse racing business. Later, and after several incidents with racing, the boys ran out of money, so they decided to rob the bank in Telluride. On June 24, 1889, Bob Parker, Matt Warner and Tom McCarty robbed the San Miguel Valley Bank of Telluride of $31,000(another account says it was about $21,0000). According to Pointer, also helping in this robbery was Daniel Sinclair Parker, Bob's next younger brother. Lula didn't mention this in her book, but it seems for good reason. (On December 29, 1889, two masked men held up the stage coach between Dixon and Rawlins, Wyoming. One turned out to be Dan Parker. He was caught and convicted, and spent time in the state pen. He later had another trial because of the mail being stolen, and spent the rest of his sentence in the Detroit House of Correction. Prison time was from October 19, 1890 to 1894. That was the last time he bypassed the law.)

During the robbery, everything went fine; no shots were fired, no one got hurt, but the boys made one small mistake as they rode very fast out of town. At a crossroads just outside Telluride, they ran into two men they knew from Telluride. But they were so nervous, thinking the law must be right behind, they didn't even stop to say hello. This obviously seemed strange to the two friends, so when the two men arrived in town and heard about the bank job, they put two and two together, and told what they knew. This incident put the names of Bob, Matt, Tom(and Dan), on the wanted lists for the first time.

After the bank job, the boys split up. The next place Bob was seen was in Milford, Utah, not far to the west of Beaver. He ran into his brother Dan(as Lula told it), who had a job there then, and they had a long visit over lunch.

It was about that time, and quite obviously after the Telluride bank job, Bob started using other names. Surely he was ashamed to use the good Parker name, so he started using the name Cassidy, after Mike, perhaps the one person more than any other who helped him get started down the wrong road.

It was likely the summer of 1889, Bob first went to Browns Hole(also known as Browns Park). Browns Hole in the 1890's got the reputation of being a great hideout or refuge for outlaws. Infact, most authors who have written about the Wild Bunch and other gangs of the west in those days, say this was the best, if not the most important of all the outlaw hideouts in the country. To the north was Hole-in-the-Wall, in east central Wyoming, and Robbers Roost was in southern Utah. These three hideouts, along with others, was connected by the legendary "Outlaw Trail". Some even called it the "Owl Hoot Trail".

Browns Hole was unique. It sat at the place where three states meet; Wyoming, Utah and Colorado. The Green River runs south out of Wyoming, into Utah through Flaming Gorge, then widens out into a large park-like valley which extends into Colorado. After flowing into Colorado, the river soon turns south, then southwest, and flows into the Canyon of Ladore, which is in Utah again. So there was a

The 17 year-old Robert LeRoy Parker. Foto taken in about 1883(Denver Public Library Western History Collection)

river valley, shut in on all sides, at the meeting place of three states, which was very isolated. And since there were very few ranchers living there, the law just didn't get out that way. It was a perfect hideout. The outlaws needed a place to rest and re-group and the ranchers needed cheap labor. As long as the outlaws were good workers(and they always were), and as long as they minded their own business, the ranchers weren't about to ask too many questions, or turn them in. In those days, and on the lonely and very isolated ranches of the west, strangers were treated like guests, and with no questions asked. So it all worked out well for both outlaw and rancher.

After a look around, Bob soon found a job at the Bassett Ranch. This was the home of Herbert and Mary Eliza Bassett, and their five children; Josie, Sam, Ann, Eb and George. According to Dora Flack, Bob felt right at home with this family. Bob was in his early 20's, and Josie the oldest daughter, was in her teens. Ann was four years younger than Josie.

The Bassett Ranch was the social hub of the valley. Mary was well educated, and had lots of books around, and the ranch was used as a church gathering place on Sundays, and well as a place to gather and have dances and horse races. At one time Bob won $3000 in one race.

Dora Flack, and probably others, believe Bob first met with Elzy Lay, who became a life long friend, while working in Browns Hole, and maybe while working at the Bassett Ranch. It was Butch and Elzy Lay who later robbed the Pleasant Valley Coal Company at Castle Gate of it's payroll. William Elzy Lay was born in MacArthur, Ohio, on November 25, 1868(making him about 2 1/2 years younger than Bob). Later, his family moved to eastern Colorado, then to Kansas. As a youngster in Ohio, Elzy had run around with a friend named William McGinnis, a name Elzy would use as an alias later in life. When old enough, Elzy left home and headed west. He landed in Browns Hole and worked for a time at the same Bassett Ranch as Bob.

After awhile, and no one knows for sure how long, Bob left to find a better paying job, this time in Rock Springs, Wyoming. He eventually found a job with William Gottsche, who owned a butcher shop. Although there are different accounts as to how Bob got the name "Butch", most seem to think it was in Rock Springs while working at the butcher shop.

While living in Rock Springs, one night he got into a bar room brawl. It turned out he somehow saved the life of one of Wyoming best trial lawyers, Douglas A. Preston. They became friends for life, and Preston in later years, was to defend members of the Wild Bunch.

At another time and in another bar, Bob(perhaps now we should call him Butch, although he was going by the name George Parker while living in Rock Springs) had another scrape with the law. He had been boozing it up with an old drinking buddy, who had been flashing a big roll of money around. About the time the friend had gotten full of grog and was fully drunk, Butch walked away, but the drunk spilled his heavy coins on the bar and floor. Later some of the money was missing, and someone pointed a finger at Butch. Dora Flack's account states that the bar tender had put some gum he was chewing on the bottom of his shoe, and walked around collecting some of the gold pieces. Butch was evidently arrested, but then apparently released, because there are no court records of the matter.

On many of the court records and in most of the books and articles written about Butch, the name George Parker is given as the real name of Robert LeRoy Parker. He may have unwittingly gotten this name in Rock Springs. At that time the marshal of Rock Springs was named Harry S. Parker, who had a son, Harry George Parker. Also in town at the same time was the brother of the marshal, George Parker. With all the George Parkers in town, this somehow could have led to Butch's use of the name, or of others applying the name George to Butch, simply because of ignorance.

At the time of the incident with the drunk, or just after and as perhaps a result of that incident, Butch and some of his friends left together and lived just outside of town a ways. Butch and friends would on occasion come into town and scare the hell out of people, but didn't take their case far enough to be arrested. Locals started calling this band the Wild Bunch, which may have been the place of origin for this famous name.

Another time, place and incident has been authenticated by Dora Flack. In the year 1892, Butch went to work for the EA Outfit in the Wind River region of Wyoming. This was in the Lander area, on the east slope of the range. Another cowpoke by the name Al Hainer worked at the ranch at the same time. They became friends and a bit later decided to homestead together. They bought a cabin on Horse Creek, northwest of Lander, which is the present day site of Dubois, Wyoming. They called their little ranch the Quien Sabe.

The winter of 1892-1893 was a severe one, and complicated by an outbreak of the flu. Butch hired himself out to various ranches in the area to help out when the owners were down and out with the bug. By doing this he evidently made a good name for himself, as in later years, people in and around Lander remembered.

It was during the winter, Butch had made special friends of the Simpson's, John C. and wife Margaret. Margaret had a simple knowledge of medicine, and as she would make up a concoction for someone, Butch would ride out to a ranch to delivery it.

During this period of time Butch made a friend, which he called in the Phillips manuscript, and in letters written later in life, his "Lander Sweetheart". Pointer says this was Mary Boyd, a half-blood from Lander. Local people think Butch and Mary had many clandestine meetings even after Butch got out of prison, and even while she was married to O.E. Rhodes. Later in life, William T. Phillips(the name Butch died with) visited the Wind River Mountains area(1934), and re-established a relationship. He later sent her several letters and his Mexican Fire Opal ring, which is discussed later.

Throughout the period of about 1891-1893, while living in the Lander area, a happening occurred which put Butch at another crossroad of life. Quoting now from Dora Flack's *Butch Cassidy, My Brother,* "Butch and Al were arrested and brought to trial for horse theft. From court records, it appears that there were two cases. A complaint dated July 15, 1892, charged George Cassidy and Albert Hainer with stealing one horse valued at forty dollars from the Grey Bull Cattle Company, on or about October 1, 1891, in the county of Fremont, Wyoming. (An interesting observation is that the complaint came almost ten months after the alleged theft.) Later, a legal notice dated March 14, 1893, gave notice for George Cassidy to appear on June 12, 1893. Chas. Staugh, Sheriff, served the papers. On June 22, 1893, the jury rendered a verdict of not guilty for both men."

The arresting officer was Bob Calverly. With the arrest warrant, they tracked Cassidy and Hainer to a cabin near Auburn, Wyoming, in the Star Valley. There was a struggle, and Butch was slightly wounded in the forehead by a gun shot. That event took place on April 11, 1892.

About this same time, another complaint was filed on June 19, 1893, charging Butch, or George Cassidy and Al Hainer with stealing a horse valued at $50, from Richard Ashworth on August 28, 1891(this was two years after the theft). Douglas A. Preston was Butch's attorney. The trial finished and the verdict read on July 4, 1894. The jury statement read:*"We the jury find the above named defendant George Cassidy guilty of horse stealing, as charged in the information, and we find the value of the property stolen to be $5.00. And we find the above named defendant Al Hainer not guilty. And the jury recommends the said Cassidy to the mercy of the court. Geo. S. Russell, Foreman.*(Flack)

No one can explain why $50 is mentioned in one record, while $5 is mentioned in another. But Lula remembered on several occasions, during Butch's visit to Circleville in 1925, he expressed bitterness over being put in jail for stealing a horse worth $5.

Butch was committed to the Wyoming State Penitentiary in Rawlins, on July 15, 1894, as George "Butch" Cassidy. The Pinkerton Detective Agency also lists and uses the name George, which must explain how and why so many writers have since used this name. It was nice for Butch and the family too, because it did not reveal the true family name.

After serving one and a half years of a two-year sentence, Butch went before Governor W. A. Richards, at the governors' request. After a lengthy discussion, and after Butch promised not to steal

A foto of Butch Cassidy or Robert LeRoy Parker, when
he entered the Wyoming Prison, July 15, 1894.
(Wyoming State Archives)

any more cattle or horses, or to rob any banks in Wyoming, he was pardoned. He was released on January 19, 1896. But he never did promise not to rob any trains in Wyoming.

As Lula Betenson puts it(in the words of Dora Flack), Butch was very bitter about the whole ordeal. He swore vengeance on Bob Calverly, the sheriff who had arrested him at the time he was sent to prison. From the seclusion of Browns Hole, he also threatened others.

It seems that time in prison did have a lasting effect on Butch, for it wasn't long after his release, he started down the outlaw trail with vengeance. During the summer of 1896, Matt Warner was in jail in Vernal on a murder charge, and his wife was sick. Butch and Elzy Lay found out about it, and it appeared to them Matt had shot in self defense; so they contacted Douglas A. Preston, Butch's attorney friend from Rock Springs, to handle the case. But they needed money. So they planned a bank job in Montpelier, in southeast Idaho.

On August 13, 1896, Butch Cassidy, Elzy Lay, and Bob Meeks rode into Montpelier. While Bob Meeks stayed outside with the horses, Butch and Elzy went inside the bank and grabbed $16,500 in gold(another account states $7,000). No one resisted, and they simply rode out of town very cool and collected, as if nothing was wrong. Outside town they headed up canyon at full speed, to where their first relay horses had been stationed. This is the same pattern they were to use over and over again; that of having several sets of horses posted at various intervals on a getaway route out of town.

It was after the Montpelier job, that Pointer thinks Butch may have gone east for a while, this according to the Phillips manuscript. He was in Michigan for a time, and nearly arrested after someone recognized him. It was also in Michigan that the first documented evidence of the existence of a Mr. William T. Phillips first appeared. That was where Phillips married Gertrude Livesay in 1908 after returning from South America. More later.

Preston defended Matt Warner, but he was found guilty anyway. He was sentenced to 5 years in the Utah State Pen. There were allegations in at least one newspaper article that part of the money from the Montpelier Bank holdup was used to pay for attorney Preston, but he flatly denied it. After Matt was in prison, Butch visited Matts wife and gave her money to live on while her husband was incarcerated.

After the holdup, and after Matt Warner was in jail, Butch and Elzy went to work for Jens Nielson who lived in Huntington, Utah, in the Castle Valley, southwest of Price. This was in the fall of 1896. It must have been about that time they were joined by Harry Longabaugh, usually known as the Sundance Kid, but no one knows for sure if Sundance joined Butch and Elzy in Huntington, or at Robbers Roost a short time later. But it is documented by several writers that during the winter of 1896-1897, the gang was at Robbers Roost, hiding out and planning their next stick-up.

During that winter of 1896-1897, there were five known figures at the Roost. Butch Cassidy, Elzy Lay, Maude Davis Lay(wife of Elzy Lay), Harry Longabaugh(Sundance Kid), and his girl friend, Etta Place. Maude Davis was from what was then called Ashley Valley(the valley area there now Is called Vernal), and she married Elzy Lay. This must have taken place in the mid 1890's. Somewhere in the Roost Country, they made camp, with one tent for Elzy and Maude, another for Sundance and Etta Place. There were other men there too, but no one knows just who. It seems logical that they were just drifters, coming and going, because it was only Butch and Elzy, and maybe Joe Walker, who pulled off the Castle Gate job.

The winter was spent planning a holdup of the Pleasant Valley Coal Company payroll in Castle Gate, just up canyon and north of Price. They also trained their horses and had everything ready by the time they broke camp in the early spring. At that time they sent the girls back to civilization.

Butch and Elzy planned this robbery very meticulously, and trained their horses too. In the week or two before, the horses were trained to hold still while Butch made a flying leap to get on board. They also took the horses into the coal mining camp daily so they would become accustomed the train whistles. All this time they posed as jockeys, as horse racing was a popular spectator sport in those days, and this gave them a reason to be in town.

The holdup took place about noon, on Wednesday, April 21, 1897. The next day the local newspaper in Price, the *Eastern Utah Advocate*, published the story. It went like this:

Bold, bad highwaymen, created consternation and excitement Wednesday noon at Castle Gate, by holding up E. L. Carpenter, the Pleasant Valley Coal Company's paymaster and making off with $7000 in gold.

The horse thieves, bandits and murderers infesting what is commonly known as Robbers Roost 60 miles(100 kms) southeast of Price on the San Rafael River in Emery Country, have in the past few years committed many an atrocious deed of daring, but none so bold and audacious as this last unprecedented and nervy holdup. This tough clique is rapidly gaining a reputation not to be envied by any except such men as composed the celebrated "James Gang" and they are invariably successful in their undertakings and in evading the minions of the law.

This last daring act of theirs is supposed to have been committed by Tom Gissell(actually Elzy Lay) and "Butch Cassidy", and it is reasonably certain at this writing that the identity of at least Cassidy, who figured about a year ago in the Montpelier, Idaho, bank robbery, can be established.

The particulars of the hold-up, robbery and flight of the desperadoes is as follows: The pay rolls, money and checks for paying the coal diggers and company's employees at Castle Gate, was sent down Wednesday from Salt Lake City on the Rio Grande Western passenger train No. 2, which reaches Castle Gate at about 12 o'clock noon. There were two sacks of silver, one of $1000, one of $860, one sack of gold containing $7000, and a satchel holding the rolls and checks for another thousand dollars, in all $9860. These were all transferred to the hands of E. L. Carpenter and a deputy clerk who were at the depot awaiting the arrival.

When No. 2 pulled out for Helper the paymaster and deputy crossed over the tracks to the Wasatch Company's store, a two story rock building about fifty yards(45 meters) distant from the depot, and were just about to carry the treasure up the stairs on the east side of the building, which led up to the P.V. Coal Company's offices, when a rough looking individual, evidently "Butch" Cassidy, stepped in front of Mr. Carpenter and exclaimed "drop them sacks and hold up your hands."

The request was backed up by a six-shooter being pushed into the astonished paymaster's face, and he naturally complied. T. W. Lewis, the clerk, noted the situation at once and made a run into the store with the thousand dollar sack of silver. The bold highwayman then cooly stooped and picking up the other two sacks and satchel handed them to his confederate who was on horse-back near at hand. Cassidy's pal rode swiftly down the road, but the former was out of luck for a few moments as his horse got loose and started away. He, however, ran rapidly and caught the animal a few feet away, instantly mounted and sped after the man ahead.

While Mr. Carpenter was being relieved of the money, the mounted bandit flourished a six-shooter and fired several shots promiscuously, and the only thing done toward preventing their escape until it was too late, was the firing of three shots from the offices of the company as they flew down the road. The robbery was accomplished with so much bravado and daring that the suddenness of the act completely paralyzed the number of men who were lounging about near the scene, and there were nearly a hundred of them around and in the store who witnessed the whole affair.

Passing safely through the lower part of town the robbers stopped a short distance north of the half-way house and cut the telegraph wires. They also examined the satchel and finding nothing of use to them in it, left it on the road. The sack containing $860 in silver had been dropped near the power house in town, no doubt on account of its being too heavy to carry, so their load now consisted only of the $7000 in gold. Reaching John U. Bryner's Ranch at the mouth of Spring Creek canyon and just north of Helper, they crossed his land and went about 2 miles(3 kms) up the canyon, where they turned south over the ridge and continued on a trail which makes a perfect circuit of Helper, Spring Glen and Price, and being only distant from them about three miles(5 kms).

It was 2:30 P.M.. when they reached the main traveled Emery county road between Cleveland and Price, and here they cut the telegraph wire, but they were too late in doing so, as messages had already gone over the line to Huntington, Castle Dale and Cleveland where posses were being organized to intercept the men.

At 4:00 P.M.. the mail carrier met them this side of Cleveland and they were then but four or five miles(seven or eight kms) ahead of Sheriff Donant's posse which left Price at 2:00 P.M. The men were described as being one about 25 years of age and the other as middle age. The younger man wore a black hat, blue coat and goggles, while the man who held Mr. Carpenter up had on a light slouch hat, denham overalls and brown coat. Both men were sun-browned and appeared more like cowboys or common hoboes than desperate highwaymen. One of the men rode a grey horse with only bridle and no saddle and the other was on a bay horse loitering around Caffey's saloon during Tuesday. They had evidently laid their plans well and were there on time to prepare for the capture of the money.

Mr. Carpenter and others followed the highwaymen down the canyon on an engine, but did not see them and came on to Price where the news spread like wild-fire."

Pearl Baker has added a few changes to the escape in her book, The Wild Bunch at Robbers Roost. As it turned out it was Joe Walker who had cut the telegraph wires in or near Price, then he headed south. Late in the afternoon Butch and Elzy met Joe Walker just south of Desert Lake, which is east of Cleveland. They all headed down Buckhorn Wash, and along the San Rafael River to Mexican Bend, arriving there at dusk. In the meantime two posses had set out after them, one from Huntington, the other from Castle Dale. In Buckhorn Wash the two posses met, and because of darkness, each group suspected the other of being the outlaws and opened fire on the other. No one was hurt, but one horse was shot.

At Mexican Bend, the outlaws had left several horses with a young boy. At that point they all split up. Cassidy and Lay rode on down to the Robbers Roost southeast of Hanksville, Joe Walker headed on over to Woodside, down the Price River then up to Florence Creek Ranch. The boy headed home to Castle Valley.

The next event in the life of Butch Cassidy may have been a bank holdup in North Dakota. In Larry Pointer's book, In Search of Butch Cassidy, where he uses the unpublished Phillips manuscript, he states that Butch may have been involved in the holdup of the bank in Belle Fourche, South Dakota, on June 28, 1897. It's from the unpublished manuscript that implies Butch was involved. People at that time thought it was George "Kid" Curry, Harvey Ray, and maybe Harvey Logan and one more man. No other writer believes Butch was involved in this one.

There are so many stories surrounding the life of Butch Cassidy, no one seems to know just where the truth ends and the story telling begins. Dora Flack, writing for Lula Betenson, used a tape recording done by Edna Robison of Hanksville, who was the daughter of Charley Gibbons, a prominent figure in the early history of Hanksville. Gibbons owned the only hotel and store in Hanksville around the turn of the century. Edna was a little girl then, but remembered the Wild Bunch well. She said they would come in looking like cowboys, and stay a few days at a time. She relates a story which surely must be true.

Once the Bunch came to stay awhile, and Butch asked Edna's mother to cook dinner for the boys, about 12 of them on that occasion. The small children were asked to go upstairs to play, while food was being prepared. When supper was ready, the boys came to eat. As Joe Walker was sitting down, his gun holster caught on a wire on the chair, turning it upside down and released the hammer. The six-shooter discharged, sending a bullet up through the ceiling and into the upstairs. Butch, who was right there, screamed "those little girls are up there". Butch dashed up the stairs to find everyone OK. Then he cursed the boys saying, "don't one of you boys ever come in this house again with a loaded gun."(Flack)

There's another story which takes many forms and is repeated often. Each time it's told, it changes a bit. This version of the story Edna Robison swears is true, and she even gives a name.

One time Butch was riding along up the valley, somewhere to the west of Hanksville, and found a lady alone and crying. When asked what was the matter she replied, the person who owns the mortgage on this property is coming by today, and we don't have the money to pay. In this particular version of the story, the amount owed was $500. Butch said, don't you worry, I can help. He went outside and got $500 from his saddle bags, and returned. He said, when that fellow comes you give him the money and be sure to get a receipt which states the mortgage is paid in full and that you now own the property. He then left, but went just up the road a ways to wait. Later, the man came to collect the bill. The woman paid, and the man left. But Butch stopped him on the way, and retrieved his $500. Edna Robison claimed the woman was Mrs. Fred Noyes.

According to the Daughters of the Utah Pioneers book, *Rainbow Views--A History of Wayne County*, the family of Fredrick Noyes Senior, lived between the small communities of Aldrich and Caineville during the 1880's, and perhaps into the 1890's. They went to church in the Aldrich branch. Aldrich began to die soon after the big flood of 1897, and was all but deserted by about 1900. It's believed the family then moved to Hanksville.

On the same tape by Edna Robison which Dora Flack used, she states a document of some kind came out about that time, saying that if the outlaws would lay down their guns and join the military in the Spanish-American War, they would all be pardoned. It was during that period of time the gang was last seen in and around Hanksville. Evidently just after that, Butch went to South America.

About a year after the Castle Gate holdup, an incident happened which only indirectly had to do with Butch. A couple of men were killed, and the lawmen in Price thought they had nabbed a big fish, Butch Cassidy. The shooting took place, according to Pearl Baker's account, in the area of the McPherson Ranch, in the middle parts of Desolation Canyon, and near the head of Hill Creek. The time was May of 1898.

After two outlaws had robbed Bud Whitmore and Billy McGuire of some cattle, a posse set out after them. Jim McPherson, of the McPherson Ranch, and a young cowhand working there, let Sheriff Allred know where the outlaws usually camped; at nearby Moonwater Spring. The young boy led them to the campsite, up one of the canyons to the east of the ranch. They arrived at dawn, and just as the outlaws were awakening. The posse opened fire even before the thieves had a chance to get out of bed, killing two of the four men there. The two who were not killed were later released.

The two men killed were taken back to Price and identified as Joe Walker and Butch Cassidy. They were buried on a Sunday, but the body tentatively identified as Butch, was exhumed the next day, Monday, for more positive identification by Doc Shores(according to Flack's account), or Evanston's Sheriff Ward and Douglas A. Preston(by Pearl Baker's account). They then agreed the body was not Butch Cassidy's, but John Herring's instead.

Years later, according to Butch's sister, Lula Betenson, he told the family that when he heard he had been killed, he thought it would be a good idea to attend his own funeral. As the story goes, Butch returned in a covered wagon, securely hidden inside, so he could peep out safely. No one knows who the wagon was driven by, and no one has tried to explain how Butch could have gotten there so fast, unless he had been living very close by.

The next event which most people attribute to Butch Cassidy and the Wild Bunch, was the train robbery at Wilcox, Wyoming. This one took place in the middle of the night, and was so cleverly done,

Prison foto of Elzy Lay(or William H. McGinnis). Taken at the New Mexico state prison, 1899.
(New Mexico State Penitentiary)

the finger automatically pointed to Butch.

On June 2, 1899, at 2:18 A.M. the Overland Flyer of the Union Pacific was stopped near Wilcox, which is on the main line between Rawlins and Laramie, Wyoming. Two armed men ordered the engineer to uncouple the express car, and to move the engine and other cars across a bridge. Then four more men appeared along side the express car, where the safe and money were at. Inside was a fellow named Woodcock. He refused to open the door, so the bandits blow it open. They then had to use dynamite on the safe as well, blowing the hell out of the car in the process. According to Larry Pointer's figures, they got away with $60,000.

After the Wilcox train robbery, the Wild Bunch headed south in a hurry. They passed by the Carlisle Ranch near Monticello Utah, as a Pinkerton detective traced Harvey Logan to that site. Then on into Arizona and finally they landed in Alma, New Mexico, just across the stateline from Arizona. Three men, Butch Cassidy(under the name Jim Lowe), Elzy Lay(William McGinnis), and Harvey Logan(under the name Tom Capehart) all got jobs on the a ranch owned by a Mr. Wilson, but managed by William French. Charles Kelly, in his book, *Outlaw Trail*, quotes French as saying, "Rustling of the WS stock stopped immediately". They also drove "a herd of cattle 300 miles(500 kms) across deserts without losing a head". They were the best cowhands he had ever had working at the WS Ranch. Apparently they hadn't worked there long as the next holdup they pulled off took place was on July 11, l899, less than 6 weeks after the Wilcox job. This they did while working at the WS Ranch. French remembers they would come and go for "business reasons". One of their business trips took them to Folsom, New Mexico.

The Folsom train robbery was carried out in typical Butch Cassidy style on the Colorado Southern line. The engine and the other cars were separated, the express car blown up, and they took off with the loot. A posse was quickly organized at Trinidad, N.M., which consisted of a number of well trained men. Part of the gang had made camp in Turkey Canyon, about 15 kms south of Cimmaron(about 50 kms south west of Folsom). The posse followed the trail into the canyon, where there was a 45 minute gun battle. Two sheriffs were killed, and Elzy Lay badly wounded. In the end Elzy Lay, going by the name William McGinnis, was sentenced to a life term in prison on October 10, 1899.

But Elzy was a model prisoner, and soon he was the driver for the warden. He was trusted to the point of being allowed to take the warden into Santa Fe on business. On one such trip, they returned to find the prison in riot, and the warden's wife and daughter being held hostage. Elzy helped to end the standoff, and had his sentence commuted to 10 years. Later, and because of good behavior, he was fully pardoned by Governor Otero on January 10, 1906.

The express car shown blown up, after the Wilcox, Wyoming robbery, on June 2, 1899(Union Pacific Railroad Museum Collection)

Upon his release from prison, Elzy went back to the WS Ranch near Alma, where he worked for two years, then went to Wyoming and got into the saloon business. Ranch manager French believed he got his start in Wyoming, from the loot taken in the Folsom robbery, since that money, some $70,000, never showed up or was recovered. At a later tIme, Elzy, who continued to use the name William McGinnis for the rest of his life, bought a ranch in Moffat County, Colorado, just east of Browns Hole, and re-married. He died in Los Angeles in 1933.

Meanwhile, after the Folsom robbery and back in Alma, Butch continued to work at the ranch for awhile, but it couldn't have been long. Pinkerton detectives in hot pursuit, traced Butch to the WS Ranch, but he had split.

Pointer, in his book, *In Search of Butch Cassidy,* where he uses the Phillips manuscript, believes Butch may have taken an extended trip to the west coast after the Wilcox robbery, but if such a trip did occur, it was more likely to have been after the Folsom holdup. According to Phillips, he got a job on the boat "Elinor," and worked his way down the coast from Seattle to Los Angeles. Trips such as this undoubtedly helped Butch come up with new ways to confuse the law of his whereabouts and how to stay undetected over the years. In the Phillips manuscript, Butch talks about taking on a new lingo(forgetting the cowpoke language), new cloths and even a new way of walking.

Because of the killing involved on the Folsom job, and with Butch's best friend almost killed, and in jail, it seems he may have taken the time to re-think his life and in which direction it was going. It was in the three months or so after the Folsom robbery, that Butch approached several people in Salt Lake City, about the possibility of getting a pardon, giving up his guns, and going straight. One man was Judge Orlando W. Powers. The problem, as Powers saw it, was that to be pardoned, one first had to be convicted of a crime. Butch's slate was clean in Utah, and they couldn't prove anything against him in the Castle Gate hyst. Judge Powers, believing Butch was on the level and really wanted to take a try at reform, suggested he might be a guard for the railroad, if they would agree(Dora Flack has good reason to believe that Butch wanted to go straight, because Butch turned in two guns to Sheriff Parley Christensen of Levan, Utah, sometime late in 1899. One was a Colt 45, #158402, which was purchased from the Ashley Valley Co-op in Vernal, in 1896. The other was a Winchester 73 44-40 Saddle Ring Carbine, Serial #64876.).

Quoting now from Kelly's *Outlaw Trail,* "After some discussion the railroad officials agreed to the plan[of having Butch be a guard for the railroad people] and authorized Powers to get in touch with Cassidy. Powers wrote to Douglas A. Preston, Cassidy's attorney at Rock Springs, who carried the message to the outlaw in Brown's Hole." When Butch got the message, he said, "sounds good to me, you meet me in ten days from today, at Lost Soldier Pass[somewhere near the Utah-Wyoming line], and bring the U.P.'s[Union Pacific R.R.] chief detective and some official with power to make an agreement." The time was in October of 1899.

Butch got there early and waited, and waited. He waited all day, and finally gave up, with storm clouds on the horizon. He left a note under a rock stating, "Damn you, Preston, you have double-crossed me. I waited all day but you didn't show up. Tell the U.P. to go to hell. And you can go with them"(Kelly). As it turned out, Preston and the two other men were delayed 24 hours by a storm. They retrieved the note seen above.

Kelly further states that "Preston rode to Browns Hole to see Butch shortly after this episode, but Cassidy wouldn't talk to him. It took him six months to square himself for what the outlaw believed was an act of treachery."

It seems Butch really had been serious about reforming and going straight, but by the time he and Preston got things straightened out, it was too late. He and the boys were already planning the next job.

That job was the Tipton train robbery. The site was 80 kms west of Rawlins, Wyoming, along the main Union Pacific line. The actual robbery took place along a steep grade about 4 kms west of the railway line station of Tipton and at a landmark named Table Rock. Five men were involved in this one, which took place about 8:00 P.M. on the night of August 29, 1900. Three were positively identified as Butch Cassidy, Harvey Logan, and Harry Longabaugh(the Sundance Kid).

As usual, the cars were separated, and the express car where the safe was located was broken into. It took three blasts to crack the safe. First accounts of the robbery said that $55,000 was taken(Larry Pointer's figures), but after a complete check, it was determined only $50.40 was missing. According to Charles Kelly, railway officials later admitted that a shipment of $100,000 was scheduled to be on that train. It was surmised the Wild Bunch had some inside information on the shipment, which as it turned out, had been delayed.

According to Dora Flack, Butch was in the process of making a few big hauls so he could leave the country and settle down elsewhere, so he could make a new start. That's the reason he made so many(five) bold robberies in a short span of two years, from 1899 to 1901.

Since it appears the Tipton job was bungled, as far as getting rich is concerned, the Wild Bunch got down to planning another holdup as fast as possible. That next job was the First National Bank of Winnemucca, Nevada.

This was one of the last holdups Butch was directly involved with before leaving for South America. But that depends on whose book you're reading. Some of the information about this holdup comes from

The interior of the express car, after it was robbed at Tipton, Wyoming, on August 29, 1900 (Union Pacific Railroad Museum Collection)

a letter written to Dora Flack from a man named Mr. I. V.(Vic) Button. He was a 10 year old at the time of the robbery, and was living at the C.S. Ranch, a few kms east of Winnemucca, on the Humboldt River.

Vic remembered three cowboys camped at a nearby haystack for about 10 days before the robbery. Each day they would ride into town, and when he was around, would ask him(Vic) a lot of questions about the town and people and the bank. Butch was riding a big white horse, which Vic liked very much. Butch said to him once, "You like the horse? Someday he will be yours."

The big day turned out to be September 19, 1900. The three men involved were Butch Cassidy, Harry Longabaugh(Sundance Kid), and Bill Carver. The holdup went fine, but on the way out, Butch dropped a sack of money, and when he turned to pick it up, some of the bank employees started firing at him. They missed.

The white horse Vic Button was crazy over, was the same horse Butch was riding the day of the robbery. A few kms down the road, and as the gang was changing to fresh horses, a posse caught up with them. Butch yelled out they would shoot it out with the posse if the posse wanted. Evidently the posse decided the odds were against them, so they turned to leave, when Butch again yelled out, "Give the white horse to the kid at the C.S. Ranch"(Flack). Vic, the kid at the ranch, eventually got the horse, and the gang got away with about $32,000, in gold and cash.

Not long after the holdup, five members of the Wild Bunch; Cassidy, Longabaugh, Logan, Bill Carver and Ben Kilpatrick(these last two men were former members of Black Jack Ketchum's Gang) found themselves together in Fort Worth, Texas. With all the money they had they decided to lay low for a while in what was then called "Hell's Half Acre." On a lark, they dressed up in derby hats and suits, and had their picture taken. But it just so happened, a man by the name of Fred Dodge, a Wells Fargo detective working in the area, chanced upon the foto, and recognized Bill Carver. Later the others were identified. Pinkertons Detective Agency was on their trail.

As another story goes, Butch sent a copy of the foto back to the Winnemucca bank, and thanked them for their contribution. This was a mistake, if in fact it did happen, because it helped put the Pinkerton boys on their trail again. Today, there is a large size picture of that famous foto hanging on the wall of the bank in Winnemucca.

The last exploit of the Wild Bunch in the USA was the holdup of the Great Northern train near Wagner(Exeter), Montana, on July 3, 1901. The exact site was 11 kms west of Malta, and 5 kms east of Wagner, near the O'Neil Ranch.

It was probably Harvey Logan who talked Butch into pulling off this one last job before going to South America. Logan was familiar with Montana, and had as one of his hideouts, a place called Landusky,

The Wild Bunch in about 1900. Left to right and seated; Harry "Sundance Kid" Longabaugh, Ben "Tall Texan" Kilpatrick, Robert LeRoy Parker, or Butch Cassidy. Standing; Will Carver and Harvey "Kid Curry" Logan (Denver Public Library Western History Collection)

just to the southwest of the robbery site, about 70 kms, as the crow flies.

This is how they pulled this one off. When the train stopped in Malta, Harvey Logan climbed aboard the blind baggage. Harry Longabaugh boarded the train as a paying passenger. Butch waited near the O'Neil Ranch. Camilla(Deaf Charley?) Hanks guarded the horses. At the right spot, Logan got to the engineer's cab, and ordered the train stopped. Logan then ordered the engineer to uncouple the express car and pull across a bridge. Butch then moved in and took over. At one point, an off-duty sheriff from Great Falls, started shooting from the rear of the train, but Longabaugh shot back. The sheriff was quiet during the rest of the stickup. It took about three shots of dynamite to blow the safe, which was full of unsigned bank notes, to a bank in Helena, Montana, and worth about $65,000. They got away clean, but the unsigned bank notes led to trouble.

Logan went to Knoxville, Tenn., where he spent some of the notes, and was arrested. He was later convicted, and sentenced to 30-90 years in prison. Still later, he escaped, but got into a gun battle with a Montana Sheriff, and was wounded. He died later near Thermopolis, Wyoming, according to Kelly.

Meanwhile, Butch and Sundance managed to exchange their hot bills, with money which was untraceable. After that they got together somewhere in Texas, and planned their departure to South America. Sundance brought along his girl friend, Etta Place.

Pointer quotes the Phillips manuscript as saying that after Wagner robbery, Butch made his way by train to Minneapolis, then Duluth. He then traveled by boat and train to Montreal, then by boat to Liverpool. He had to wait only a week in Liverpool, before boarding a boat to South America, making stops in the Canary and Cape Verde Islands, Pernambuco(Recife), and Rio De Janerio. He ended his journey in Montevideo, and waited for his friends.

By whatever way he made it to South America, it was to begin a new life for Robert LeRoy Parker, at least for the next four years or so.

Harry Longabaugh (the Sundance Kid) and Etta Place. Foto taken in New York City, in about 1901, before leaving for South America(DeYoung's Studio-New York, and Pinkertons)

South America

Getting information about the life of Butch Cassidy in South America must have been a real job for those writers who got deeply involved. But much of what we know comes from Butch himself in letters written home to various friends. In other cases, other gringos who knew him there have contributed information.

Some dates are fixed on records. The Wagner holdup was on July 3, 1901, and according to government land office records in Buenos Aires, Butch, Sundance and Etta, received four square leagues of land in Cholila District, Province of Chubut, on October 16, 1901. According to Pointer, all three used their real names while in Argentina; Robert LeRoy Parker, Harry Longabaugh, and Etta Place, indicating they were serious about settling down and forgetting the past.

Many writers have published a letter from Butch to the mother of Maude Davis Lay(Elzy Lay's mother-in-law), dated August 10, 1902. The address given was, Cholila. Ten Chubut. Argentina Republic. S. Am. In this letter Butch describes the conditions of life and where he was. He said he was over 400 miles(650 kms) from the nearest sea port in Argentina, 1600 miles(2500 kms) from Buenos Aires, and 150 miles(240 kms) from the Pacific Coast.

The letter states that the Chilean Government had plans to cut a road across the frontier to Argentina, making the route for him and cattle much shorter to Puerto Montt, than to San Antonio, Argentina, on the Atlantic Coast. The route he speaks of must be the route from the area of Bariloche, the famous ski resort, over a pass to the northwest, and on to Osorno in Chile. But that would have been a lot longer than the four days to the port he talks about(This author has been in that area several times, once walking from Argentina to Chile, via the summit of a prominent volcano, Tronador, which took about 3 days, trailhead to trailhead.). No evidence exists that tells of Butch ever taking cattle over to the Chilean side for sale.

One supposedly reliable source of information about Butch's life and adventures in South America comes from an article in *Elks Magazine* for April, 1930, written by Arthur Chapman, titled "Butch Cassidy".

Apparently Butch, Sundance and Etta lived on a ranch in the upper valley of the Chubut River not far from the Chilean Frontier, and in the same area as a colony of old Confederate veterans who migrated there after the Civil War. Everything went fine for about 4 years. But then they got one new neighbor, who had been a deputy sheriff from somewhere in the western USA. He recognized Butch and Sundance and contacted local authorities, probably with the idea of collecting a big reward. After awhile, Butch and Sundance, who were getting letters from home in the states, heard that detectives were on their way to arrest them. They hurriedly sold their holdings and headed for Chile, and were on the loose once again.

It was at about this time, while Butch was still on a ranch, or about the time he went back to some of his old ways, that his mother died. She had gotten ill at home in Circleville, but was taken south to Panguitch to be under the care of a doctor. She died on May 1, 1905 in Panguitch, but was taken back to Circleville to be buried on the 5th of May. Her grave is in the Circleville cemetery, just north of town, with the rest of the immediate family members(near the middle of the cemetery).

The way her daughter Lula talks about her mother in the book, *Butch Cassidy, My Brother,* she literally died of a broken heart because of what her son, Robert LeRoy, had done with his life, and the embarrassment he brought to the family.

According to Arthur Chapman, South America began to experience a rash of bandit raids, bank robberies and train holdups like had never happened before. This must have began about 1905 or 1906. Chapman claims the three were joined about this time by someone from the States named Dey. In between holdups, they apparently worked on ranches, as they had done in the States. There were plenty of old expatriate Yanks in South America at the time, so finding work was easy.

Pointer, who uses the Phillips manuscript, gives Cassidy credit for about six robberies in Argentina, before leaving for either the States or Bolivia. Pointer also uses information from an Argentine journalist who did research on Cassidy while he was in Argentina. The journalist named Justo Piernes, believes Cassidy was responsible for the robbery of the Bank of Laudres and Tarapaca at Rio Gallegos, on February 11, 1905, and a bank robbery in Mercedes on March 2, 1906. Piernes also states there were other minor robberies in this same time frame, committed by gringos, but were likely not the work of Cassidy. They didn't seem to fit his style.

One experience Chapman mentions is the employment of Butch and Sundance at the Concordia Tin Mine(it was somewhere in the mountain range called the Tres Cruces, between Cochabamba and La Paz). They were there working under a Mr. Rolla Glass for a time, and doing well. But then Longabaugh(Sundance), got drunk once, and spilled the beans about some of their previous outlaw escapades. Word spread, and they headed down the trail again.

Another holdup was of the Bolivian Railway pay train at Eucalyptus, near Cochabamba. This time Cassidy and Longabaugh were assisted by a man named McVey. They robbed it in Cassidy style, which included blowing up the express car and safe. The railway employees were so happy not to be

BUTCH'S ARGENTINA(PHILLIPS)

ADOPTED FROM "IN SEARCH OF BUTCH CASSIDY", BY LARRY POINTER

robbed themselves, they made no attempt to chase the "ladrones". After this robbery, Cassidy and Longabaugh made their headquarters for a time at the old abandoned Jesuit mission of Cacambaya, somewhere on the headwaters of the Amazon.

The next identifiable location where Butch is known to have been was at Huanuni and the mines there. These mines were operated by the Scotch firm of Penny & Duncan. Butch got on so well with these fellows, that he forgot all about robbing the place, which was his original plan, Instead, he got a job being in charge of a crew of watchmen. Nothing was stolen while he was there.

Using Dora Flack's sources again. She says Etta Place became ill and all three of them returned to the States for her medical attention. This must have been in about 1906, or thereabouts. (However, Pointer in his book, who uses Pinkerton Detective Agency records, states that detective Frank Dimaio, traced Sundance and Etta back to New York to a hospital. They left B. A. in March, 1902, and returned on August 9, 1902. This would explain why, in the letter to the mother of Maude Davis, dated August 10, 1902, Butch writes about being alone.) Dora Flack has a letter from Cowboy Joe, some kind of circus show performer from earlier in this 20th century, who states he was a wrangler for Butch and Sundance, somewhere in Wyoming near Rock Springs, between 1906 and 1908. But then it appears that in 1908, Butch and Sundance went back to South America and to Bolivia.

According to one source, when they returned to Bolivia, they went to work at the Concordia Tin Mines, where Rolla Glass was the manager. It's not clear from the different sources this author has, if this was the second time they worked at the Concordia Mines, or whether dates have been mixed up. It could be that they worked there twice, in 1905 and 1906, and in 1908. Or their employment could have been during one period around 1908. It seems certain they were there during this last time frame.

Another boss at the Concordia operation was a man by the name of Percy Siebert. Arthur Chapman quotes Siebert as saying, "when Cassidy worked for me at the Concordia Mines, where I was a manager in 1908, on coming into the sitting room he would invariably take a seat on a small sofa which was placed between two windows. This seat gave him a survey of three doors and one window. He always seemed to be cool and calculating, and protected his back very well. Although he always went armed with a frontier model .44 Colt, this weapon was usually stuck in his trouser belt in such a way as to be inconspicuous. I never saw him under the influence of whiskey except once, and then he seemed to be very much ashamed of himself because he could not walk straight."

Siebert goes on to say, "Longabaugh was somewhat distant and did not make friendships easily. But Cassidy seemed to be good natured, pleasant, and entertaining. He used good language, was never vulgar and was liked by all the women who made his acquaintance. To Mr. Siebert he talked freely of his former outlaw career in the States, stating that he had come to South America to make a new start because he knew it was only a matter of time before he was captured or killed in his former territory, as the officers were getting familiar with his tactics and his hideouts. In Bolivia, Cassidy traveled under the names of James or Santiago Maxwell or Jim Lowe", and Mr. Ryan.

In the weeks just prior to the famous San Vicente gun battle, in which it had been widely claimed(but now totally disputed), that Butch and Sundance died, they apparently pulled off a robbery of the mine payroll of the Aramayo Mines, near Quechisla, in southern Bolivia. Then, according to Kelly, they proceeded to Tupiza(on the main rail line in southern Bolivia), where they took employment for a transportation company. Soon someone pointed a finger at them as the perpetrators of the previous robbery, and they again left in a hurry. It was just after this that the San Vicente gunfight supposedly took place, but since they both came back to the USA, Kelly's description of it won't be discussed.

Here's another story of "the final gunfight" as told by Phillips. In the book by Pointer, again using the Phillips manuscript, it states that Butch and three others, including Sundance(under the name of Maxwell) had left La Paz and were going northeast into the Beni Region(the Bolivian Amazon area, east of La Paz), when they met a mule caravan. They began to hold it up, but then a Bolivian cavalry unit came around the corner. There was a long gun battle and Butch's three companions were killed, and most of the soldiers too. When darkness came, and there were no more shots, Butch planted on the body of a companion, a small folder of his with identification inside. Then he took one mule and left for the jungles below. Left at the scene of the gun fight, were three dead bandits, one with Butch's I.D., and three mules.

He made his way down river to Villa Bella, and hence on down the Amazon. At Pernambuco he took a boat to Liverpool, thence to Paris. He entered a private hospital where he had a minor face lift. Then he returned to the States, to begin a new life. Again, this according to the Phillips manuscript.

Quoting from Lula Betenson now, and in the words of Dora Flack, "I do know from Butch's own words that they were not responsible for all they were accused of. Other pairs and gangs of outlaws copied their methods in South America as they did in the United States."

There seems to be three accounts(maybe more) of how two dead gringos were identified as being Butch and Sundance. Quoting Dora Flack's detailed research again, "Kerry Ross Boren has proven without a doubt that the reported gun battle at San Vicente in 1909 had not occurred. However, in 1911 there was a gun battle at Mercedes, Uruguay, where two outlaws were killed. A salesman from the

BUTCH'S BOLIVIA(PHILLIPS)

ADOPTED FROM "IN SEARCH OF BUTCH CASSIDY", BY LARRY POINTER

United States was in his hotel room in Mercedes and overheard a soldier say, 'Come down and see the dead Americanos Bandittos.' The salesman went down and was convinced the outlaws were Butch and Sundance. A year later(1912?) he returned to the United States and went to see Frank Dimaio(of Pinkertons), to whom he told his story and assured Dimaio the dead men were Butch and Sundance. On this flimsy evidence, the file was closed."

Another story comes from the memory of Lula Betenson. When Butch came home in the fall of 1925, they quizzed him about San Vicente, and he said, "I heard they got Percy Siebert from the Concordia Tin Mines to identify a couple of bodies as Butch Cassidy and the Sundance Kid all right. I wondered why Mr. Siebert did that. Then it dawned on me that he would know this was the only way we could go straight. I'd been close to Siebert--we'd talked a lot, and he knew how sick of the life I was. He knew I'd be hounded as long as I lived. Well, I'm sure he saw this as a way for me to bury my past along with somebody else's body so I could start over. I'd saved his and Mr. Glass's lives on a couple of occasions, and I guess he figured this was how he could pay me back."

Butch Goes Home

In the fall of 1925 Robert LeRoy Parker went home to Circleville, Utah. He was driving a new black Ford touring car. He stopped at the old ranch house, where he found his brother Mark fixing a fence. It took a moment for Mark to recognize the man, but then he knew it was Bob. They both got into the car and went to the family home, then in town, 3 kms away. Bob had gone straight to the family farm south of Circleville, but things had changed in the 41 years since he had been gone. By 1925, the family lived in Circleville.

That reunion is told in one long chapter in Dora Flack's book, *Butch Cassidy, My Brother, by Lula Betenson*. He visited with his father, who was 81 years old at the time. Also there during his homecoming were his brothers Eb and Mark and sister Lula. As Lula remembers, he spent about two days in town with his father, then rode by horseback out to a cabin and stayed with his brothers, Mark and Eb for about a week. He then returned to town and stayed a few more days with his father, before leaving, never to return home again. Bob occasionally wrote to his father, but the letters were all carefully destroyed to protect Bob's whereabouts. Bob's brother Dan who was living in Milford at about that time, also got a number of letters from Bob. He also destroyed the letters, to conceal Bob's fake name.

During his visit, Bob revealed many things about his past. One would assume he would surely be telling the truth to his family, even though he was one of the most notorious criminals of his time. But at the same time, one could also assume he would guard his words carefully, and may not have told all. One must also be aware that Lula was recalling memories that were 50 years old at the time her book came out in 1975. While Dora Flack spent 5 years researching to write the entire book, the last chapter is from the memory of Lula Betenson, and memories tend to fade and become distorted with time.

One of the things Bob revealed, was that he had gone straight for the past 16 years, from 1909, when he was allegedly killed, until the present(1925). Being considered a dead man certainly helped him get out of the rut he had been in for so long. He hadn't returned home sooner because he felt ashamed.

He revealed that he had traveled widely. He of course had seen most of South America, and had spent time in Europe, mostly in Spain and Italy, where his knowledge of Spanish certainly must have helped. He had spent a lot of time in Mexico, some of which was in states of Chihuahua and Sonora, and in the Mormon colonies, namely Juarez. He had spent a year or two in Alaska, trapping and prospecting, but spent much of the time among the Eskimos. He was mad as hell at the way speculators had been dishonest and had cheated the Indians out of land.

Lula remembers vividly how Butch had talked about his mother. Whenever the conversation veered, he always came back to asking questions about her. Because she was dead, and because he hadn't seen her since he left home in 1884, he was saddened that he had lost the chance to see and talk to her one last time.

Bob revealed that he and Sundance hadn't come back to the States together after they were supposedly killed. They were getting ready to leave and Bob got a badly swollen leg, perhaps from the bite from a scorpion. He was to meet with Longabaugh later at a rendezvous, but was unable to meet him, and they couldn't contact each other(This is much different from the story in the Phillips manuscript, which means he was a great story teller, or a great lier). Bob said an Indian woman took him in and cared for him until his leg became better. After that he drifted into Mexico, where he moved from job to job.

He recalled the time he met Sundance and Etta Place for the last time. He was sitting in a bar in Mexico City, just minding his own business, when he felt someone place a hand on his shoulder. For a split second, many thoughts ran through his head. He thought Pinkertons had found their man. But he turned to see Etta Place. It was a grand reunion. They went back to Etta's home and met Sundance, and sometime later the three went to a bullfight. Bob was sickened by it, as he never did like bullfighting. Finally in disgust, he stood up and said "three's a crowd", and left. That was the last he had seen of them.

As far as the Parkers in Circleville were concerned, and as far as they knew, Bob never did get married and never had children. At least Bob never told them any of these things. To quote Lula again on her account of the death of Butch Cassidy, she said in her book:

"One day Dad received a letter from one of Bob's friends, reporting that Bob had died of pneumonia. The letter assured Dad that his son was 'laid away very nicely.' It was signed simply 'Jeff'. Robert LeRoy Parker died in the Northwest in the fall of 1937, a year before Dad died. He was not the man who was known as William Phillips, reported to be Butch Cassidy." This is how Lula and the rest of the Parker family wanted it, to keep the burial place and Bob's assumed name at the time of death, a family secret. But there are other accounts by other authors, namely Larry Pointer.

All throughout Lula's book, *Butch Cassidy, My Brother*, it is evident she and the family were ashamed of Bob's behavior, and really didn't like talking about him. Lula seems always to be protecting him, and is always trying to make him a better person than he outwardly was. Surely the family members didn't want to be associated with a criminal, and they certainly didn't want others to know one of the most famous outlaws in America came from their home!

Throughout all books on the subject, Butch is depicted as a great guy whom everyone liked very much, and that in many ways he was like Robin Hood. He stole from the rich only, never robbing the poor; he drank only moderately, and used good language; he helped people in hard times, etc, etc. But bad memories of difficult times fade; good memories last forever. So maybe all the letters quoted in Flack's book from people who heard of Butch through friends or relatives, or who recalled him as a child, are merely choosing the positive side of the man, who was one of the most wanted criminals in American history.

Pearl Baker has a different ending than Lula's. After coming back to the USA for the last time, Butch "then tried to live in Seattle, but the climate and city life galled him. He had some money, but was only in his 60's, and could and did work as a rule. He drifted around and finally settled in Spokane, where he took the name of Roy or LeRoy Phillips. He died in the late 1930's unknown and alone--of pneumonia, Carl Hanks tells me. Butch Cassidy's brothers and sisters in Circleville have always been closed-mouthed about him. I knew the family for years, and finally became good friends with Lula Betenson. She tells me the reason the Parkers have always had nothing to say about Butch was not because they were ashamed of him, or because they didn't know anything--they got tired of being quizzed and the story(and pay) falling into someone else's hands."

Then there's the story written by Larry Pointer, *In Search of Butch Cassidy*.

William T. Phillips

All the evidence in this section of the book concerning the name and whereabouts of Butch Cassidy after he returned from South America, is from the rather well researched and well documented book by Larry Pointer, *In Search of Butch Cassidy*.

The first documented evidence that a William T. Phillips ever existed was when he married Gertrude Livesay in Adrian, Michigan, on May 14, 1908. Prior to this date nothing exists to prove Phillips ever existed. But obviously more research needs to be done.

In 1938, Charles Kelly wrote a letter to Gertrude, and in the reply she said of her late husband, he "did mural decorating in New York City for two or three years; at one time had a machine shop in Des Moines, Iowa, for about seven or eight years." Pointer tracked down these leads, and no evidence ever showed up in either place showing Phillips' ever existed. In later years, Phillips adopted son Billy, told Pointer of how his mother had purposely misled Kelly about her husbands past to protect him.

The last reported proof that Butch Cassidy was in South America, was in the form of a letter. Percy Siebert, the man who worked at the Concordia Tin Mine, and who knew Butch well, had died before Pointer got on the track, but he left behind in the care of his son, a scrapbook of letters from his tour in South America. There were two letters, both written by Cassidy. One letter, signed by Gilly(his grand parents were named Gillies), was sent from Argentina on February 16, 1908. The handwriting was checked and matched with other known documents written by Cassidy. This left three months for him to get from Argentina to Michigan.

The courtship of William and Gertrude was short, and her parents objected. They were married by a Methodist minister, with two witnesses. After a short honeymoon, they settled down in Arizona for awhile, on account of her asthmatic condition. He worked on ranches and in house construction. He also spent a short hitch with Pancho Villa in Mexico, around 1911 or 1912, but that must have been after they had established themselves in Washington State. They settled in Spokane, after Phillips got a job for the Washington Water Power Company. The city directory of Spokane, first listed him in 1911.

In 1912, he went to Alaska with another man, where they did many things, including prospecting for gold and trapping, but according to Lula, his sister, it was too cold for him.

In 1915, he started his own business, the Phillips Manufacturing Company. The company made adding machines. It must have been a successful business, as the Burroughs Company considered buying the patent for one of his machines at one time. Phillips made a trip to Detroit in 1916 to discuss the matter. In 1918, he opened a small machine shop, which later did contract work for the Riblet Tramway Company, which specialized in building ski lifts and mining tramways. By 1925, the business was doing very well. One question which has always bugged researchers over the years is, if Phillips was Cassidy, how or where did he learn about drafting and machine work and about adding machines?

For many years William and Gertrude had tried to have children, but without success. There were several miscarriages. Finally in 1919, they adopted a six-month old boy, who they named William Richard, but who they called "Billy Dick". In 1987, Billy(William R. Phillips) is still alive in Spokane.

During the years in Spokane, Phillips or Cassidy, made friends with two men he had known in Wyoming. One was William C. Lundstrom, who had been a bartender in Sheridan for the White Owl Saloon, which was owned by the second friend, Charles F. "Fred" Harrison. Both of these men had known Phillips in Wyoming as Butch Cassidy.

One of the former employees of the Phillips Manufacturing Co., Athol Evans, was alive and was interviewed by Larry Pointer in 1976. According to Evans, it was common knowledge around the small company, that Phillips had once been one of the leaders in the Hole-in-the-Wall gang in Wyoming, and that Phillips had gone by the name of Cassidy in those days.

Evans recalled the only time anyone recognized him as Butch Cassidy, outside the small circle of friends who knew him well. It was one of the bartenders at the Clausen & Schutte Saloon. When Clausen mentioned to Phillips that he was Butch Cassidy, Phillips asked how he knew. The bartender then showed him a wanted poster, with his foto on it. Then Phillips asked him why he hadn't turned him in. Clausen said, the reward wouldn't be paid, because the statute of limitations had run out. Phillips then knew Butch Cassidy was a free man.

An interesting event happened in 1925. One Riblet official asked Phillips to go to Bolivia to help put up a tramway, but he refused to go. However, since the business was doing well, he used this as excuse to get away from family life awhile. He told Gertrude he was going to South America, but instead he headed to Wyoming and Utah and other parts, to visit old friends. It was at this time he paid his visit to his family in Circleville. The last chapter in Lula Betenson's book, *Butch Cassidy, My Brother,* centers on that two week visit.

Because of the depression and by 1930, Phillips had virtually lost his business. He had to give it up to pay his employees. Things were bad. In that summer, he made a trip to Wyoming, but it wasn't a vacation. He was looking for some of the money he had hidden a way in his outlaw days. No evidence exists that he ever found any.

Things were so bad, that in 1931, he had to give up their big home on Providence Street in Spokane, and buy a smaller home on Kiernan(the exact addresses are found in Pointers book).

During a period of time from about 1933, Phillips and Bill Lundstrom made a living doing odd jobs and looking for gold along the Colombia River

In 1934 Phillips made an extended trip to Wyoming. A Mrs. Ellen Harris, who had known and socialized with the Phillips in Spokane, helped to finance the trip. She took her son, Ben "Fitzharris."

Ben Fitzharris was interviewed in his North Hollywood home by James Dullenty in 1973. Much of the information on that 1934 trip comes from him. Ben was told Phillips was going to look for a certain gold deposit, obviously one of his outlaw caches. Ben remembers the time they first arrived in Lander. He and Phillips had walked from the trailer court, where they were camped, into town, and met with people who had known Phillips earlier in life. Everybody was exited to see him after so many years, and they kept called him "George" and "Cassidy."

Later, Phillips, Mrs. Harris, and Fitzharris, were helped into the Wind River Mountains by Will and Minnie Boyd, and Bert and Jesse Chamberlain. There they made camp, and stayed from May until about October 1, 1934. They camped at Lake Mary and were to do some prospecting. Will Boyd was so happy to see Butch, that he sent for his sister, Mary Boyd Rhodes, who had been Butch's "Lander Sweetheart", back in the good old days. Along with her came her teen-age granddaughter, Ione Campbell.

Throughout the packtrip and while camping at Lake Mary, Ben Fitzharris remembered Phillips told some of the stories of his early life. One was the story about how he had been falsely accused of stealing cattle, while he lived at the little ranch on Horse Creek, which he called Quien Sabe. This is where Dubois is today. Because of those accusations, he landed in the Wyoming Penitentiary.

Fitzharris also remembers how well Phillips could shoot and his expert marksmanship. Another thing he remembered was the Mexican Fire Opal ring Phillips wore. This ring later helped Larry Pointer find out Phillips' true identity.

The party left Lake Mary about October 1, because of snow and cold weather. After they had left the mountains, other people in the area noticed he had done some peculiar prospecting. In the area between Lake Mary and Moccasin Lake, a series of holes were found; each was at the base of a tree and always on the north side. It's quite obvious that he had been looking for one of his caches made in the area. Phillips later complained to Will Boyd, that the country had changed, and it wasn't the way it used to be.

When Phillips returned to Spokane, his finances worse than ever, he decided to write the story of his life. So in the fall of 1934, and surely extending into 1935, he wrote the manuscript, *The Bandit Invincible, the Story of Butch Cassidy.* He submitted the manuscript to publishers and the movie industry, but it was rejected. The movie people apparently didn't want a movie with a "Latino" connection.

In 1935 and very desperate financially, Phillips concocted a plan to kidnap for ransom, one of the rich folks in town, a man by the name of William Hutchinson Cowles. He had tried to get his friend Bill Lundstrom involved, but he didn't succeed. Nothing ever came of the incident.

In 1936 Phillips began to lose his health. He had been treated by a doctor from Pendleton, Oregon, and later was in contact with a cancer sanitarium in Missouri. It was about this time he wrote a letter to his "Lander Sweetheart", Mary Boyd Rhodes. That letter was signed, "Geo" and "W. T. Phillips." It is reprinted in Pointers book. In the letter it is apparent he is near the end, and tells Mary about his failing health and that he may not see another Christmas. In the letter he indicates he is afraid of his letters not getting through, and beyond his wife Gertrude.

In January, 1936, owing to the lack of money, Gertrude went to work as a clerk and librarian at an elementary school in Spokane. In the summer of 1936, Phillips made one last trip to Wyoming and the Wind River Mountains to find a cache of gold, but returned empty handed.

In early 1937, Phillips' health became worse, and Gertrude, being unable to handle the situation, sent him to a resthome. It was a pretty bad place and Phillips about went crazy. It was from the rest home he wrote his last letter to Mary Boyd Rhodes on April 8, 1937. With that letter he also sent his Mexican Fire Opal ring which he had worn for 35 years. On the inside of the ring Phillips had inscribed "Geo C. to Mary B." That ring and letter are now in the possession of Ione Campbell Manning(who author Pointer interviewed).

Phillips stayed in the rest home until July 10, 1937. On that day he was taken to a better place, the Broadacres, the county poor house at Spangle, a few kms from Spokane. He was transported there by ambulance hired by Bill and wife Blanche Lundstrom. On July 20, 1937, William T. Phillips died of stomach cancer.

His body was cremated by the Hazen and Jaegger Mortuary, which was followed by a Rose Croix memorial service conducted by the local Masonic Lodge. There is no grave stone, as Gertrude Phillips scattered his ashes over the Spokane River, according to her husbands' wishes.

Larry Pointer has much in his book which he believes is proof that William T. Phillips is or was indeed, Butch Cassidy and Robert LeRoy Parker. Some of Phillips possessions went to his friends Bill and Blanche Lundstrom. Among the items were two Colt revolvers, similar to those used around the turn of the century, and a .22 Derringer. Carved on the handle of one pistol was the unmistakable brand used by Cassidy, the reverse E, and box E(ƎⵑE).

Concerning the manuscript, *The Bandit Invincible, the Story of Butch Cassidy*. The story goes; as Phillips finished each section of the writing, he would send it to Mrs. Ellen Harris, who was living in California at the time. She would type it up as it was, including the misspelled words and errors in punctuation and grammar. Then she discarded the hand written copy. She gave one copy to her son, Ben Fitzharris, who was doing some bit acting and prop man work in Hollywood, to help market it in movie industry. It apparently was rejected on account of the South American part. A second copy was sent back to Phillips.

Later, the Lundstroms got a look at the typewritten manuscript in possession of Phillips, but that copy was apparently lost or discarded. Shortly after Phillips death, the Lundstroms contacted Ellen Harris about her copy of the manuscript. Harris sent them her copy, and Blanche, with the help of her daughters, hand copied the total manuscript. Although the Harris copy was later lost, the Lundstroms' hand written copy was kept in a trunk. Nearly 40 years later, in 1973, when reporter Jim Dullenty, who wrote for the *Spokane Daily Chronicle*, began doing a series on the controversy of the true identity of William T. Phillips, she remembered the manuscript, and contacted Dullenty. Sometime later, Larry Pointer was given the manuscript.

Larry Pointer, with the aid of the Phillips manuscript, traveled to many locations around the west, and found many sites to be as Phillips described them. It could only have been written by someone who had been there at many locations at the turn of the century. The manuscript is written in third person, Phillips not wanting to expose himself, but in two places he slipped into first person.

Even though the Phillips manuscript was not in his handwriting, it was still examined by Jeannine Zimmerman, a Master Certified Graphoanalyst and Questioned Document Examiner, from Aurora, Colorado. Also included for examination was the August 10, 1902 letter from Cassidy in Chubut Province, Argentina, to Mrs. Davis in Ashley Valley, Utah; and the letter written to Mary Boyd Rhodes(Butch's "Lander Sweetheart"), from William T. Phillips on December 17, 1935, which is presently in the possession of Ione Campbell Manning.

Zimmerman stated that in her opinion these letters were written by the same person. Also, in examining the Phillips manuscript, it was found to have similar sentence structure, spellings of words, and the same writing style as in the letters. Apparently the letter written to Percy Siebert from Butch in Bolivia in February, 1908, had the same hand writing and style, and it was otherwise known to have came from Butch Cassidy.

By the handwriting examination, the places and locations of sites mentioned in the Phillips manuscript, the Mexican Fire Opal ring, the hand gun with the double reverse E on the handle, the fact that William T. Phillips appeared from thin air beginning in April, 1908, the fact that many people knew him as Butch Cassidy when he returned to Wyoming, and the fact William T. Phillips told many people, some of whom are still living, that he was Butch Cassidy, seems to point in the direction that these two men and the "Bandit Invincible," were one and the same person. It appears Larry Pointers research has closed the book on Butch Cassidy.

William and Gertrude Phillips, and another man(middle), shown inside the Phillips Manufacturing Company, in Spokane Washington. Foto was taken in March, 1916.(William R. Phillips foto)

Robert LeRoy Parker, Butch Cassidy, or William T. Phillips of Spokane, Washington. Foto was taken in Spokane about 1930, at 64 years of age.(William R. Phillips foto)

History of Mining in the Henry Mountains Region

Gold Mining

Perhaps the most colorful part of the history of the Henry Mountains has to do with the legends of gold and the old Lost Spanish Mine, sometimes known as the Lost Josephine Mine.

It's not clear exactly how the legend got started, but it seems to have been refined by a man named Edwin T. Wolverton. Wolverton was a mining engineer from the state of Maine, who had been born in Canada. He first visited the Henry Mountains in about 1900, and after years of exploring and mining in the Henry's, wrote a book, or rather a manuscript, in about 1928. This manuscript is now in the B. J. Silliman collection. Wolverton died in 1929, at the age of 67.

The Lost Spanish Mine

Here's a story Wolverton tells in his manuscript. It seems that a rancher in southern Utah, who remains nameless, used to run cattle on the western slopes of the Henry mountains, and more specifically the southwest slopes of Mt. Pennell. The time was the 1860's. In those days it was difficult to find help running cattle, as other farmers were always busy, especially in the summer months. So because of the lack of any anglo cowhands, the rancher hired Indian boys to help herd his cattle.

One time when the rancher was camped at Pipe Springs, on the southwest slopes of Pennell, the Indian boy pointed to the mountain and said, "Plenty gold up there." He said his people had told him many stories about the gold and the Spaniards, but when the rancher ask the boy to take him to the mountain and show him the site, the Indian said,

"Many years ago the Spaniards dug gold out of the mountains. They made the Indians do the work and treated them badly. They were forced to labor from dawn to darkness, and often beaten and kicked like dogs. One day the surrounding hills were filled with warriors and a terrible battle was fought. Many of the Indians were killed, but all the Spaniards were slain, their shelters burned, and the mine carefully filled in. As the Indians were covering the mine, the Medicine Man placed a great curse on the place. If anyone ever opened the mine again, his blood would turn to water, and even in his youth he would become as an old man. His squaws and papooses would die, and for him only poison weeds would grow instead of corn."

Sometime later, in 1868, and at the Desert Springs stage station somewhere in southwestern Utah, a man by the name of Burke came in asking for aid. He stated that he had been prospecting for gold in the mountains to the east, and that the Indians had stolen his horse, and had told him to leave the country. Burke had some ore samples which he thought had come from an old Spanish Mine. The owner of the stage station, a man named Bowen, had glitter in his eyes, so he sold the stage station as soon as possible, and joined Burke.

Later, Bowen and Burke went to Minersville, where they outfitted themselves and set out to find their fortune. In Rabbit Valley(where lies Loa and Bicknell), they hired a man named Blackburn to help guide them and take care of the horses and to cook. Arriving on the mountain, they camped on Corral Creek(the first canyon north of Straight Creek), on the eastern side of Mt. Pennell.

The first day, Burke and Bowen set out to find the mine, while Blackburn watched after the horses. They found the mine, and took some ore from it. They packed up some 400 lbs of the ore, then set out for Minersville again, presumably to get blasting powder.

Their route back to Minersville went through Pennellen Pass, and from there it appeared to be an easy ride straight across the desert to the Waterpocket Fold. But it wasn't. They got lost in the maze of canyons and became very thirsty. They came to a waterhole, but the water was stagnant. The two men decided to drink, over the objections of Blackburn. They were soon very ill. Finally they arrived in Rabbit Valley and at Blackburns home, where they rested a few days.

When they gained strength, they returned to Minersville. They later learned the ore which had been brought out of the mountains and sent to Salt Lake City, had assayed out at $6000 a ton. Some friends they had made in Minersville, helped to outfit them once again, and off they went to dig for gold, even though Bowen had heard of the Indians curse, and was a little reluctant to go on this second trip. Their first stop was Rabbit Valley to pick up Blackburn, but just after arriving, Bowen perished. Four days later, Burke also died. That stagnant water had done them in. All of their grubstake and outfit was returned to Minersville. Although their friends who had helped to finance their trip, had made fun of Bowens concern about the Indians curse, none of them every went in search of the gold.

Blackburn however did go back to the mountains, but as he was arriving on the mountain, a messenger caught up with him, saying one of his children had an accident. He returned without relocating the mine. It is said that from those days on, bad luck followed Blackburn every step of the

The Wolverton Mill on Straight Creek, as it looked about 1930 (Enid Wolverton foto).

The water wheel of the Wolverton Mill, being transported out of the mountains to Hanksville, for reconstruction(BLM foto)

Close-up of the original waterwheel of the Wolverton Mill. Now it's next to the BLM office in Hanksville.

Wolvertons' cabin, as it is today, next to where the old mill once stood.

way. Finally he moved to another part of the state.

After several years, Blackburn did manage a return to the mine area, where he found the tools, but not the rock ledge where the ore had actually come from. Many years passed by, and finally in 1921, Blackburn and several other men again went back to Mt. Pennell. They found the cabin of Edwin T. Wolverton on Straight Creek. Upon arriving, Blackburn who was now a very old man, collapsed, perhaps because of the altitude, and was cared for overnight. The next day, and without ever showing his friends the site of the Burke-Bowen diggings, returned home. Blackburn never returned to the mountain.

The Wolverton Mill

Edwin T. Wolvertons first experience with the Henry Mountains was in 1900. On that first visit he found old mining camps and a number of old timers prospecting for gold. At that time there hadn't been much in the way of development, although sometime in the 1890's, it's said that a Camp Ruth was set up along upper Straight Creek on the east side of Mt. Pennell.

It was about this same time he learned of the story of the old Spanish Mine, so he became interested in the Henry Mountains, and especially of the mining sites on the eastern slopes of Mt. Pennell. On that first visit to Pennell, the ground was covered with claims, so he could do nothing at that time. He apparently returned to the mountain again in 1912, but found the place still under other peoples claims. Finally in 1915, he returned once again to find claims had lapsed, and the ground free to stake new claims. He therefore re-staked the claims, calling them the Rico, Rico 1 and the Rico 2.

Wolverton officially filed the claims in 1915, but did little in the way of mining until 1921. In that year, and presumably after the visit of Blackburn, he started development. With the help of his two sons, he built a fine cabin and began a mill on the upper part of Straight Creek, in the big canyon coming off the eastern slopes of Mt. Pennell.

Wolverton, who was trained as an engineer, built a mill with a 6 meter high water wheel. He also built an aqueduct or flume made of lumber, which brought water from Straight Creek to the mill. The water turned the mill wheel, which in turn rotated a grinding stone, which ground ore brought off the mountain. It appears he didn't grind much ore, and he never got rich. It seems most of the work done by the mill was to cut logs from Mt. Pennell into lumber. Lumber from the mill was used to build cabins throughout the Henry Mountains and even as far away as Hanksville. Most of his pay was in the form of barter goods, such as flour, coffee, tobacco, and bullets.

Wolverton, who was a true believer in the Indians story of the old Spanish Mine, was also a believer in the Medicine Mans curse upon the mine. One day while dragging logs off the mountain with horses, he had an accident, and was thrown against a tree. Sometime later, Riter Ekker came upon Wolverton

Inside the re-constructed Wolverton Mill at the BLM office in Hanksville.

crawling to the stream with a bucket in his mouth, trying to fetch water. Ekker rode to the Trachyte Ranch, which at that time was owned by Brinkerhoff and Smith, where a wagon was found. Wolverton was taken off the mountain, and eventually to Fruita, Colorado, where he underwent surgery. He apparently survived the surgery, but died a few days later of pneumonia. He is now buried in the Elgin Cemetery near Green River, Utah(this cemetery is on the east side of the Green River. To get there, drive east out of Green River town to the east side of the river. Then drive north on Hastings Road a km or two to the cemetery on the east side of the road).

Wolvertons sons, Thatcher(Ted) and Norville, brought from the mountain a piece of granite to mark the grave. That granite slab is said to be part of the drag stone, or the arrastre, from the mill at Camp Rico on Mt. Pennell.

Sometime later, the Rico claims were relocated by Kay Hunt of Hanksville. He apparently never got rich either. In later years, the mill became famous around southeastern Utah, and many visitors drove up Straight Creek to see it. Eventually there was vandalism of the mill and nearby cabins and property of Hunts, so he requested the BLM to do something about the situation. The plan was made to take the mill and water wheel out to the BLM office area in Hanksville for preservation. Most people would agree, it would have looked much more impressive in it's original location, but the BLM had no other choice but to relocate the mill.

In 1974 the project began. Fotos and measurements were taken of the mill, then it was dismantled piece by piece. A helicopter was brought in and the mill wheel was taken out intact. Other important and better preserved parts of the mill were also airlifted out to trucks waiting below, then hauled to Hanksville. The move took two months, and for several years the mill parts were in storage. But as monies became available, the mill was finally reassembled beginning in 1983, immediately next to the BLM office. In the fall of 1986, the mill reconstruction was essentially completed. Slowly but surely, more work is being done to make it into Hanksville's only tourist spot.

At the old Wolverton Mill site today, one can see parts of the old flume, the foundation of the mill itself, and the cabin Wolverton lived in nearby. The cabin is still standing.

To get there, drive along State Road 276, the main link between Highway 95 and Bullfrog, on Lake Powell. Between mile posts 4 and 5, turn west onto a very good gravel road. This road passes the old Trachyte Ranch, the burned down Trachyte Ranch house, some old mining buildings and cars and trucks; crosses Trachyte Creek twice, then heads up to the Coyote Benches. From there it heads straight for the mountain. At the base of the mountain, and at the junction, turn south about a km, and park where the road crosses Straight Creek. From there, walk west on an old trail along side the creek to Hunts Cabins. Continue west along the north side of the creek on an old track, 'till you see the remains of the mill site, about one and a half kms from where you parked. Any kind of vehicle can make it to Straight Creek, with care. It's a well traveled road these days. Depending on the year, you can make it to the mill site from about May 1 to perhaps Thanksgiving time.

Gold Mining in Glen Canyon

The story of gold mining in the Henry Mountains actually began in Glen Canyon along the Colorado River. Glen Canyon is that part of the Colorado River Gorge lying between the mouth of the Dirty Devil River and Lee's Ferry, at the mouth of the Paria River. Most accounts of the history of Glen Canyon state the discovery of gold in the year 1883, but Charles B. Hunt in his USGS professional paper, *Geology and Geography of the Henry Mountains*, believes it was in 1882. That's when Carl Shirts joined the Hall family at Hall's Crossing on the Colorado River, just south of the present day Bullfrog Marina. He prospected the nearby Burro Bar in 1882.

But the man who really put gold on the map of Glen Canyon was Cass Hite. He arrived at the Colorado River on September 19, 1883. Hite had fled Arizona in a cloud of dust because of troubles with the Navajo. He had been hanging around the Navajo Nation for some time trying to locate the legendary Peshliki Gold Mine, which had been used by the Navajos for centuries. The young bucks were threatening to kill Hite, but one of the leaders named Hoskinini, who Hite had made friends with, warned him of an impending bushwhack. Hoskinini told Hite of the whereabouts of a long-time Navajo route to, and across, the Colorado River. Hite took the advice and found the route to the river via White Canyon.

Slowly but surely news spread of the discovery of gold in Glen Canyon, but there were never more than a few hundred souls in the canyon at any one time(one historian estimates no more than 1000 miners were in the canyon at the peak of the gold rush). Most of them were old timers living a dream. Cass Hite worked over the gravels at Dandy Crossing(the actual crossing place at Hite's Ferry), and later moved down stream to Ticaboo(where he later built the Ticaboo Ranch) and Goodhope Bars. In 1888, four California prospectors, including Haskell and Brown, found and worked the New Year and California Bars. They built and used an 80 horse power boiler on the California Bar, using coal they had mined at the head of Hansen Creek, on the south slopes of Mt. Hillers. It was their fairly good success, which helped more than any other event, to create the Glen Canyon Gold Rush. A man named Kohler started work on the North Wash Bar near what later became known as Hite. Eventually he and Cass Hite had some differences, which ended in the shooting of Kohler.

One of the Colorado Rivers sandbars which saw a lot of action was the Goodhope Bar, located about 5 kms below Ticaboo. It was first worked by Cass and John Hite(brothers) and George and Frank Gillam. When they gave it up, Bert Seabolt and Goss built a 12 meter high water wheel and a flume. The water from the wheel and flume went into a large reservoir, and from there to sluice boxes for the recovery of gold. Virtually all large sand bars along Glen Canyon saw prospectors.

Because of the isolation and the lack of a real good strike, most prospectors were local farmers, who would settle in along the river when farm work would allow, which was usually in the spring and fall. Between the sand bars and sod bustin', the farmers of the region just barely managed a living.

Gold mining in Glen Canyon is covered in greater detail in another part of this book, History of Glen Canyon.

Mt. Ellen and Bromide Basin

Because many of the streams entering Glen Canyon came from the direction of the Henry Mountains, it wasn't long before some of the prospectors began to cast their eyes to the mountains. Jack Sumner, who had been with Powell on the 1869 expedition, along with J. W. Wilson, began prospecting the benches along Crescent Creek just to the east of the South Ridge part of Mt. Ellen. They gradually worked their way up stream, and in 1889, found a gold-bearing fissure at the head of Crescent Creek. They named the fissure and the surrounding basin Bromide, because it reminded them of some Bromide ore they knew in Colorado.

This discovery launched a second gold rush, this time in the Henry Mountains to the west and northwest. Word spread, and before long a small town began to grow about 3 kms below and east of the entrance to Bromide Basin. This was Eagle City. The town was located along Crescent Creek at the foot of the mountain. At the time of it's hayday, the town had a dozen or so homes, a hotel, two saloons, a dance hall, three stores and post office. This was in about 1893.

Meanwhile, the Bromide Mine was in full operation in 1891. A five-stamp mill was constructed to handle the ore, and one source states that $15,000 worth of gold was removed between 1891 and 1893. Another report in the Desert News of October 5, 1893, stated the Bromide had produced $8,000 worth of ore between May 15 and October 1 of that year. At that time, about a 100 men were in the basin area working at several mines.

Things looked so promising, the Denver & Rio Grande Western Railroad made a preliminary survey of a route from the main line at Green River to Eagle City in anticipation of building a branch line. They

The ruins of an old cabin, said to be part of Eagle City.

MINING AND MINERALIZED AREAS

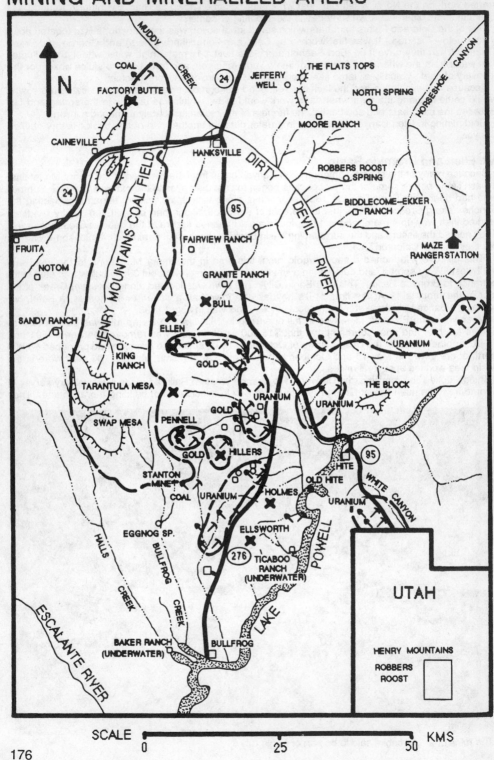

N

MUDDY CREEK

COAL
FACTORY BUTTE

CAINEVILLE

(24)

JEFFERY WELL

THE FLATS TOPS

NORTH SPRING

MOORE RANCH

HANKSVILLE

DIRTY DEVIL RIVER

HORSESHOE CANYON

(24)

HENRY MOUNTAINS COAL FIELD

(95)

ROBBERS ROOST SPRING

BIDDLECOME—EKKER RANCH

FRUITA

NOTOM

FAIRVIEW RANCH

GRANITE RANCH

MAZE RANGER STATION

SANDY RANCH

BULL

ELLEN

KING RANCH

GOLD

URANIUM

TARANTULA MESA

URANIUM

THE BLOCK

GOLD

URANIUM

SWAP MESA

PENNELL

GOLD

HILLERS

STANTON MINE

COAL

URANIUM

HITE

(95)

HALLS CREEK

EGGNOG SP.

BULLFROG CREEK

OLD HITE

HOLMES

URANIUM

WHITE CANYON

(276)

ELLSWORTH

TICABOO RANCH (UNDERWATER)

LAKE POWELL

UTAH

ESCALANTE RIVER

BAKER RANCH (UNDERWATER)

BULLFROG

HENRY MOUNTAINS

ROBBERS ROOST

SCALE

0   25   50   KMS

176

GOLD—BROMIDE BASIN & CRESCENT CK.

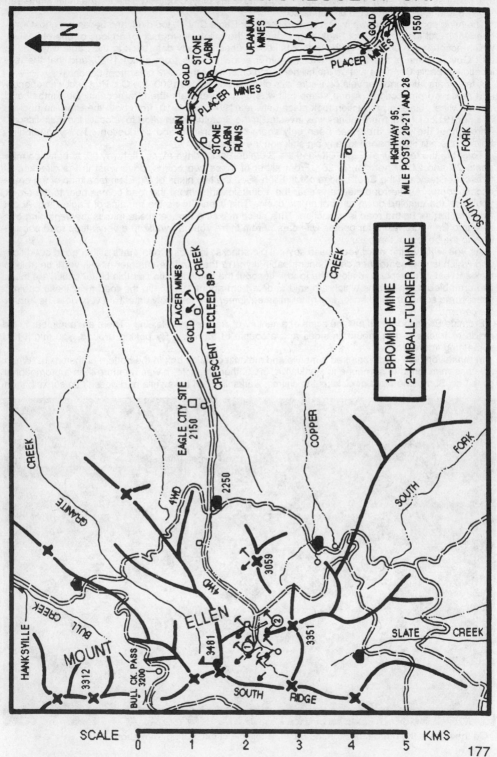

N

URANIUM MINES

GOLD STONE CABIN

PLACER MINES

GOLD PLACER MINES

1550

CABIN

STONE CABIN RUNS

PLACER MINES

HIGHWAY 95, MILE POSTS 20-21, AND 26

SOUTH FORK

CREEK

PLACER MINES

GOLD CREEK

CRESCENT LECLEED SP.

1—BROMIDE MINE
2—KIMBALL-TURNER MINE

EAGLE CITY SITE 2150

COPPER CREEK

2250

SOUTH FORK

GRANITE CREEK

4WD

3059

SLATE CREEK

BULL CREEK

HANKSVILLE

MOUNT ELLEN

4WD

3481

3351

3312

BULL CK. PASS 3200

SOUTH RIDGE

were hoping the mines would produce 100 tons of ore daily. But the railway tycoons were big dreamers too, because shortly after that newspaper report, the veins played out. Apparently the main tunnel ran straight to a fault, and the vein disappeared.

The mine soon closed down, which spelled doom for Eagle City. It too died, and became a ghost town overnight. All that remains of Eagle City today are the fallen down and rotted logs of one old cabin, which according to one source the author talked to, doesn't really date back to the Eagle City time at all. Guy Robison of the Fairview Ranch, said it actually dates from about 1925, and that the real location of Eagle City, was just up the hill north and on or near the ridge crest from the cabin.

A few years later another vein or fissure was discovered. About 1900, the Oro Prospect was opened and achieved production. A one stamp mill was built. Eventually the Oro became the Kimball and Turner Mine. Limited production took place between 1900 and 1910, from both the Bromide and the Oro. In 1912 or 1913, more money was invested in the Bromide in an effort to relocate the main fissure. Throughout the years there has been only sporadic exploration and production. Today, geologists believe there is little chance for any big strike on the mountain.

To get to the remains of Eagle City and the Bromide Basin, drive along Highway 95, to between mile posts 20 and 21; or near m. p. 26. From either of these two points, drive west in the direction of Crescent Creek and the South Ridge of Mt. Ellen. See the two hikes of Mt. Ellen for a map of the entire access route. As the road steepens near the mountain, and where the road comes near to the creek, you'll see the tumbled down ruins of an old cabin. This is said to be the remains of Eagle City. About two kms further up the road is a junction. This place makes a fine campsite, and is the beginning of a hike into Bromide Basin, for people with cars. From there you can walk up a very steep road about 3 kms to the bottom of the basin.

As you walk up the road you'll pass several old shacks, including one that's still in good condition, and which is now someones deer hunting cabin(if you're there in late summer or fall, you'll be able to pick and eat wild raspberrys along the road). In about the same location as this better cabin, are found two crumbled down cabins which are said to date from about 1910. On the road near these cabins, you'll come across a large boiler and other mine equipment, which likely date from very near the turn of the century.

Bromide Basin today still has the scars of a century of digging and blasting. There are a number of old roads or tracks up the mountain sides and a couple of tunnels. By poking around, you might find something interesting.

In the fall of 1986, someone had a mobile and motorized sluice box in the bottom of the basin. When this was mentioned to someone in Hanksville, the author was told, it was no more than a promotional scheme. Some one buys or obtains the claims, works like hell for awhile and doesn't do so well, then

On the road at the bottom of Bromide Basin, is this old cabin, dating from about 1910.

A miners cabin, at the entrance to Bromide Basin.

Bromide Basin and the Bromide Mine. Seen from the top of one of the southern peaks.

Motorized sluice box, as it sat in Bromide Basin, in the fall of 1986.

Wild raspberries, picked in September, along the road leading into Bromide Basin.

sets things up to make it look like a real operation. Then he sells it to the next sucker. And the game goes on and on. When it comes to gold, and the possibility of getting rich, there's a sucker around every corner it seems.

Down along Crescent Creek, which is the part between the site of Eagle City and where South Fork enters, are a number of placer mining sites. There has also been some activity around Lecleed Spring and further down in the vicinity of the stone cabin. There has also been work done in the area where Crescent, Copper and South Fork Creeks meet. In the past it was Neilus Ekker and Frank Lawler who did most of the work, or someone who leased it from them. This property has been worked with hydraulic equipment about every year that enough snow has fallen on the mountain to provide the necessary water.

One of the biggest problems associated with placer gold mining in the Henry Mountains is the very fine gold particles, which often float away during sluicing or panning. This is the same problem the miners experienced in Glen Canyon. Another problem is the lack of a good year-round and adequate water supply to work the gravels.

Gold on Mt. Pennell and Hillers

At the same time mining in the Bromide Basin was at a peak, there was activity on Mt. Pennell. When Wolverton saw the mountain in 1900, there were mine claims plastered everywhere. Butler(a geologist who made surveys of the region) wrote in 1920, he observed one active mine known as the Baby Ruth, about 3 kms west and up-canyon from the present Wolverton Mill site. His observations took place in 1913. At that time, and in about the same general area as the present Wolverton Mill site, he noted an arrastre(mill stone for grinding out ore) which he believed had milled several tons of ore.

The U.S. Bureau of Mines and Minerals Yearbook series states that a small amount of ore was removed from the Rico Mine between 1925 and 1927. This must have been Wolvertons doings. In the 1960's and 1970's someone invested money in equipment to bulldoze a number of short roads and made some exploratory pits in the upper Straight Creek Basin. The recorded value of the ore removed, was $263. According to Doelling, the recorded value of all ore taken from Mt. Pennell over the years, couldn't be more than about $1000(value at the time of production)!

Most evidence of work done on Mt. Pennell is seen on Bulldog Ridge, the big ridge south of Straight Creek. At least 8 adits(exploratory mine pits) have been found there, either along quartz-filled fissures or along diorite porphyry contacts with sedimentary rock. If you end up climbing the mountain, you'll see along the southwest summit ridge, several shallow adits very near the top. There has been some exploratory placer mining along Straight Creek east of the mountain, but nothing of value has been recorded.

Along the road and near the entrance to Bromide Basin, is this old mining equipment, dating from about 1910.

181

Southeast of Mt. Pennell at the very end of Bulldog Ridge, and next to Mud Spring, are some recent workings. This is called the Viola V Mine. Exploration adits were run along the contact zone between the shale and the diorite porphyry. No ore was ever taken from this operation, but there is still an old cabin, a tent foundation, and a water storage tank still standing at the spring. This work was done during the 1960's and 1970's. Mud Spring is located on the rough, but barely passable road, running between Mt. Pennell and Straight Creek, and the road running up to Cass Creek Peak and the old Star Mine on Hillers.

Not much ever happened on Mt. Hillers. According to Hunt, "Soon after the decline of the Bromide Mine, Al Star started a mine at the head of Mine Canyon(this is now called Cass Creek on the USGS maps) on Mt. Hillers but no production was obtained. There was no further development of fissure mines until about 1900 when Woodruff prospected the south side of Mt. Hillers by driving an adit 360 feet(110 meters) into the shatter zone at the edge of the Mt. Hillers stock." In the hiking section of this book, are descriptions on how to get to each of these two mines.

Today at the Star Mine you'll see a shaft, which was buried under snow at the time of the authors visit. It must be fairly deep, because above the shaft is a windlass used to haul out ore samples. And there are a few more artifacts lying about, in addition to the remains of three old cabins in the canyon below. Someone still has the mineral rights, as seen by the claim notices plastered around the canyon.

The author spent half a day just climbing the cliffs around the old Woodruff Mine area, but found no shaft or tunnel. At one spot not far above the crumbling old stone cabin, it appeared there might be an adit, but now it's covered with rocks. If someone does find evidence of a mine, please contact the author. One old timer in Hanksville told the author that Woodruff never did have an actual mine. He was just an old hermit who found a spring on the mountain and was doing a lot of dreaming and hoping. He was apparently committed to an institution by a sister, as the story goes.

Henry Mountains Coal Field

Not many people are aware of the fact there's a good sized coal field immediately west of the Henry Mountains. The field is about 30 by 80 kms, and extends from about Factory Butte in the north to a point just west of Mt. Hillers in the south.

Because of it's isolation, lack of a nearby market and poor road conditions, not much actual mining has taken place in the region. The first known mine was located just south of Mt. Hillers in the upper Hansen Creek area. It was cut in the Ferron Sandstone Member of the Mancos Shale. It opened sometime after 1888, probably by Haskell and Brown, who used the coal to run a boiler on the California Bar In Glen Canyon. It was used for about three years, then abandoned. Later, the same mine apparently was used by Stanton when he began operations in Glen Canyon with his famous dredge.

A placer mining operation on lower Crescent Creek, near where South Fork enters.

182

MOUNT PENNELL GOLD MINES

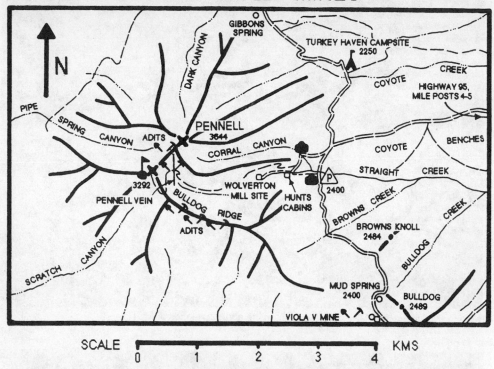

SCALE |0—1—2—3—4| KMS

An old stone cabin, dating from early in this century. Near the middle part of Crescent Creek.

The entrance to the Star Mine, which is high on the northern slopes of Mt. Hillers.

This is all that remains of the Woodruff stone cabin on the south slopes of Mt. Hillers. It sits at the location known by some as the Woodruff Mine.

That was about 1900. More on that in the History of Glen Canyon.

Just north of Highway 24, and just east of Caineville, is Factory Butte(drive north on a good road from between mile posts 106 and 107). The Factory Butte Coal Mine was opened in the Ferron Sandstone coal beds in 1908 to supply the needs of the local towns in the Fremont River Valley. More openings were cut into the Emery Sandstone Member of the Mancos Shale in 1914. According to Doelling, this mine or mines operated intermittently until about 1945. According to Barbara Ekker, Hanksville historian, the company or outfit doing the mining at Factory Butte was called the Atlas-Dirty Devil Coal Operation. They shipped most of the coal to the Nevada Power Company.

Notice the geology cross section named *Geology Below Tarantula Mesa*. Two of the five members of the Mancos Shale Formation have major coal deposits, the Emery and Ferron Sandstone Members. Just below the Mancos Group is the Dakota Sandstone. It has minor coal seams.

History or Glen Canyon

This book centers on the Henry Mountains, and areas to the east, including the Robbers Roost Country. The boundaries for the area covered are: Highway 24 in the north, the Orange Cliffs in the east, the Waterpocket Fold and Capitol Reef National Park in the west, and Lake Powell to the southeast. Prior to the mid 1960's the part of what is now Lake Powell, was the canyon of the Colorado River. And that part of the Colorado River from the mouth of the Dirty Devil River down to Lee's Ferry, was known as Glen Canyon.

Glen Canyon had quiet waters for it's entire length, as there were almost no rapids. What rapids there were, were just riffles, compared to what lay upstream in Cataract Canyon. Because of the quiet waters, Glen Canyon was more hospitable to man; as a result, there's a fair amount of history to tell in this section of the Colorado River. This part then concentrates on the history of Glen Canyon before the waters of Lake Powell covered it.

The first white men to enter this great gorge(first documented entry) was John Wesley Powell and an expedition of geologists and geographers. They left Green River, Wyoming on May 24, 1869, and sailed all the way down the Colorado to the mouth of the Virgin River. Powell's diary has entries of the time they passed into and through Glen Canyon.

On July 28, 1869, as he entered the region just above the Dirty Devil River he states,........*Floating down this narrow channel and looking out through the canyon crevice away in the distance the river is seen to turn again to the left, and beyond this point, away many miles, a great mountain is seen. Still floating down , we see other mountains, now on the right, now on the left, until a great mountain range is unfolded to view[obviously the Henry Mountains]. We name this Narrow Canyon, and it terminates at the bend of the river below.*

As we go down to this point we discover the mouth of a stream which enters from the right. Into this our little boat is turned. The water is exceedingly muddy and has an unpleasant odor. One of the men in the boat following, seeing what we have done, shouts to Dunn and asks whether it is a trout stream. Dunn replies, much disgusted, that it is "a dirty devil," and by this name the river is to be known hereafter.

Some of us go out for half a mile[800 meters] *and climb a butte to the north......and beyond these cliffs is situated the range of mountains seen as we came down Narrow Canyon.*

Narrow Canyon was an 8 km stretch of the Colorado River, between Cataract Canyon to the north, and Glen Canyon below. Here is a list of some of the more important sites and events in Glen Canyon, the history of which spans the years 1869 to the mid 1960's.

Just below where North Wash entered the Colorado, was one of many placer mining bars. At one time it was called Crescent City, but there was only one cabin and several tents at the site. At that time the creek was named Crescent Creek.

In the early history of the region, Trachyte Creek Canyon was the original route used between Hanksville and the Colorado River, but it was good only for pack horses. Later, North Wash became more popular, because wagons could make the route easily.

Not far below North Wash once stood the "Kohler Cabin". Just before the lake covered the site, there were two chimneys standing. This likely belonged to a man named A. H. Kohler, who was a miner in the canyon beginning in the late 1880's. It seems he and Cass Hite didn't get along. As the story goes, while Kohler was on a trip to Denver, he discouraged capitalists from investing in Cass Hite's mining properties. Later, and in Green River, Utah, Kohler made threats on Hite's life. Hite confronted Kohler about the threats, a gun fight followed, and Kohler was killed on Sept. 9, 1891. Hite was tried for murder in late February and March of 1892, and sentenced to 12 years in prison for 2nd degree murder. He was later pardoned by Gov. Caleb W. West on November 29, 1893.

According to Crampton, who interviewed Art Chaffin in 1960, the first white occupant in the Hite area was Joshua Swett, a squaw man, who allegedly stole horses on one side of the river and sold them on the other. He had arrived in 1872 and built a cabin at the mouth of Swett Creek, a south fork of Trachyte

GLEN CANYON--BEFORE LAKE POWELL

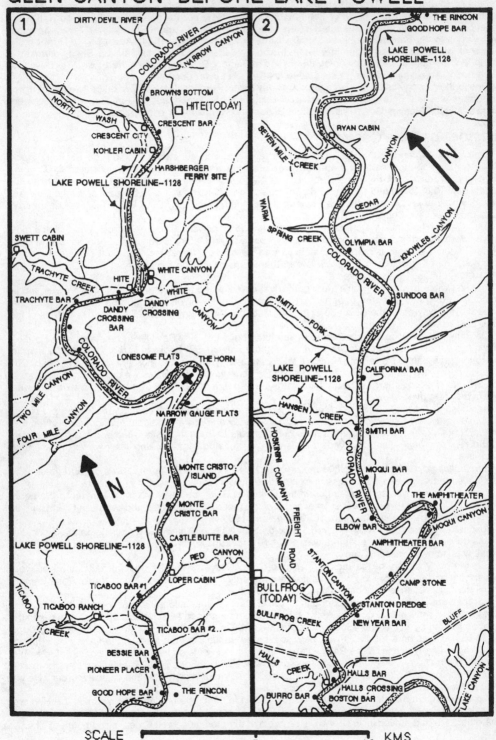

① DIRTY DEVIL RIVER
COLORADO RIVER
NARROW CANYON
NORTH WASH
BROWNS BOTTOM
□ HITE(TODAY)
CRESCENT BAR
CRESCENT CITY
KOHLER CABIN
HARSHBERGER FERRY SITE
LAKE POWELL SHORELINE--1128
SWETT CABIN
TRACHYTE CREEK
HITE
WHITE CANYON
□ WHITE
TRACHYTE BAR
DANDY CROSSING BAR
DANDY CROSSING
WHITE CANYON
COLORADO RIVER
LONESOME FLATS
THE HORN
TWO MILE CANYON
FOUR MILE CANYON
NARROW GAUGE FLATS
N
MONTE CRISTO ISLAND
MONTE CRISTO BAR
CASTLE BUTTE BAR
LAKE POWELL SHORELINE--1128
RED CANYON
LOPER CABIN
TICABOO BAR #1
TICABOO CREEK
TICABOO RANCH
TICABOO BAR #2...
BESSIE BAR
PIONEER PLACER
GOOD HOPE BAR
THE RINCON

② THE RINCON
GOOD HOPE BAR
LAKE POWELL SHORELINE--1128
RYAN CABIN
SEVEN MILE CREEK
KNOWLES CANYON
CEDAR CANYON
WARM SPRING CREEK
OLYMPIA BAR
COLORADO RIVER
SUNDOG BAR
SMITH FORK
CALIFORNIA BAR
LAKE POWELL SHORELINE--1128
HANSEN CREEK
SMITH BAR
COLORADO RIVER
MOQUI BAR
HOSKINNIN COMPANY FREIGHT ROAD
THE AMPHITHEATER
ELBOW BAR
MOQUI CANYON
AMPHITHEATER BAR
STANTON CANYON
CAMP STONE
BULLFROG (TODAY)
STANTON DREDGE
BULLFROG CREEK
NEW YEAR BAR
BLUFF
HALLS CREEK
HALLS BAR
BURRO BAR
HALLS CROSSING
BOSTON BAR
LAKE CANYON
N

SCALE
0   5   10 KMS

186

Creek, about 6 or 7 kms from the Colorado. When Hite arrived in 1883, Swett left. Then Hite moved the Swett Cabin to the river, where it stayed until Lake Powell covered it.

The town of Hite was founded upon the arrival of Cass Hite to Glen Canyon on September 19, 1883. He had fled Arizona under threats of being scalped by Navajos, and had entered the area via White Canyon on the east. Chief Hoskinini of the Navajos had told him of gold in the canyon. The location where Cass Hite first settled, and what was later known as Hite City, is about 8 kms south or downstream from present day Hite Marina.

When Hite first reached the Colorado from the east through White Canyon, he found a good place to cross, which he called Dandy Crossing. As it turned out, it was the best crossing of the Colorado in all of Glen Canyon. The normal way through southeastern Utah in those days was to pass through Hanksville and go down North Wash, cross at Dandy Crossing, then go on up White Canyon and on to Blanding or Bluff.

Soon after Hite arrived, he discovered gold in the sand bars of the Colorado. This led to two minor gold rushes, one lasting from about 1884 until around 1890, the other from about 1893 until 1900. C. Gregory Crampton believes there were probably no more than a thousand men in the canyon at any one time, so the Glen Canyon Gold Rush wasn't of the same magnitude as the California or Yukon Gold Rushes.

As it turned out the gold was very hard to get out of the sand. It was in the form of fine gold dust, which tended to float away in the panning process. Another problem miners encountered was the lack of water. It proved difficult to get river water up to the higher bars, where most of the gold was located. There were a few side canyon streams, but they flooded periodically, washing everything away. Water wheels were used in a place or two, but with little success, and pumping the muddy water out of the river quickly wore out the pumps. The best way to get the gold was simply with a shovel, some form of sluice, and a pan.

Hite apparently brought the Swett Cabin down to the river, and was soon followed by his two brothers. The family ran a store for many years, and the post office, which opened in 1889. The Hite brothers stayed in the canyon until Cass Hite died at his ranch at Ticaboo in 1914.

Cass Hite may have put his name on the town and ferry crossing, but he never did build or operate a ferry himself. For years those who wanted to cross just swam their animals over, or floated their wagons across on drift logs found along the river. It was never really a ford, because animals always had to swim.

In 1907 or 1908, a man named Harshberger built and operated the first real ferry boat at Hite, but it was about 5 kms upstream or north of the later Hite Ferry. The boat itself measured about 4 x 9 meters. At the time, the price of copper was high, and Harshberger found some in White Canyon and established a mine. With the use of the ferry, he was able to take the copper to the railway at Green River, via North Wash and Hanksville. Apparently the ferry service stopped, when the price of copper dropped after only a year or two.

There is no record of regular ferry service at Hite again until 1946. Arthur L. Chaffin moved to Hite in 1932, and ran a farm. It was he and other local people who, over the years, opened a real road from Hanksville to Hite. Finally the state got involved, and built a road from Hanksville to Blanding. It was Chaffin who supplied the last link. He opened the first auto ferry service at Hite on September 17, 1946. This ferry, along with a small store, ran continuously until June 5, 1964, when the rising waters of Lake Powell forced the closure.

Because of the opening of the road and ferry, more mineral exploration began in the area. Uranium was found in White Canyon, and in 1949, the Vanadium Corp. of America and the AEC opened an experimental mill just across the river from Hite, at the mouth of White Canyon. Shortly after, a one-room school opened with 30 pupils, as well as a post office. The school closed about the time the mill shut down in 1954, but the post office stayed open until 1964.

There were a number of petroglyph panels in the area and all along the Colorado River, as well as ruins. Right at the mouth of White Canyon, was an Anasazi ruin, sitting right out in the open on a little bluff. J. W. Powell was the first white man to see and describe it(in 1869). In later years it was Hite's best tourist attraction. It was called Ft. Moqui, because of its location and shape.

Before leaving the Hite area, it must be noted there was more than just the ferry crossing and store, and the uranium mill on the White Canyon side. There were several homesteads, one of which belonged to Ruben Nielsen(in the 1960's). It covered about 8 hectares(20 acres), some of it under cultivation. Raised there were grapes and fruits of various kinds.

Look at the map, *Glen Canyon--Before Lake Powell*. There was a road from North Wash to Hite, which came in to being during the gold rushes. Another road runs downstream from Hite to The Horn or Cape Horn. This section was built in 1898-1900, by Robert Brewster Stanton of the Hoskinini Company. (The entire story of Stanton, the Hoskinini Co. and the dredge is discussed later in this chapter). Notice also, the trail from The Horn downstream to Sevenmile Creek. This was the main foot and horse trail used by the miners when going to Hite for supplies and mail. It went up Sevenmile Creek to the mesa

The Hite Ferry, as it looked in July, 1963. (Crampton foto).

Ice on the Colorado River in Glen Canyon, in January, 1898. (Stanton foto).

top, and headed toward the upper part of Hansen Creek.

Between Hite and Ticaboo Creek, there weren't many landmarks of consequence. The map shows all the major sand bars. But just up stream from Ticaboo Creek was the Bert Loper Cabin. This was a 3 x 5 meter cabin made of squared logs, with a stone fireplace. No one knows for sure who built it, but Albert "Bert" Loper lived in it from 1909 to 1914. One has to wonder if the death of Cass Hite had anything to do with his moving. Bert called the cabin his "Hermitage".

Loper is said to have dammed nearby Red Creek, in order to have water to run his placer mining operation on the bar, and to irrigate a small farm of about one hectare(2 acres). Loper had brought several pieces of farm equipment to the canyon. In later years(1952) it was reported by a river runner that a family was living in the cabin and doing a little farming themselves.

Years later Bert Loper became a river guide, and took many people down the Colorado. He did this until he was 80 years of age. In July of 1949, he was drowned in the Colorado River somewhere in the Grand Canyon.

After several years at Hite and that area, Cass Hite moved to Ticaboo Creek. He built a cabin, later known as the Ticaboo Ranch, and stayed there most of the time between 1883 until his death in 1914. More details on this ranch are in the section on Ranches.

Going down river, the next point of interest was the Good Hope Bar. Gold was discovered there, and a company founded by Cass Hite and J. S. Burgess, in February of 1887. It was one of the major gold mining bars in Glen Canyon. At some point in time, Burgess and Hite built on the rivers edge, a 12 meter high water wheel. This was connected to a flume, also about 12 meters high, which took water to a reservoir a distance away, then the water was used in the placer mining operation. In later years, when uranium prospecting was in full swing, there was a landing strip built along the bar.

When Stanton was laying out claims along the river on December 29, 1897, he came to what is usually referred to as the Ryan Cabin. Although Stanton mentions the names of Ryan and O'Keefe, he referred to the cabin as "O'Keefe's Lone Star rock house." The cabin was probably built in 1895, when O'Keefe and David Lemmon located the Lone Star placer mine on the nearby bar.

Olympia Bar was another important placer mining site dating back to as early as the 1890's. When Crampton was there in the 1960's studying the archeology of the canyon, he noticed extensive placer mining operations had occurred. At one point, a water wheel had been placed in the river to lift water to a flume, which carried it to a nearby gravel bar. Hunt, who was there in 1953, reported this same wheel was the one originally located at Good Hope Bar, further up stream. It was moved there in 1910, and was called the Bennett Wheel, according to Frank Bennett.

California Bar was another important placer mining site in Glen Canyon. The earliest records list it under White Canyon Mining District as early as 1888. It was first worked by four Californians; Hawthorn, Brown, Keeler, and Haskell. They reached the bar via Hansen Creek. In the upper part of

The Bert Loper Cabin before lake waters covered it. (Crampton foto).

Hansen Creek these men opened a coal mine in the Mancos beds, and used the coal to run a boiler at the bar.

Crampton reported seeing many remnants of machinery, largely built from automobile parts, scattered about the place. Also, at one time Bert Loper and Louis Chaffin worked this bar. When R. B. Stanton passed that way in 1899, he learned there had been $30.000 worth of gold taken from the bar during it's history.

Hansen Creek was an important canyon to the miners in Glen Canyon in the early days. Hansen Creek offered an easy route to the Colorado from the Henry Mountains. A wagon road(good enough for trucks) was opened as early as 1888. Hansen Creek was the only easy and usable route into the canyon between Hite and Halls Crossing. It served three important mining locations; California, Smith and Moqui Bars.

Perhaps the most important site in Glen Canyon, as far as mining history is concerned was the Hoskinini Company operations at Camp Stone and Stanton Canyon, and the Stanton Dredge. Robert Brewster Stanton was an engineer, educated at U. of Miami, in Ohio. One of his first jobs was in Colorado, working on a railway line to Leadville. Surveying potential railroad grades became his specialty. He once met a Frank M. Brown, who in 1889, founded the Colorado Canyon and Pacific Railroad Company, for the purpose of constructing a watergrade railroad from Grand Junction, Colorado, to the seaboard, through the canyons of the Colorado River, connecting the coal fields of the Rocky Mountains with southern California(Crampton, 1962).

Brown hired Stanton to help assess the potential route. During the survey, in 1889-90, and while boating the Colorado, Brown and two others were drowned near Navajo Bridge in the upper part of Marble Canyon. That ended those big plans. But Stanton remembered the gold mining in Glen Canyon.

After a few years, Stanton and several interested business men, went back to Hite and Glen Canyon, and made some tests of the gold diggings. They thought they had something, so on March 28, 1898, the Hoskinini Company was founded, with Stone, Mills, Brooks, Morton and Ramsey as owners and investors. Robert B. Stanton was brought into the firm as a vice president, engineer and a superintendent.

In the year 1898, a crew made the trip from North Wash to Lee's Ferry, and re-staked all old claims. In all, the company had 145 continuous claims from about 3 kms above Hite to Lee's Ferry, a distance of 265 kms.

Early in 1900, a contract was let out to Bucyrus-Erie of Milwaukee, to build a gold dredge. Later in the spring it was shipped by rail to Green River, Utah. Moving the dredge the 160 kms, required the building of a road from the areas between Granite and Trachyte Ranches, up Benson Creek to South or Stanton Pass between Mt. Hillers and Pennell, and down Hansen Creek, passing Stanton Mine on the way.

Dredging equipment and supplies at the head of Stanton Canyon, 1900. (Stanton foto).

190

Camp Stone, where the Stanton Dredge was assembled, in 1900. (Stanton foto).

The Stanton Dredge under construction, 1900. (Stanton foto).

From lower Hansen Creek, it went south over the mesa and down Stanton Canyon to the river. It took about 25 men and several wagons, with 4 to 8 horses each, and 75 to 100 horses total, to haul the dredge to the river. It took 8 days.

For some reason, Stanton ordered the dredge to be assembled not at the mouth of Stanton, where a dugway was built out of solid rock, but at a site about 1.5 kms up-river. This site was called Camp Stone. The dredge was built on a barge measuring about 12 x 25 meters. The construction started in June of 1900, and took about 7 months to complete(January, 1901). The dredge worked for about 6 months and quit, a total failure. It failed because the equipment was unable to separate the fine gold dust from the sands. Estimates on the total costs to the company were between $100,000 and $350,000.

Sometime later, the dredge was moved down stream to the mouth of Stanton Canyon, where it gradually sank in the river. For many years it was a regular stopping place for river runners on the Colorado. It now sits below about 100 meters of water.

The last historic site in Glen Canyon covered in this book is the area around Halls Crossing, where Halls Creek enters the Colorado. Some authors have stated that because of the ferry, which began operating in 1881, gold was likely first discovered near the crossing in 1882. That's unconfirmed, but later in the 1880's and 1890's, there was activity along Halls, Boston and Burro Bars.

But the most important site in these parts was Halls Crossing. The crossing was situated about 1 km upstream from where Halls Creek enters the river. The history of this ferry crossing really begins further down stream at the Hole-in-the-Rock. Hall was a carpenter living at Escalante, when the San Juan Party made its epic journey through the Hole-in-the-Rock on its way to Bluff, in 1879-80. He was called to build a raft or ferry for the party, which he did. He then stayed on the Colorado operating the ferry through 1880, but the route to the river was so incredibly difficult, almost no one gave him business.

In the spring of 1880, a man named Platte D. Lyman, who apparently lived at Lake Pagahrit at the head of Lake Canyon, walked down Lake Canyon and viewed the crossing for the first time. It appears this is how Hall got wind of a better crossing up stream, because later he scouted the region, then moved his ferry to the site, which became known as Halls Crossing and Halls Ferry.

The approaches to Halls Crossing were much easier than to the Hole-in-the-Rock crossing. From Escalante, the route went down Harris Wash to the Escalante River, up Silver Falls Creek to the Circle Cliffs, then descended Muley Twist Canyon to Halls Creek, thence to the river. On the east side, the route ascended the sand flats and slickrock slopes in the area between Moqui and Lake Canyons, then joined the Hole-in-the-Rock Trail to the east, which led to Bluff on the San Juan River.

The ferry is said to have been built with materials from Escalante, some 80 kms away. It consisted of two pine logs, with planks spanning the logs. It measured about 3 x 10 meters. Ferry

The completed Stanton Dredge, 1900. (Stanton foto).

192

charges were usually about $5.00 per wagon and $.75 per horse. Hall operated the ferry from 1881 to 1884.

Two events led to the ferry closing. The completion of the Denver, Rio Grande, and Western Railroad across Utah in 1883 greatly eased communications between the settlements on both sides of the Colorado. Also, the ferry broke loose from it's moorings during high water and was not replaced. Hall then left the area.

Hall lived up stream along Halls Creek, about 3 kms above the Baker Ranch, for at least part of the time he was at the Crossing. Read more on this under the history of ranches.

Uranium and Vanadium

The Henry Mountains have a short but colorful mining history. While that actively started with gold, by far the most profitable mineral mined have been uranium and vanadium. It was in the year 1898 that uranium bearing ores were first discovered on the Colorado Plateau. Shortly after this discovery, uranium was first discovered in eastern Garfield County(the Henry Mountains region), but it was a while before any serious mining took place in these parts, on account of it's rugged and desolate nature and lack of roads.

The first real "uranium boom" took place with the sudden demand for radium for the treatment of cancer and because of the discovery and production of luminous paint. This took place around 1912. Shortly after this industry-wide boom, significant discoveries were made along lower Crescent Creek, and in the Trachyte and Del Monte areas of the Henry Mountains. Ore shipments began in 1913, and have continued intermittently to the present day.

Between the years 1924 and 1935 there was very little activity going on. This was a result of far richer radium ores being found in the Belgian Congo(now Zaire).

In the late 1930's, and with the approach of World War II, another boom began. During this period, only ore bodies rich in vanadium were mined. Not much happened in the Henrys during this time, but there was one small mill constructed to concentrate the low grade ore near the Trachyte Ranch in the early 1940's. It was built by Cornelius Ekker and Ray Bennett and operated for a short period of time in the Trachyte District. The mill concentrated the ore so it could be shipped more economically to Naturita, Colorado for further milling. The big handicap for local miners was two fold; a long haul to distant mills and markets, and very poor roads.

It was in 1948, when the vanadium "boom" declined, that the demand for uranium began. The U. S. Atomic Energy Commission lunched a drive to stimulate discovery and development of uranium on the Colorado Plateau. Again, mining began in the Henry Mountains. In 1951, the first mill designed and constructed in the U.S., exclusively for the production of uranium, was built in Grand Junction, Colorado. At the same time Union Carbide built a buying station at Thompson, Utah, and a bit later built an upgrading plant in Green River.

New areas were discovered, such as in the lower Poison Spring Canyon, the Orange Cliffs, and Hatch Canyon. This was the biggest boom yet, but it only lasted until about 1954. That's when government stockpiles grew to enormous proportions, and all mines shut down.

Since the early 1950's boom, there has been only sporadic mining in the Henry Mountains. In recent years the demand for uranium is mainly the result of the world wide constuction of nuclear power plants.

In more recent times, Plateau Resources Limited, a subsidiary company of Consumers Power Co. of Michigan, built a concentrating mill and small company town in the lower end of Shitamaring Canyon. Both the mill and the nearby town are known as Ticaboo. Construction on the mill was began in 1979, and completed in June of 1982. It ran for three months, then was shut down in August 1982. Apparently the only reason for opening the mill, was to give it a good test run, to try out new equipment. Evidently, the price of enriched ore dropped during the two years while plant construction was underway. Today(1986), it costs about $30 a pound to mine and mill the ore concentrate, called yellow cake, but the going price is about $17 a pound!

The company had such a large investment in the mill, it had to keep it ready and available and protected for future use, so while the mill itself was closed from 1982 until 1984, a skeleton crew was still on board. All this time some mining continued, and ore stockpiled. Finally in March 1984, mining stopped completely. As of the fall of 1986, there was only a skeleton office crew and guards at the mill and mine. The mill and mine will again open, but only when the price for yellow cake rises above the cost of production.

To date, uranium and vanadium deposits of economic importance in the Henry Mountains region have been found only in the Jurassic Morrison Formation, and its Salt Wash Member; and the Moss Back and Monitor Butte Members of the Chinle Formation of Triassic age. Minor occurrences of uranium minerals have been found in other formations(Moenkopi) and in intrusive igneous rock(Mt. Pennell), but by far the vast majority of ores in the Henrys have come from the Salt Wash Member of the Morrison

EAST HENRY MOUNTAINS MINING AREAS

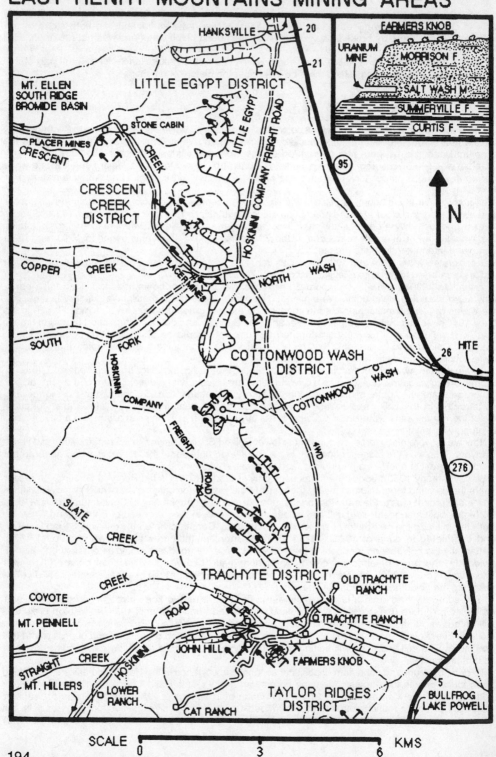

HANKSVILLE • 20
• 21

LITTLE EGYPT DISTRICT

MT. ELLEN
SOUTH RIDGE
BROMIDE BASIN

STONE CABIN

PLACER MINES
CRESCENT

LITTLE EGYPT

CREEK

HOSKINN COMPANY FREIGHT ROAD

95

CRESCENT
CREEK
DISTRICT

N

COPPER CREEK

PLACER MINES

NORTH WASH

SOUTH FORK

26 HITE

HOSKINN

COTTONWOOD WASH
DISTRICT

COMPANY

COTTONWOOD WASH

FREIGHT

4WD

276

SLATE

ROAD

CREEK

TRACHYTE DISTRICT

OLD TRACHYTE
RANCH

COYOTE

CREEK

ROAD

TRACHYTE RANCH

MT. PENNELL

4

HOSKINN

JOHN HILL

STRAIGHT CREEK

FARMERS KNOB

MT. HILLERS

LOWER
RANCH

5

CAT RANCH

TAYLOR RIDGES
DISTRICT

BULLFROG
LAKE POWELL

Inset:

FARMERS KNOB

URANIUM
MINE

MORRISON F.

SALT WASH M.

SUMMERVILLE F.

CURTIS F.

SCALE
0   3   6   KMS

Formation.

In the report, *Uranium Deposits of Garfield County, Utah,* by H.H. Doelling, a list is made of the characteristics of deposits of economic interest in the Salt Wash Member. They are: (1)The largest ore bodies have been found where sandstone-mudstone ratios approach equality. (2)The largest ore bodies lie in thicker(up to 20 meters) sandstone lenses. (3)Very commonly, uranium ore is associated with carbonaceous material in sandstone, apparently deposited along side former stream channels. Logs and other vegetal materials in the centers of the channels generally are silicified. Simplified, this means the ore is found in petrified logs which were deposited on the banks of former river beds. For example, a log jam. (4)And lastly, plant indicators--such as Astragalus, a variety of loco weed with beanlike pods--are particularly numerous on surfaces near uranium ores in the Salt Wash Member.

Also listed are characteristics of uranium deposits in the Chinle Formation(Orange Cliffs Mining Areas). (1)Most commonly, uranium mineralization is associated with sandstone-filled Chinle channels cut into the upper Moenkopi Formation. (2)They occur mostly in intermediate-size stream channels. (3)Uranium mineralization is associated with carbonaceous trash(logs and limbs of trees), clay galls and slump debris along the edges, banks, and bottoms of former stream channels where permeable rock layers alternate with impermeable rock layers. (4)Copper minerals, iron sulfides and stains of limonite occur with uranium minerals, and can serve as guides.

The Doelling report goes on. Reliable information as to the source of uranium ore and the how's and why's of its deposition would be important when searching out new deposits. Several theories have been proposed to explain how uranium ores are deposited and distributed. The theories are: (1)Uranium, which is in low concentrations in many different rock strata, was later redistributed and concentrated as deposits by ground water. (2)Uranium was leached from immediately overlying clays or tuffs of volcanic debris and distributed by percolating ground water. (3)Uranium deposits were derived from igneous(or intrusive) bodies, such as the Henry Mountains. (4)Uranium was leached from sources in the Precambrian basement rock and re-distributed to favorable formations by later percolating water. (5)Uranium ores were derived from deep seated sources and carried upward by rising hydrothermal solutions to favorable rock strata for deposition. This last theory of how uranium deposits come about, the hydrothermal theory, is the most widely accepted.

Apparently uranium, like iron and manganese, is a very mobile element, easily moved by ground water. Because the proportion of uranium in ground water is small, large quantities of water must pass through a favorable rock layar to produce a heavy concentration of the metal. Presumably, organic material and/or bacteria could be the precipitating agents. Areas of permeable and impermeable materials slow the passage of uranium-bearing water, allowing time for chemical reactions to take place. This may explain why intermediate-sized former stream channels or funnels, and trough-shaped aquifers provide the most favorable situation for the precipitation of ore. Small, thin, or poor aquifers do not allow enough mineral-bearing water to pass, and large aquifers distribute the available water over too much material for significant concentration to take place.

Uranium Mining Districts

This author and others have divided the Henry Mountains region into three mining districts. They are: East Henry Mountains Mining Area; South Henry Mountains Mining Area; and the Orange Cliffs Mining Area.

East Henry Mountains Mining Area

The northern half of this area has two parts, the Little Egypt (named after some formations similar to those in Goblin Valley), and the Crescent Creek Districts. To reach these locations, leave Highway 95 between mile posts 20 and 21, and drive south to near North Wash, then west and north. Only one or two kms north of where South Fork meets Crescent Creek, there's a road running east to some mine tunnels or adits. Just north of this minor turnoff, you'll see several tunnels right next to the creek bed on the east side of the road. Further north, and near where you'll see an old stone cabin(which dates from about the turn of the century), look for a road running east to the mines overlooking Little Egypt. The author hasn't seen these, except from the old Hoskinini Company Freight Road.

In the center of the mapped area is the Cottonwood Wash District. The easiest way to reach these mines is to leave Highway 95 just north of the Bullfrog Turnoff, and very near mile post 26. Drive northwest and west to a road junction and turn south onto an unmaintained road running towards the Trachyte Ranch. At or near Cottonwood Wash, you can then walk west and into a cove where a spring is located. On the cliffs above are the old mines. But it might be easier to actually reach the tunnels if you attempted to come into the cove from above, and from a south fork of North Wash. The author hasn't been on that old track, but you can always walk it from North Wash.

By far the easiest mines to reach, and the ones which produced the most ore, are those in the

Old miners cabin, found along Trachyte Creek, just below Trachyte Ranch diversion dam.

Petrified log in a mine tunnel at John Hill. Uranium is found in vegital trash heaps, like this.

Petrified log, one that apparently didn't register on the geiger counter. Below John Hill.

Mine tunnels along the base of John Hill, with Mt. Hillers in the background.

Trachyte District. To get there, drive State Road 276, the paved highway running to Bullfrog. Between mile posts 4 and 5, and near Trachyte Creek, turn west and proceed towards the Trachyte Ranch, and past some old mining buildings with several old cars and trucks lying about. Cross Trachyte Creek on a well maintained road, which goes to the occupied Cat Ranch. Just to the south of the creek ford is Farmers Knob, and to the west of it, John Hill.

These two mining sites are easy to get to and have lots of old relics lying around. Park on the road in any number of locations, then walk a short distance to the mine tunnels or adits. You can see many old fossilized or petrified logs in ore heaps, presumably some which didn't register on the geiger counter. Upon entering some of the tunnels, few of which are long enough to need a flashlight, it's easy to pick out the old petrified logs and trash heaps still in the walls and ceilings.

As you wander about, remember all or most of these mines or claims are still active. You will also see the claim notices posted in various locations. Please don't disturb.

Farmers Knob has an interesting history. It apparently was one of the first places where uranium was discovered, and one of the places, over the years, which has produced the most ore. Some of it's first ores mined went to Europe and France for Madam Curie.

Standard Chemical Company was the first to prospect and stake out claims in the district, but they allowed the ownership to lapse for failure of assessment work. The claims were then restaked by Cornelius Ekker of Hanksville, and later sold to the Vanadium Corporation of America. Today, all mines in the Trachyte District are owned by the Foote Mineral Company. To the south of Farmers Knob is the Taylor Ridges District, which has seen very little activity.

All uranium ore bodies found in the East Henry Mountains Mining Areas are located in the Salt Wash Member of the Morrison Formation.

South Henry Mountains Mining Areas

The second generalized region for uranium mining is found in the southern part of the Henry Mountains. The Woodruff Spring District is located just a few kms northeast of Star Spring Campground, but it has never been a big producer, mainly just an area of exploratory adits.

The second district is the Del Monte Mine area. It has been a moderately large producer, and there are many tunnels and adits to explore. To get to this mine or mines, drive along State Road 276 to a point about 200 meters north of mile post 20. At that point you will see a road running downhill and to the west. It ends at the mine and at a pond, which was built as a water supply to the mines. This road is a little rough, but the author got his VW Rabbit down in and back out several times.

The Del Monte Mine, or mines, are a group of tunnels cut into the hill-side facing south. As in the whole of the east and south parts of the Henry Mountains, the ore bodies here are in the Salt Wash Member of the Morrison Formation.

By far the biggest producing mining region in the Henry Mountains in recent years is the Shitamaring Canyon complex. Before advancing further, the story behind this canyons' name must be told. The story, which is surely true, goes back to late last century or perhaps early in this century. Early day ranchers in the region gave the canyon it's name. It apparently started because of the water supply. It seems the water found in the area acts as a laxative, on both cattle and man. When cattle drank it, the next thing that happened was a big soosh, and a splat. The splat on the ground, caused a ring-like configuration. Thus the name Shit-am-a-ring Canyon.

This is the name used on all USGS maps. However, there are always those who miss the joke and have tried to change the original title. On a number of geology and mining reports done in recent years, the name *Shootering Canyon* is used. Even some BLM employees try to soften the impact by using this latter name.

The new mine-mill complex in lower Shitamaring Canyon has already been discussed. The present day mine(or mines) in the canyon is called the Tony M Mine, which has been changed from the original Lucky Strike Mine. If you drive into the canyon, you'll see a number of piles of uranium ore waiting to be concentrated in the mill, if and when the price of yellow cake or uranium ore, goes back up. All along the canyon walls are hundreds of adits and tunnels, some old and no longer in use, some new and recently opened.

High on some cliffs just to the north of the mill itself, are some old adits which are no longer in use. This place where the mill is actually located is called Lost Spring Canyon.

To get to the Shitamaring Canyon mine-mill complex, drive along State Road 276, which runs between Highway 95 and Bullfrog. About half way between mile posts 23 and 24 is a paved road running southwest to the mill and to the entrance to the canyon. If you'd like to visit the mining area, it's best to stop at the mill offices and ask if it's alright to proceed further. Most of the newer mines in the canyon are now fenced off and protected. Daily patrols are also made.

South of the Plateau Resources Ltd. mill about 7 kms, is the small company town of Ticaboo. As you drive south along State Road 276, and between mile posts 27 and 28, you'll see a large hotel-resturant

One of several old cars and trucks along Trachyte Creek, in the Trachyte Mining District.

Blasting caps box, found inside one of the tunnels at Farmers Knob.

SOUTH HENRY MOUNTAINS MINING AREAS

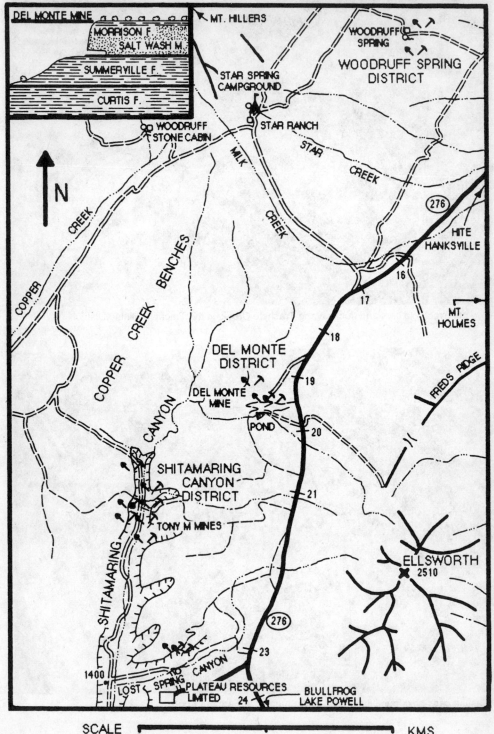

DEL MONTE MINE

MORRISON F.
SALT WASH M.

SUMMERVILLE F.

CURTIS F.

MT. HILLERS

STAR SPRING CAMPGROUND

WOODRUFF STONE CABIN

WOODRUFF SPRING

WOODRUFF SPRING DISTRICT

STAR RANCH

N

STAR CREEK

MILK CREEK

COPPER CREEK

COPPER CREEK BENCHES

276

HITE
HANKSVILLE

16

17

18

MT. HOLMES

DEL MONTE DISTRICT

DEL MONTE MINE

POND

19

20

FREDS RIDGE

CANYON

SHITAMARING CANYON DISTRICT

21

TONY M MINES

SHITAMARING

ELLSWORTH
2510

276

1400

LOST SPRING

TO CANYON

PLATEAU RESOURCES LIMITED

23

24

BLULLFROG
LAKE POWELL

SCALE

0   4   8   KMS

ORANGE CLIFFS MINING AREAS

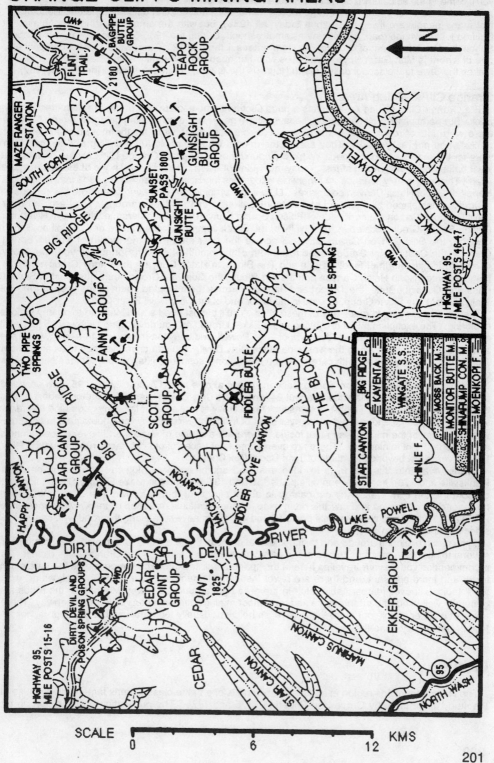

SCALE |0   6   12| KMS

complex. If you make a sharp turn to the west at the hotel, and drive about 2 kms from the highway, you'll come to the actual town of Ticaboo, located behind a low hill.

This town consists of one rather large mobile home park, and several offices of Plateau Resources. Not many people are living in Ticaboo today(fall 1986), but with the small permanent population at Bullfrog just down the road, it does have a small school. During the 1986-87 school year, the Ticaboo School had an enrollment of 41 students, from grades 1 through 12. There were four school teachers, one of whom is Mrs. Garth Noyes, who lives with her husband and family at the Cat Ranch, and who makes the drive to the school daily. Garth Noyes is the towns part-time Justice of the Peace(1987).

Orange Cliffs Mining Area

The Orange Cliffs Mining Area covers a huge section in the eastern half of the area covered by this book. But perhaps it's a bit misnamed, because there never was much mining going on there. For sure there were lots of roads graded into several canyons, but these were for the most part merely "cat tracks", and not really roads. They served the miners who did exploratory drilling and testing, then were for the most part, abandoned. Within the boundaries of the map, Orange Cliffs Mining Area, are at least half a dozen old landing strips. Today, not many of these old tracks, and none of the airstrips, are used. They are merely scars on an otherwise wilderness landscape. Even 4WD's can't make it into the Happy or Upper Hatch Canyon complexes. Little if any uranium ore was ever taken from this region.

Doelling has placed all these old exploratory locations into 10 different groups. They are: the Dirty Devil Group, found on the north side of Poison Spring Canyon where it enters the Dirty Devil River; the Poison Spring Group, located in the vicinity of the Black Jump, near the bottom end of Poison Spring Canyon; the Star Canyon Group, situated across the river east from the mouth of Poison Spring Canyon; the Cedar Point Group, found just south of the mouth of Poison Spring Canyon; the Scotty Group, found just north of Fiddler Butte and The Block, in Hatch Canyon; the Fanny Group, which is found between North Hatch Canyon and the Big Ridge; the Gunsight Group, found just east of Sunset Pass and Gunsight Butte; the Teapot and Bagpipe Groups, both located south of the area of the Flint Trail; and last, the Ekker Group, located in the lower end of the Dirty Devil River Gorge.

There's no easy way to reach any of these sites. You'll almost need a 4WD vehicle to do any serious exploring. The exception might be getting to the Ekker Group. As you drive along Highway 95 just west of the bridge over the Dirty Devil River arm of Lake Powell, and between mile posts 44 and 45, you'll see a dirt road running north along the west side of the Dirty Devil. You can drive this road to its end, about 7 or 8 kms, with any car(but with care). As you drive along, scan the cliffs to the west for signs of adits or tunnels.

Another entry point is Poison Spring Canyon. Right at mile post 17, on Highway 95, turn east and proceed down canyon, a distance of about 24 kms to the Dirty Devil River. The author made it a third the way down with his VW Rabbit, but was lucky and crazy to make it that far. Any good high clearance vehicle should be able to make it to the river most of the time. From there you should plan to do some walking to any of the mine sites in that locale. There are a couple of shacks and several good tunnels at the Cedar Point mining site. There are even some faint traces of old cat tracks running up the Dirty Devil River to just beyond the mouth of Twin Corral Box Canyon.

A third way into this region is to drive east and southeast from Highway 24(running between Hanksville and I-70), from between mile posts 136 and 137. Drive to the Maze Ranger Station first, then go south to the Flint Trail. Any car can go to about that point, but not down The Trail. 4WD's can however drop off the top and use this often used, but never maintained road or track, which runs on to Highway 95, meeting it between mile posts 46 and 47. From anywhere along this road, you can hike to selected mine exploration sites.

If you're out exploring around and taking a look at some of these old uranium mining sites, remember several things. Summer time temps are usually very warm, especially in the Orange Cliffs district. It's recommended you do your traveling here in the spring or fall season. The temperatures then are much lower and more pleasant, and there are fewer insects. Remember, take plenty of fuel, water, extra food, tools, a shovel, jumper cable, etc. In the area right around the Henry Mountains, the roads are generally well used and often maintained, and most mining sites aren't too far off the highway. There are a lot of other people out there these days, so help isn't usually too far away, but go prepared for any kind of emergency none-the-less.

Geology

The Henry Mountains region in southeastern Utah is one of the classic areas in geology because of the study made there by Grove Karl Gilbert in 1875 and 1876. The publication on his report on the

Inside one of the tunnel openings of the Del Monte Mine.

Stockpiled uranium ore in Shitamaring Canyon, awaiting the price of uranium to rise.

203

Mine equipment at the Cedar Point Group uranium mines.

mountains was among the first to recognize that intrusive bodies can deform host rock. His report also brought to light and made famous features called *laccoliths*, or *laccolith mountains*. The *Report on the Geology of the Henry Mountains,* was published in 1877 by the U.S. Geological Survey, which at that time was headed by John Wesley Powell,

The Henry Mountains Region was a blank on all maps of Utah and the western USA prior to 1869. This was the year J. W. Powell made his epic journey by boat down the Green and Colorado Rivers. At the time of discovery(at least by white men)by Powell, the mountains were the center of the largest unexplored district in the territory of the continental USA, a district which by its peculiar ruggedness had turned aside all previous travelers. While camped at the mouth of the Dirty Devil River, John F. Steward, a geologist and member of the Powell party, climbed the cliffs near the mouth of the river and approached the eastern base of the mountains. This was the very first investigation of the range by any white man. At that time, Powell named the mountains after an associate, a professor Joseph Henry, a distinguished physicist.

During the 1872 Colorado River expedition, a professor A. H. Thompson, in charge of geographic work of the Powell Survey, crossed the mountains by the Penellen Pass and ascended some of the principal peaks.

In 1873, E. E. Howell, who at the time was a geologist for a division of the Wheeler Survey(which did most of the early surveys of the western USA), traveled to within 20 kms of the western base of the mountains, and observed the unique character of the region.

It was then in 1875, that G. K. Gilbert traveling from Salt Lake City, down through the Sevier Valley, spent two weeks in the mountains doing a preliminary study. That trip was followed in 1876 by the same group which spent two full months in the region. The report of these two trips was published the following year by the USGS. His study and report have since become a landmark in geologic investigation.

In discussing the Henry Mountains, it's perhaps best to quote directly from Gilberts publication, and from the chapter on "Eruption versus Irruption". He states that *it is usual for igneous rocks to ascend to the surface of the earth, and there issue forth and build up mountains or hills by successive eruptions. The molten matter starting from some region of unknown depth passes through all superincumbent rock beds, and piles itself up on the upper most bed. The lava of the Henry Mountains behaved differently. Instead of rising through all the beds of the Earth's crust, it stopped at a lower horizon, insinuated itself between two strata, and opened for itself a chamber by lifting all the superior*

HENRY MTNS. GEOLOGY CROSS SECTION

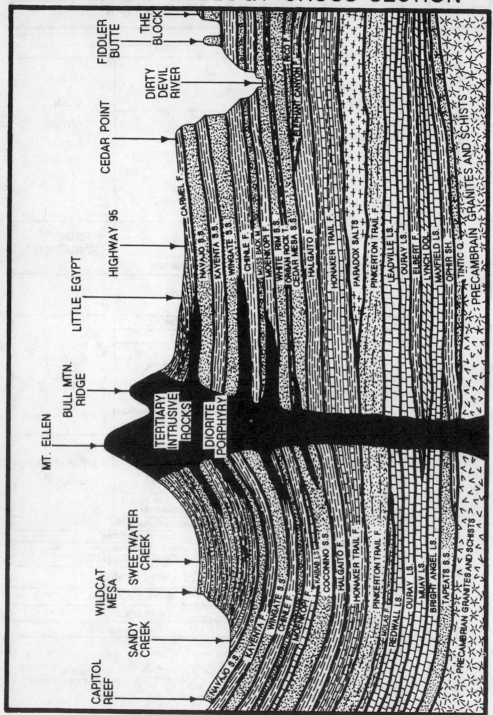

GEOLOGY BELOW ROBBERS ROOST

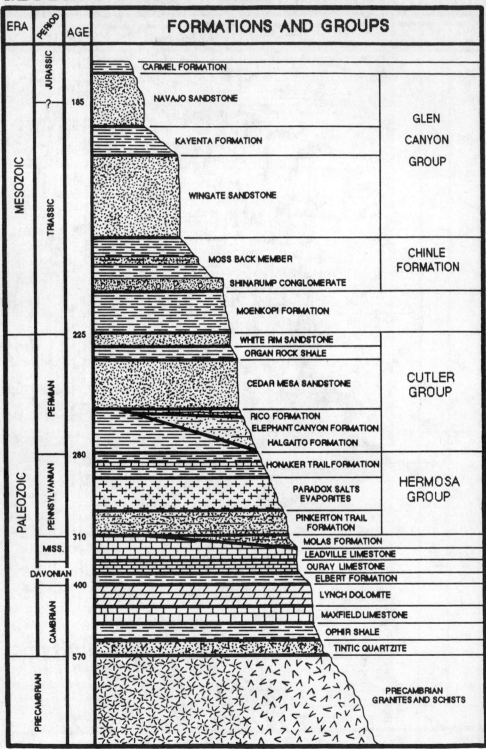

ERA	PERIOD	AGE	FORMATIONS AND GROUPS	
MESOZOIC	JURASSIC		CARMEL FORMATION	
	?	185	NAVAJO SANDSTONE	GLEN CANYON GROUP
	TRIASSIC		KAYENTA FORMATION	
			WINGATE SANDSTONE	
			MOSS BACK MEMBER	CHINLE FORMATION
			SHINARUMP CONGLOMERATE	
			MOENKOPI FORMATION	
PALEOZOIC	PERMIAN	225	WHITE RIM SANDSTONE	CUTLER GROUP
			ORGAN ROCK SHALE	
			CEDAR MESA SANDSTONE	
			RICO FORMATION	
			ELEPHANT CANYON FORMATION	
		280	HALGAITO FORMATION	
	PENNSYLVANIAN		HONAKER TRAIL FORMATION	HERMOSA GROUP
			PARADOX SALTS EVAPORITES	
			PINKERTON TRAIL FORMATION	
	MISS.	310	MOLAS FORMATION	
			LEADVILLE LIMESTONE	
	DAVONIAN		OURAY LIMESTONE	
		400	ELBERT FORMATION	
	CAMBRIAN		LYNCH DOLOMITE	
			MAXFIELD LIMESTONE	
			OPHIR SHALE	
		570	TINTIC QUARTZITE	
PRECAMBRIAN			PRECAMBRIAN GRANITES AND SCHISTS	

GEOLOGY BELOW TARANTULA MESA

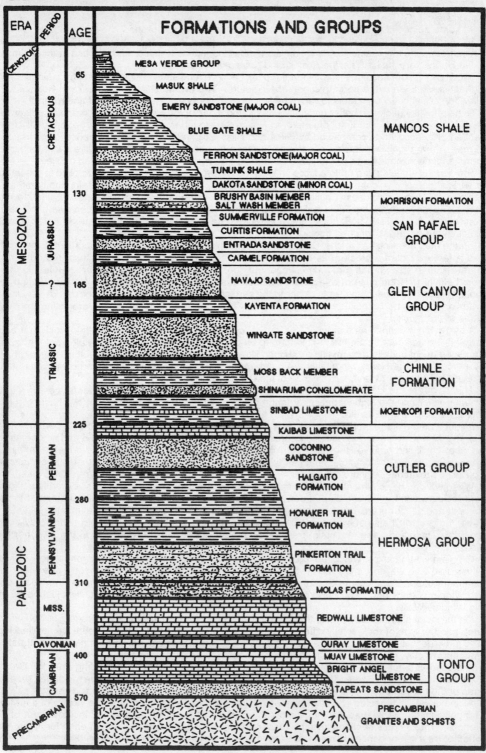

ERA	PERIOD	AGE	FORMATIONS AND GROUPS	
CENOZOIC			MESA VERDE GROUP	
	CRETACEOUS	65	MASUK SHALE	MANCOS SHALE
			EMERY SANDSTONE (MAJOR COAL)	
			BLUE GATE SHALE	
			FERRON SANDSTONE (MAJOR COAL)	
			TUNUNK SHALE	
MESOZOIC		130	DAKOTA SANDSTONE (MINOR COAL)	
	JURASSIC		BRUSHY BASIN MEMBER / SALT WASH MEMBER	MORRISON FORMATION
			SUMMERVILLE FORMATION	SAN RAFAEL GROUP
			CURTIS FORMATION	
			ENTRADA SANDSTONE	
	?	185	CARMEL FORMATION	
			NAVAJO SANDSTONE	GLEN CANYON GROUP
			KAYENTA FORMATION	
	TRIASSIC		WINGATE SANDSTONE	
			MOSS BACK MEMBER	CHINLE FORMATION
			SHINARUMP CONGLOMERATE	
		225	SINBAD LIMESTONE	MOENKOPI FORMATION
	PERMIAN		KAIBAB LIMESTONE	
			COCONINO SANDSTONE	CUTLER GROUP
		280	HALGAITO FORMATION	
PALEOZOIC	PENNSYLVANIAN		HONAKER TRAIL FORMATION	HERMOSA GROUP
			PINKERTON TRAIL FORMATION	
		310	MOLAS FORMATION	
	MISS.		REDWALL LIMESTONE	
	DAVONIAN	400	OURAY LIMESTONE	
	CAMBRIAN		MUAV LIMESTONE	TONTO GROUP
			BRIGHT ANGEL LIMESTONE	
		570	TAPEATS SANDSTONE	
	PRECAMBRIAN		PRECAMBRIAN GRANITES AND SCHISTS	

207

beds. *In this chamber it congealed, forming a massive body of trap. For this body the name laccolite will be used. The laccolite is the chief element of the type of structure exemplified in the Henry Mountains.*

At some point during the last century since Gilberts' report was published, the term laccolite, seems to have evolved to laccolith. The name laccolith is now used in all the literature when referring to the structure and the mountains they form. In Utah, other mountains which are formed in a manner similar to the Henrys, are the La Sals, the Abajos, and Navajo Mountain.

The Henry Mountains consist of five major peaks and several smaller and minor outcroppings. The highest is Mt. Ellen in the north, rising to 3512 meters. The two most southerly peaks of Holmes and Ellsworth are about 1000 meters lower. The two other major peaks are Mts. Pennell and Hillers.

To help the lay geologist better understand the foundations of the Henrys, several maps and diagrams have been prepared. But first some terms. Notice the sketch from Gilberts report of an ideal cross section of a laccolith, accompanied by dikes and sills. Sills(called sheets by Gilbert and others) are formed when a molten intrusion penetrates between two layers of rock, in this case sandstone, and forms a thin horizontal body. If the intrusion forms a thin vertical body, it's then called a dike.

The vertical shaft leading up to a laccolith is called a vent. This is also the name applied to the throat or vertical part of a volcano leading to the Earth's surface. Think of a laccolith as being the same as a volcano, but one which doesn't quite reach the surface. Instead of reaching the surface, and blowing its top, the magma(very hot liquid rock inside the earth) is stopped somehow, and because of pressure from below, forces itself horizontally into the rock strata to be uplifted and deformed. Later erosion exposes the event like an open book.

On the map showing Laccoliths, Stocks and Bysmaliths, you'll notice that each mountain in the range has a feature called a stock at its center. A stock is an intrusive body of rock less than about 65 square kms in size. It has a rounded shape, but does not have the narrow vent or shaft leading to it from below, as is the case of a laccolith. A stock is a bulging of the Earth's crust, thus bringing the molten matter from within the earth closer to the surface, to be eroded and later exposed. A very large intrusion is called a batholith. Laccoliths then, in this case, are smaller bodies projecting from the sides of the stock.

A bysmalith is defined as a more or less *vertical cylindrical* body of igneous(liquified) rock that cuts through the adjacent sediments and is formed by pushing up the overlying strata along steep faults. Thus you might think of a bysmalith as shaped like a tall glass, as opposed to the flatter, saucer shape of a laccolith. The Henry Mountains are one large cluster of stocks, laccoliths and bysmaliths riding along in a sea of sandstone, in the center of the Colorado Plateau.

Hikers out in the Henrys doing some foot work, will notice a number of different types of rocks, whether you're on the highest peaks, or in the lower canyons. What you'll see are two basic types of rocks; sandstone and granite.

If you're on the higher summits, you'll be walking atop a granitic type rock called diorite porphyry. It is the speckled rock, having a salt and pepper appearances. Some of it is very solid and smooth, such as what you'll find on The Horn. In other places it'll be broken or brecciated, and rather crumbly. If you're close to the contact zone, that part lying near where the granite intrusion meets the sandstone, you'll find the granite very broken up.

When walking down almost any of the canyons featured in this book, you'll often see granite boulders and rocks, which have been carried down canyon from the peaks above. It's quite a contrast to see the salt and pepper granite rocks scattered among the red rock canyons. If you get into the Dirty Devil River Gorge, you'll also see on occasion, the black volcanic cobblestones brought all the way down from the Thousand Lake Mountain area, located much further to the west, and in the area north of Torrey and Bicknell.

On most canyon hikes, which are mostly along the Dirty Devil and the former canyon of the Colorado River, you'll be walking into real "Red Rock Country". Almost all of the rocks you'll see there are members of the Glen Canyon Group, which includes the Navajo Sandstone, Kayenta Formation, and the Wingate Sandstone. You'll also be confronted with the Chinle Formation, which lies just below the big Wingate Walls.

On the other side of the range, in this case the northwest part of this books coverage, you'll be walking atop another type of rock, totally different from the two just mentioned. On the South Caineville Mesa and in Sweetwater Creek drainage, you'll be aware of the Mancos Shale and it's several contrasting members of clay, shale and sandstone.

Included, is a full page geology cross section of the Henry Mountains, extending from the Capitol Reef to the Dirty Devil River. This gives you a generalized look at the whole region. Included on each map of the canyon country, is a small geology cross section of that particular hike and canyon.

Also included is a geology cross section below the Robbers Roost Country in the vicinity of the Maze Ranger Station, as well as another, below the surface of the Tarantula Mesa, located west of Mt. Pennell. These cross sections give the reader an idea of the physical makeup of each formation and whether it's a cliff or bench-maker. This is an important facit to know for the canyon hiker.

LACCOLITHS, STOCKS, AND BYSMALITHS

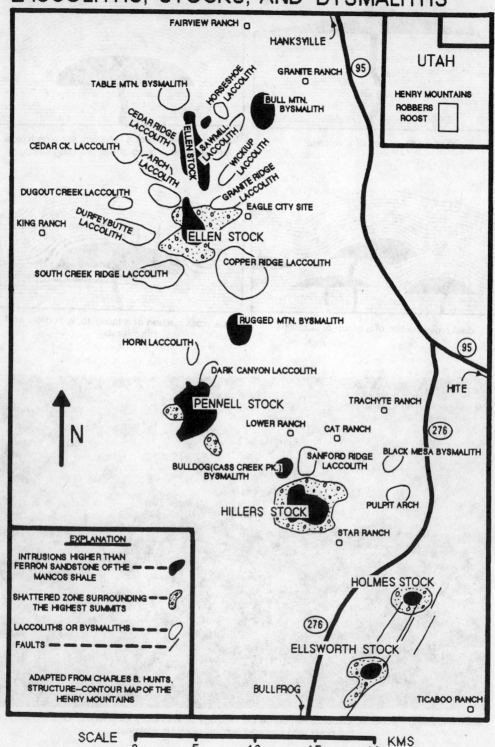

FAIRVIEW RANCH ▫

HANKSVILLE

GRANITE RANCH ▫

95

UTAH

HENRY MOUNTAINS
ROBBERS
ROOST

TABLE MTN. BYSMALITH

HORSESHOE LACCOLITH

BULL MTN.
BYSMALITH

CEDAR RIDGE LACCOLITH

SAWMILL LACCOLITH

ELLEN STOCK

WICKIUP LACCOLITH

CEDAR CK. LACCOLITH

ARCH LACCOLITH

GRANITE RIDGE LACCOLITH

DUGOUT CREEK LACCOLITH

EAGLE CITY SITE

DURFEY BUTTE LACCOLITH

KING RANCH ▫

ELLEN STOCK

SOUTH CREEK RIDGE LACCOLITH

COPPER RIDGE LACCOLITH

RUGGED MTN. BYSMALITH

HORN LACCOLITH

DARK CANYON LACCOLITH

N

PENNELL STOCK

TRACHYTE RANCH

HITE

95

LOWER RANCH ▫

CAT RANCH ▫

276

BULLDOG (CASS CREEK PK.) BYSMALITH

SANFORD RIDGE LACCOLITH

BLACK MESA BYSMALITH

HILLERS STOCK

PULPIT ARCH

STAR RANCH ▫

HOLMES STOCK

EXPLANATION

INTRUSIONS HIGHER THAN
FERRON SANDSTONE OF THE ---
MANCOS SHALE

SHATTERED ZONE SURROUNDING ---
THE HIGHEST SUMMITS

LACCOLITHS OR BYSMALITHS ---

FAULTS --- --- --- ---

ADAPTED FROM CHARLES B. HUNTS,
STRUCTURE—CONTOUR MAP OF THE
HENRY MOUNTAINS

276

ELLSWORTH STOCK

BULLFROG

TICABOO RANCH ▫

SCALE

0   5   10   15   20   KMS

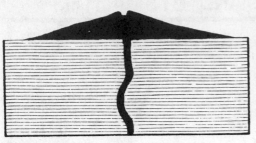

Ideal cross section of a volcano.

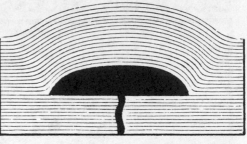

Ideal cross section of a laccolith, showing typical form and the arching of the overlying strata.

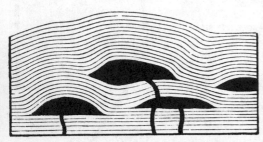

Ideal cross section of a group of laccoliths.

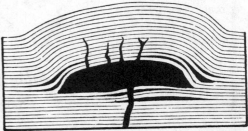

Ideal cross section of a laccolith, with dikes and sills(sheets).

Scetch drawing from G. K. Gilberts, Report on the Geology of the Henry Mountains. Looking south at the north face and northern valley on Mt. Holmes.

A typical set of potholes, which are common throughout the canyonlands part of this book. These are in the Navajo S.S., and on the lip of upper Twin Corral Box Canyon.

Concretions which have eroded out of the Navajo Sandstone along the Burr Point route to the Dirty Devil River.

Vegetation of the Henry Mountains Region

From the top of Mt. Ellen at 3512 meters to the surface of Lake Powell at 1128 meters(high water mark), a distance of about 40 kms, there is a range in elevation of 2400 meters. Despite the small size of the Henry Mountains Region, a range in elevation exists to allow development of vegetative types from nearly all the major vegetation zones of Utah. Only the Creosote Bush Zone, from the area around St. George, is missing.

Vegetation Zones

1. **Alpine Zone** This zone exists only on the summit ridges of Mt. Ellen above about 3350 meters. It's that part of the mountain above timberline, which has the typical alpine tundra type of vegetation, as well as blocky sections of frost-heaved boulder fields.

2. **Subalpine Zone** This zone is well developed only on Mt. Ellen, within the altitudes of about 2900 to 3350 meters. This zone is sharply divided into two vegetation types--the *subalpine forest*. dominated by Engelmann spruce and subalpine fir. It has the occasional limber pine on exposed ridges(not to be confused with bristlecone pine which is in a similar zone) and even a few scattered groves of aspen which occupy special niches. And the *subalpine grassland*, dominated by species of *Poa* and *Festuca*.

3. **Montane Zone** This zone covers the higher parts of Hillers, Pennell and Ellen, between the altitudes of about 2600 to 3200 meters. In shaded areas where snow stays on the ground longest, is a dense mixed forest of Douglas fir, white fir, blue spruce and aspen. Douglas fir is by far the most common tree in this zone, and has a very wide altitudinal range. The author has seen two small stands of Douglas fir in the Middle Fork of Robbers Roost Canyon in two large alcoves and at approximately 1375 meters elevation. Aspen often are found to be the first trees to grow in a burned area. On more exposed sites, the forest gives way to a highland sagebrush and grassland community.

4. **Ponderosa Pine--Mountain Brush Zone** This zone is generally between about 2450 and 2750 meters, but the zone can descend to about 2100 meters on north facing slopes, and rises to as high as 3000 meters on the dry south exposures of Mt. Hillers and Mt. Pennell.

The mountain brush community is dominated by oak brush, or gambel oak. It can be seen and is most apparent in the gap between Mt. Hillers and Mt. Pennell, and to a lesser extent on the south slopes of Mt. Ellen.

The Ponderosa pine occupies the rockier, steeper and cooler sites, and tend to be in small and scattered stands with open space between trees, allowing sunlight to reach the ground. These stands of Ponderosa pine are best seen around Mt. Hillers, but they are also seen on Mt. Pennell and Mt. Ellen in scattered sites. According to Neese in the book *Henry Mountains Symposium,* the bristlecone pine is also in this zone. This tree is seen in a number of locations on the south ridges of Mt. Hillers, and to a much lesser extent on Mt. Pennell.

5. **Pygmy Forest Zone** This zone has a wide altitudinal range, from about 1800 to 2450 meters, and includes areas which receive more than about 30 centimeters of precipitation yearly. In the Henry Mountains, this zone covers all the foothills between the desert lowlands and the upper montane zones. The trees involved here are the pinyon pine and juniper trees, more commonly called the pinyon-juniper forest, or PJ for short.

All the higher parts of the Robbers Roost Country, especially areas to the east of the Biddlecome-Ekker Ranch and in the area around the Maze Ranger Station, are covered with this forest. South of the Roost Country, and on top of The Block, this forest is also dominant.

On the two southern most mountains of the Henrys, Mt. Holmes and Mt. Ellsworth, this forest covers the entire mountain, right up to the summit, with only a small protected place or two where ponderosa or limber pines are found.

It's this pinyon-juniper forest which has been cleared in many places with bulldozers and large chains, to create an open environment for grasses to grow. These chained areas have been created for the benefit of ranchers who have grazing permits in the mountains. Most chained areas are on the eastern slopes of Mt. Pennell(Coyote Benches), and between The Horn and Mt. Ellen. Buffalo or bison take advantage of the new grasslands as well, and they can be seen in the areas of The Horn and Mt. Ellen in summer time.

6. **Cool Desert Shrub Zone** This major zone covers more area than any other in the Henry Mountains Region. It ranges from 1500 to about 2100 meters, and covers all soils, saline to neutral. It occupies all areas between the Pygmy Forest down to the Warm Desert. This larger zone covers eight sub-zones, each with it's own micro environment.

First, the *Little Rabbitbrush--Mixed Desert Shrub*. It occupies the higher deserts, where precip is greater than about 18 to 20 cm per year. The dominant species is little rabbitbrush. Next is the *Galleta--Three-Awn Grassland*. It occurs in slightly sandy soils, and is dominated by a spotty turf of galleta and three-awn, intermixed with shrubs of shadscale and blackbrush.

The third sub-zone is the *Big Rabbitbrush Desert Wash*. This zone lies in the small and sandy desert washes, where on occasion the land is flooded by runoff. This added moisture makes for healthier plant growth. The dominant plant is big sagebrush. Next is the *Saltgrass Meadow and Salt Marsh*. This vegetation group occurs where water ponds on occasion, causing saline soils to generate. Saltgrass is the dominant species.

The fifth sub-zone is the *Cottonwood Floodplain*. This zone is along canyon bottoms where perennial streams flow. The dominant specie is Fremont poplar, but also willows, tamaracks, rabbitbrush, sagebrush, cliffrose and service berry occur. Next is the *Greasewood Flats*. Greasewood grows along the bottoms of broad valleys and in areas of saline soils. Greasewood grows near the water table, such as along the Dirty Devil River.

The seventh sub-zone is *Mat Atriplex Clay Barrens*. It occurs northeast of Mt. Ellen in the Blue Hills area, and on the weathered badlands of the Mancos Shale Formation. Vegetation is almost nil, the dominant specie perhaps being the beavertail cactus. The eighth and final sub-zone is the *Shadscale Salt Desert*. Shadscale is the dominant specie. This zone covers the lower part of the major zone, and where precip is lowest, usually less about 15 cm per year. This zone occurs most noticeable north and west of the mountains.

7. **Warm Desert Shrub Zone** The vegetation in this zone is noticeably different from that of the cool desert areas. Occurring in the lowest, driest and generally the warmest areas of the Henry Mountains Region, vegetation in this zone is a transitional type between the Creosote Bush or Lower Sonoran Zone, and the Cool Desert Shrub or Upper Sonoran Zone. This zone is best developed south and east of the mountains. Formerly it occupied the lower canyons of the Colorado River drainage. It still does, but the lowest parts are now under the waters of Lake Powell. This zone covers areas generally below 1500 meters, and along the Dirty Devil River, North Wash, and Trachyte, Ticaboo, Bullfrog and Halls Creeks. The plants include arrowweed, seepwillow, and dogweed. In other areas you'll see sandsage, Mormon tea, yucca and blackbrush.

Wildlife in the Henry Mountains Region

Buffalo or Bison

The history of Utah's modern day free roaming buffalo herd began in 1941. In was in that year the Utah Fish and Game Department transplanted 18 head of bison from Yellowstone National Park to the Henry Mountains Region. This initial herd consisted of 3 bulls and 15 cows. They were released somewhere north and west of the Robbers Roost Spring and north and east of the Dirty Devil River.

Because of some unknown factors the herd dispersed In all directions, to the point of the bulls separating themselves from the cows. Some apparently moved north and east of the transplant site, while others stayed in the general area where they were introduced. Because of this, the decision was made to bring another 5 bulls to the Robbers Roost area the following year, 1942. This plant was successful, and the herd stayed together. Later they moved south across the Dirty Devil River, and made their home in the Burr Desert, in the area west of the Angel Trail. From there the herd moved to the Henry Mountains in the summer, returning to the Burr Desert during the winter months.

The first sanctioned buffalo hunt was held in 1950, but there wasn't another hunt until 1960. No reason has been given as to why there was no hunt during this 10 year period, but it's assumed the herd didn't do as well as anticipated. Blood samples taken in 1961, 1962 and 1963 indicated brucellosis was present in the herd. Brucellosis is a disease which causes females or cows to lose or abort their embryo or fetus. Because the disease effects both cattle and buffalo, it became necessary to inoculate the herd.

In 1963, a two phase brucellosis eradication program got underway. The job consisted of rounding up the herd, placing them in a corral, then vaccinating them. In March of 1963, 12 calves were vaccinated. In November the same year, the rest of the herd was rounded up, tested, and vaccinated. In all, 10 buffalo were deemed to have the disease. These were marked and culled during the hunt which took place later. This particular hunt was the only one where the DWR got directly involved with some kind of supervision. During all other hunts, the permit holders had to find, shoot and remove the buffalo, as they would with any other big game animal.

During the years 1964 and 1965 there were no hunts. This was needed to allow the herd to build in numbers. During this period when no hunts took place, and because of the roundup and corralling in 1963, the herd headed for greener, if not safer pastures. They moved to the western slopes of the Henry Mountains, which is where they spend most of their time today.

During the summer months, the buffalo head for the higher and cooler country. They can be seen on all the higher slopes of Mt. Ellen, but mostly on the north, west, and south slopes, and to a lesser degree, on Mt. Pennell. Bull Creek Pass, is one of the better places you can drive to in order to have a chance to view the herd. Along the way to Bull Creek Pass, you'll drive through Nasty Flats(west of the South Ridge of Mt. Ellen), which is also a good viewing area. Another possible location to see the herd in summer is in the area of The Horn. They spend lots of time in the chained areas there. Since they eat grass, you can often spot them in open meadows.

Most of the herd heads southwest for the winter, to the Swap Mesa area, located to the west of Mt. Pennell. Some may locate themselves on Tarantula Mesa and Cave Flat as well. These two locations are also west of Mt. Pennell.

During the month of November, when most of the hunts have taken place in the past, the biggest part of the herd is located near The Horn, Airplane Springs, Tarantula Mesa and Cave Flat. In 1986, the buffalo hunt was divided in two time periods; one part was in mid-October, before the deer hunt; the other in November, after the general deer hunt.

In the years since 1974, the herd has done very well, and the hunts have been very successful. An agreement has been reached between the BLM, the Utah Division of Wildlife Resources, and the local ranchers who have permits to graze cattle in the area, to keep the herd at about 200 head. Cattle and buffalo occupy the same ecological niche, so the more buffalo there are, the less feed there will be for cattle.

Notice the table, *Utah's Buffalo Harvest*. In 1974, only 10 permits were issued, but in 1985, 45 permits were sold. Of the 45, four went to out-of-state residents. They paid big money for the buffalo permits($1000). One permit was let out to the highest bidder. Utah hunters have to pay $200 for the privilege to hunt, and they only get one permit per lifetime. It seems obvious from the increase in permits issued, that the herd is doing better, and the brucellosis eradication program in 1963 was successful.

As you might imagine, this little herd of bison is a real treasure and a pet of the Dept. of Wildlife Resources. Lots of time has been spent studying the herd, in order to maintain it's good health, and to keep poachers in check. Much of what we know about this herd was gained through the research done prior to the 1963 brucellosis problem. Some interesting facts were learned at that time and in subsequent studies.

It's been learned that buffalo have virtually the same diet as cattle. They are primarily grass eaters, although they supplement their diet with forbes and shrubs. Buffalo do not seem to require a daily water supply. But if water is nearby they'll use it. Unlike cattle, when buffalo satisfy their water needs, they will leave the watering area. This means the herd is more widely dispersed and have a larger daily range than cattle.

Buffalo take about 8 years to fully mature, but they sometimes breed at about three years of age. The rutting season is generally from about late July through early September. The calves are dropped any time from April to June, after a 9.5 month gestation period.

This is part of the Henry Mountains wild buffalo herd (Larry Sip foto)

During the hunt in 1962, researchers found the live weight of males or bulls was about 385 kgs, whereas the weight of the females or cows was about 330 kgs. These weights seem to be rather similar to that of a large elk or a moose.

Buffalo of all ages like to wallow in the dust, and these wallows are in the same areas where they feed. Researchers have never speculated as to why they do this, but the removal or prevention of insects seems a logical conclusion. Buffalo, like cattle, have rubbing posts. They like to rub against trees or posts, presumably scratching themselves because of insects.

The Henry Mountains Region at the present time is an ideal location for a buffalo herd, from the standpoint of the short distance between the summer and winter ranges, and a lack of fences in the area. Also, a wide variety of plant life on both the summer and winter ranges appears to meet the dietary needs of the bison.

Utah's Buffalo Harvest

Year	Hunt?	Permits Sold	Harvest Total	% of Success
1950	yes	10	10	100
1951	no	–	–	–
1952	no	–	–	–
1953	no	–	–	–
1954	no	–	–	–
1955	no	–	–	–
1956	no	–	–	–
1957	no	–	–	–
1958	no	–	–	–
1959	no	–	–	–
1960	yes	10	10	100
1961	yes	12	12	100
1962	yes	20	20	100
1963	yes	14	7	50
1964	no	–	–	–
1965	no	–	–	–
1966	yes	10	10	100
1967	yes	10	10	100
1968	yes	15	10	100
1969	yes	10	8	80
1970	yes	10	6	60
1971	yes	15	10	67
1972	no	–	–	–
1973	no	–	–	–
1974	yes	10(9 hunters)	7	78
1975	yes	10(9 hunters)	9	100
1976	yes	10	10	100
1977	yes	10	10	100
1978	yes	22	21	95
1979	yes	27	27	100
1980	yes	27	23	85
1981	yes	27	25	93
1982	yes	28**	28	100
1983	yes	28**	28	100
1984	yes	36**	35	97
1985	yes	45**	41	91
Totals		416	382	92%

*Beginning in 1978, nonresident permits were available.
**Includes one bid permit.

A 1963 foto showing buffalo being corralled and vaccinated for brucellosis (UDWR foto)

Deer

Of all the big game animals in the Henry Mountains Region, the mule deer has the largest numbers and has the widest range of habitat. Most of the deer live in the Henry Mountains proper. They make the higher altitudes their summer range, and the pinyon-juniper and cool desert sagebrush areas their winter home.

Prior to the early 1950's there weren't large numbers of deer in the Henry Mountains Region. Since then their numbers have grown. The reason for the recent increase, was the introduction of the poison "1080", and the use of cyanide guns. These were used to kill coyotes, which more than any other animal besides man, kept deer numbers down. That allowed the deer herd to increase in size. However, in more recent years, with the ban of these poisons, there's been an increase in coyotes again, therefore the deer numbers seem to have taken a drop.

Other areas where deer are found include the higher portions of the Robbers Roost County, and on the highlands in all directions from the Maze Ranger Station. Much of this area is moderately high elevation and covered with a dense forest of pinyon-juniper. Deer make their home there the year-round, but during winters with heavy snowfall, will move down into the lower canyons. The deer numbers are small, so it's not worth the effort to go hunt them there.

The author has seen tracks, presumably that of deer, in almost every canyon he has hiked. This, during the summer and fall seasons. It's assumed these deer make these canyons their home on a year-round basis. In Robbers Roost and Fiddler Cove Canyons, the author actually drove deer up-canyon in front of him, and had them trapped in the upper tributaries. One was a huge 4-point buck.

Antelope

There are several areas or ranges for antelope in the scope of this book, but you'll likely not see any of these animals while hiking. You may however see them as you drive across the region. Most of the antelope are in the area north of the Robbers Roost Country, and in the areas around North Springs, the Moore Ranch, and Jeffery Well. This is in the southern part of the San Rafael Desert.

Another region where habitat is favorable for antelope is the area between Hanksville, Mts. Ellen and Pennell, and the Dirty Devil River. This includes favorable sites like Burr and Cedar Points. Another place where sightings occasionally occur is in the Cane Spring Desert, which lies between Mt. Ellsworth, Lake Powell, Bullfrog and State Road 276.

In years past there must have been even more antelope than the area has today, which is about 75 head, according to a BLM report. Pearl Biddlecome Baker saw many as a child, and has fond memories of them. In her book, *Robbers Roost Recollections,* she writes about antelope, "they are curious and friendly and they play regular games of their own. One game is outrunning anything and dashing in front of it. This was fun when the roads were first put into the Roost and cars could travel a little faster than horses. The antelope herd would swoop down from sidehill, or up from a swale, run alongside the road and finally, after a real burst of speed, cross in front of our vehicle. It was a game with us, too, and we speeded up as much as we dared in the more or less parallel cow trails which served for roads, and made them really lay to the ground to outrun us. It cost us springs, but it was worth it!"

Antelope tracks are similar to deer tracks, but are more delicate and the toes are more slim and pointed. Pearl remembers antelope as making a kind of "stud pile", similar to that done by wild horses. "We thought they marked out boundaries to their territories. As they crossed a trail, they pawed out a slight depression, the long, fine scratches running out sometimes as much as two or three feet(up to meter) from the center of the "hole" into which they planted their sign, a pile of manure." This is surely the work of a mature buck.

Pearl also states that antelope seem to share her own hatred of rattlesnakes. "Apparently wherever an antelope buck ran onto a rattlesnake, that snake was immediately stamped not only to death, but also into minute pieces."

Elk
Elk were transplanted to the Henry Mountains in 1950, but they just didn't do well. It's been years since any have been seen. No one seems to know just what happened to the herd, whether they moved to the highlands to the west, or just died off.

Big Horn Sheep
Big horn sheep have always inhabited this region, but early in this century their numbers almost reached zero. On every panel of petroglyphs in the region you'll see these magnificent animals depicted. So they have been around a long time, and in apparently great numbers.

In recent years the Utah Division of Wildlife Resources has transplanted a number of these animals to areas around the Little Rockies; Mt. Holmes and Ellsworth. Today they range from the summits of these two peaks, to the canyons leading to Lake Powell. Big horns also range along the cliffs and walls of the Dirty Devil River Gorge, the cliffs and escarpments of The Block, and along the areas just to the east of the area covered by this book(The Maze District of Canyonlands National Park).

In the early 1980's, a BLM report suggested there might be 30 to 40 head of big horn sheep in the territory the Hanksville office is responsible for; that's roughly the same land area covered by this book.

Beaver
A recent BLM report made a list of places where beaver may be found in the Henry Mountains Region. About half the locations they list have about zero possibilities of having a beaver population at present. That list includes Ticaboo, Four Mile, Two Mile, and Poison Spring Canyons. This author believes there are no beaver in these canyons today, although at one time, there may have been. The list also suggests Crescent and Halls Creeks, as possibilities. It is possible, but not probable.

The list also states that some beaver may be in the Fremont and Dirty Devil Rivers, and in Beaver and Trachyte Creeks. In these cases the report is right, there are beaver in these four streams or side canyons(as is the case of Trachyte Creek and Maidenwater Canyon). This author has either seen live beaver, or has seen fresh sign of beaver in all of these four streams.

The Beaver Creek Canyon population is unique because it has constructed several dams using desert vegetation rather than willow and cottonwoods. It is believed that the last beaver inhabiting the Henry Mountains proper, was trapped from Bull Creek in 1963. In recent years the population of Beaver in the region seems to be on the increase.

Feral Goats
Actual census data for feral goats(descendents of formerly domesticated goats) is not available. In recent years small bands have been observed in the Burr Point, Cedar Point, and the Little Rockies areas. Because of these sightings, the BLM puts the population at about 50 for the entire region. However, the last official sightings were in 1976 and 1977(from a report issued in about 1980).

Wild Burros
The wild burros of the region probably began in the 1940's and presently inhabit the area east of the Roost County, and north of the Maze Ranger Station. This is in the Horseshoe Canyon drainage, which

includes Bluejohn, Horseshoe and Spur Fork. Sightings have also occurred in Millard Canyon, the first canyon east of Spur Fork.

The most recent BLM inventory of the herd, conducted in the fall of 1981, located 16 mature animals and 3 colts. The herd seems to build up to about 35 animals quite fast but apparently dies back every few years.

The summer range for burros is from the Head of the Spur and across the head canyons of Horseshoe Canyon. In winter, the burros drop down into Horseshoe Canyon. Starvation during the winter months may be a major factor preventing the herd from sustained expansion, because there is plenty of forage on the high country above the canyons.

The Wild Horse and Burro Act of 1971 mandates that BLM consider wild burro equally with other resource values in developing resource management plans. This includes providing sufficient forage to maintain a healthy population at the level determined desirable through the multiple-use planning system.

This author has seen fresh tracks of wild burros in the area of Trail and Wildcat Springs and in Spur Fork. The hoof prints are oblong, but almost round, and are about the same size as a track of a large mule deer. The prints have line features, in a kind of star pattern, which slightly resemble the logo used by the Chrysler Corp.

Wild Horses

In the northern parts of the Roost Country, and in the southern part of the San Rafael Desert, one may see a herd of wild horses. The BLM has no figures on the numbers of wild horses in the area, but it seems there are very few today. It's likely the wild ones you may see are only semi-wild and which belong to a local rancher, as is the case of the herd in Robbers Roost Canyon.

But in the early days of settling this country, there were many of these *broomtails* around. Broomtail was the name applied to the wild horses, because their untrimmed tails reached the ground.

Pearl Biddlecome Baker in her *Recollections* book states, "The few horses at the Roost were dropouts from Butch Cassidy's Wild Bunch, or from J. B. Buhr's fine stock, but those on the San Rafael Desert were from further back(from the days of the old Spanish Trail). They had been there fifty years or more before we went to the Roost; they were inbred, with the only size given to them by Percheron forebearers, which added little to their value as saddle stock."

Life for these wild horses on the San Rafael Desert must have been tough; the summers were extremely hot, the winters cold, and it's about as dry as any place in the state. As a child on the Joe Biddlecome Ranch, Pearl had many experiences with these wild horses. She remembers, "A desert stud(stallion) was about the toughest animal alive; he had to be, to get to the position of leader and hold

Semi-wild horses in Robbers Roost Canyon. A fence across the mouth of the drainage keeps them in this box canyon.

it. His bunch of mares, some fifteen or twenty head, was his harem, and their welfare was his first concern."

One interesting feature of the wild horse range are stud piles. "Studs had their territory, marked on the boundaries and on the high lookout points by piles of manure, which were added to every time the owner passed. We called these stud piles(when my mother wasn't around to hear us!) and sometimes they would be two or three feet(up to a meter) high, hold ten or twelve bushels of manure above ground, and who knows how much the sand had covered over the years while these had served as boundary markers."(Baker)

Other Wildlife

Other animals you may see, or see the tracks of, if hiking either in the mountains or canyons may be coyotes, bobcats, foxes, cougars or porcupines. Coyotes are on the comeback now after near extinction, due to the use of "1080 poison." You'll see their tracks everywhere, and at night, if you're camping in the backcountry, you'll hear them yelping everywhere.

Pearl Biddlecome Baker comments on coyotes and foxes in her book. She says, "Coyotes were plentiful, and a real menace to the calves for many years until "1080" and cyanide guns thinned them almost to the vanishing point. The biggest mistake of this campaign was the killing of the foxes, which allowed the seed-eating rodents to overrun and almost denude the ranges. Foxes didn't bother calves, but this was not true of their bigger cousins, the coyotes."

You may also see tracks of bobcat, especially in the mud of the canyon bottoms, but they are not nearly as plentiful as coyotes. Pearl remembers bobcats while she was growing up on the Biddlecome Ranch. "Coyotes are not much of a threat to our house cats, but for some reason bobcats will kill every house cat they get a chance at. Bobcats put us out of the chicken business from time to time, too. They couldn't get into the coop, but all they had to do was wait until morning and out would come a hen for feed or water, and then nail her. This must have been a great treat; a fat hen was much bigger than a skinny jack rabbit, and much easier to catch."

One larger animal inhabiting the region, but in very few numbers, are mountain lion or cougar. You'd be lucky to find a dozen in the whole country.

Some innocent little fellows you'll surely see if you do much hiking in the canyons, are porcupines. The author has seen several, all in the side canyons of the Dirty Devil River Gorge. You'll see their tracks in the sandy creek beds, especially in those canyons which have some running water, and where there's a presence of willows and cottonwood trees. The tracks are easy to pick out, because of the swishing movement of their tails overlaying the deeply dented tracks that look like they could be made by tiny human feet.

Those who do much hiking in the canyons will surely see one of these small fellows, a porcupine.

Wilderness Study Areas(WSA's)

Within the arbitrary boundaries of this book, are a number of wild, rugged, and scenic areas. In the past several years a number of these places, which are essentially road-less, have been studied and have been set apart for both further study and consideration by the general public and the BLM(Bureau of Land Management), for possible inclusion into Americas wilderness system. Within the scope of this book, are 8 such regions under consideration.

First is the *Blue Hills-Mount Ellen WSA*. It covers the South Caineville Mesa, the Upper Blue Hills, most of the Sweetwater Creek drainage, and the northern ramparts of Mt. Ellen and Bull Mtn. Besides including some high forested mountains, this WSA includes some unique geology and desolate desert scenery. Most of the northern portion of this area, including the Blue Hills, is made up of the Mancos Shale Formation. It's divided into 5 members, with the Blue Gate Shale Member being the layer which gives the Blue Hills their name.

Next is the *Mount Pennell WSA*. It covers Mt. Pennell and The Horn, as well as lowland areas to the west and south. Included here is Swap Mesa, one of the normal winter grazing areas of the wild buffalo herd of the Henry Mountains.

The smallest WSA in the region is *Mount Hillers*. It covers the mountain itself, plus, it extends to the northeast and includes the Black Mesa Bysmalith, otherwise known as the Black Table.

The *Little Rockies WSA* includes, as you might expect, the Little Rockies peaks of Mts. Holmes and Ellsworth, as well as parts of the Trachyte Creek drainage. Canyons included in this WSA are; Maidenwater, Trail, Woodruff, Swett, Fourmile, and all forks of Ticaboo Creek Canyon. The eastern boundary is the Glen Canyon National Recreation Area.

The *Fiddler Butte WSA* includes Butler, Stair and Marinus Canyons, as well as Fiddler Butte and much of the Hatch and Fiddler Cove Canyon drainages. It also includes The Block, an isolated remnant butte of the higher mesa to the north.

Located to the south and west of the Maze Ranger Station is the *French Springs- Happy Canyon WSA*. This includes the eastern and northern portions of Happy Canyon. The eastern boundary is the Glen Canyon National Recreation Area.

The area to the north and northwest of the Maze Ranger Station is included in the *Horseshoe Canyon WSA*. Perhaps it should be called Upper Horseshoe Canyon WSA, as there is still another separate WSA, covering the lower or northern half of Horseshoe Canyon, that part northeast of the small Horseshoe Canyon sector of Canyonlands National Park.

The last area to be nominated as a WSA, is the *Dirty Devil WSA*. It covers the northern part of the Dirty Devil River, and the bottoms of many side canyons such as(from north to south); Buck, Pasture, Robbers Roost, Beaver, No Mans, Larry, Twin Corral Box, and finally Sams Mesa Box Canyon. While there may be a few *ways* or *vehicle tracks* on the mesa tops between some of these canyons, the bottoms are still as wild and wooly as any canyons you'll find.

Within this region, there are other areas which are under appeal as WSA's. These are not included on this map, as their chances of making it through Congress aren't very good. Some time in the 1990's, Congress will take up and decide the matter of what will officially be wilderness, and what will be open to motor vehicles and ORV's.

Topographic Maps

Those who are considering spending a lot of time in the Henry Mountains or the Robbers Roost Country, should also plan to buy and use some better maps than are in this book. The author of course has tried to make his maps as good and as accurate as possible, but there's nothing like the real thing. In this case maps from the USGS or the BLM.

Covering this region of Utah are basically two types of maps, or rather two sets of maps at different scales. First, the maps most of us are familiar with, the 15 minute quadrangles, or those at 1:62,500 scale. These maps are very good for hikers, because they are at a large scale, and show good detail. Most people prefer this scale of map for hiking. But there are two problems with these maps. One, they are old, most dating from the early 1950's. While the canyons change little if any, the roads and other man-made features on the landscape do. So this particular group of maps are outdated and difficult to use at times, mainly because they don't show the newer roads. The second problem is, you often must have two, or maybe three maps to cover one hike, especially a longer hike. It's nice when the hike you're planning fits neatly in the middle of one of these 15 minute maps, but they seldom do. For those just driving about and looking at historic sites, these maps aren't too good.

Beginning about 1980, a new set of maps began to appear. These are at the scale 1:100,000, or as

WILDERNESS STUDY AREAS(WSA)

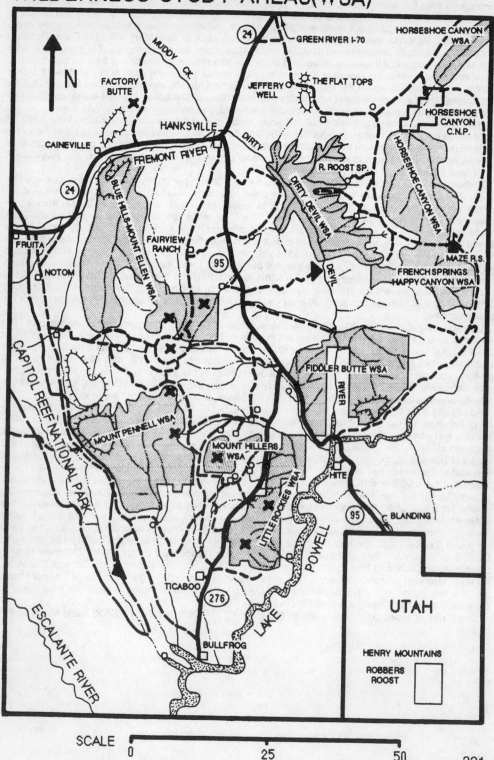

N

MUDDY CK.

24 GREEN RIVER I-70

HORSESHOE CANYON WSA

FACTORY BUTTE

JEFFERY WELL

THE FLAT TOPS

HANKSVILLE

HORSESHOE CANYON C.N.P.

CAINEVILLE

FREMONT RIVER

DIRTY

R. ROOST SP.

HORSESHOE CANYON WSA

24

FRUITA

BLUE HILLS-MOUNT ELLEN WSA

FAIRVIEW RANCH

95

DIRTY DEVIL WSA

DEVIL

MAZE R.S.

FRENCH SPRINGS HAPPY CANYON WSA

NOTOM

CAPITOL REEF NATIONAL PARK

FIDDLER BUTTE WSA

RIVER

MOUNT PENNELL WSA

MOUNT HILLERS WSA

HITE

95

BLANDING

LITTLE ROCKIES WSA

POWELL

TICABOO

276

LAKE

ESCALANTE RIVER

BULLFROG

UTAH

HENRY MOUNTAINS

ROBBERS ROOST

SCALE

0   25   50

221

some might say "30 x 60 minute quads". This scale is considered intermediate. These maps cover a larger area than the older 15 minute quads, and aren't as detailed. However, this author uses them all the time and doesn't mind this one deficiency. There are some advantages in using this series of maps. First, one map covers a number of different hikes, rather than having to have two or three maps for one hike. So these maps show a larger area. In the case of the Henry Mountains and Robbers Roost area, basically two of these 1:100,000 scale maps cover the entire region. They are Hanksville and Hite Crossing. For the extreme western fringes of this region you must use the Loa and possibly Escalante maps. Also, for access to the Robbers Roost area, you might want to buy and use the San Rafael Desert map. It shows the first(or northern) part of the road leading to the Maze Ranger Station. But having this map is not a necessity. So the big advantage of this series of maps is that carrying two is a lot better than lugging around 10 or 12. In many cases, you can drive all day on one map.

The second advantage of these 1:100,000 scale maps is that they are all new, dating from 1980, at least in the case of the those just mentioned. So you have a map which shows all or most of the roads as they are on the ground. If they haven't shown a particular road on the map, it's usually because of choice, not because the road was built after the map came out. In most cases, only the very recent ORV type tracks are not shown, all others are.

These new 1:100,000 scale maps come in two series. One is put out by the USGS, the other by the BLM. The USGS maps are white in color, but show forested areas in green. This is a good feature. When you first begin using them, it's difficult to locate the roads, but with use, it becomes easy. Sometimes roads and contour lines look alike. The BLM maps are virtually the same as the USGS maps, and covering the same area, but are colored different. The background is yellow, with red lines as dirt roads. This also takes getting used to, but you do with time. The one bad feature about the BLM maps, which this author hasn't gotten used to yet, are the several different background overlays used for land ownership. These maps show general public land, forest service land, private land and land under lease, such as for mineral rights. It's this last part, where the overlay of the leased land is placed over and covers up the other symbols of the map, which makes the maps difficult to read. Otherwise, the BLM maps are good. At least you know whether you're on somebodys private land or on public domain.

One last thing about these 30 x 60 minute maps. They are metric. Most people will hate this part. But for some strange reason the maps are set out in grids or little squares of one square mile each, same as the 1:62,500 scale maps. These are the section lines which show ownership, and date back to when maps were first made in the USA. So even though these maps are metric, with all altitudes given in meters, you can still use these little squares showing the land laid out in one mile lengths. About the only complaint this author has had with his books, which are also in metric, is the fact that all car odometers register in miles and the distances in his books, including this one, are in kms.

Admittedly it's a little confusing, this metric business, but in 1975 the US Congress initiated a plan to bring America into the mainstream of the world standard in weights and measurements. Then in 1980, with the first coming of Ronald Reagan, the plan was abandoned by the White House. This now leaves the good old USA, along with Burma and Brunei(a small British ex-colony on the northwest coast of the island of Borneo) as the only 3 countries on earth that still use the old English system of measurement. The rest of the world uses *metric*.

Besides the USGS and BLM topo maps, there's another series of maps which are helpful and handy, especially for the non-hiker. These maps are put out by the Utah Travel Council, an organization whose job it is to promote travel and tourism in the state. They have a series of 8 maps covering the entire state of Utah, which are sold wherever tourists are found, and especially at national park visitor centers. These maps are at 1:250,000 scale and have contour lines. The scale is obviously too small for hikers, but the maps do show the major side roads and many features which might be of interest to tourists or travelers. Two of these maps cover the area discussed in this book. They are Map 1, Southeastern Utah; and Map 2, Southeastern Central Utah. For those not too familiar with this state, it's recommended you always carry a Utah state highway map, both of the Utah Travel Council maps, and the two metric maps, Hanksville and Hite Crossing. With these maps in hand you'll be ready to drive and/or hike in virtually any location covered by this book.

The index of topographic maps shows the metric 1:100,000 and the 1:62,500 scale maps of this region.

INDEX TO TOPOGRAPHIC MAPS OF UTAH

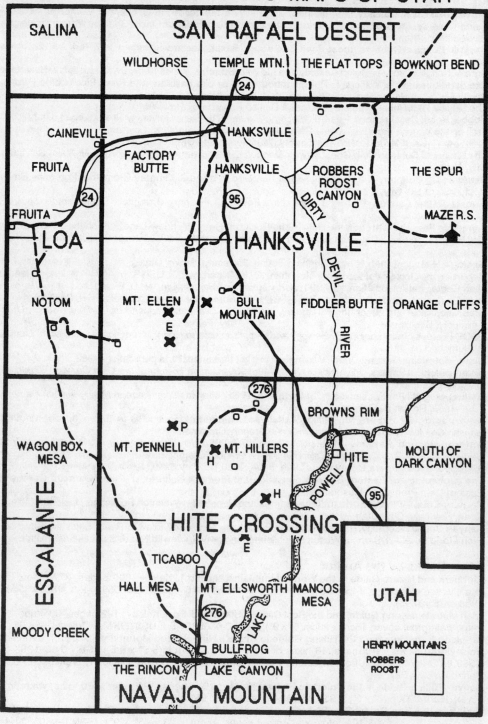

SALINA		SAN RAFAEL DESERT		
	WILDHORSE	TEMPLE MTN.	THE FLAT TOPS	BOWKNOT BEND

SALINA — WILDHORSE — TEMPLE MTN. (24) — THE FLAT TOPS — BOWKNOT BEND

CAINEVILLE — HANKSVILLE

FACTORY BUTTE

FRUITA

HANKSVILLE

ROBBERS ROOST CANYON

THE SPUR

(24)

FRUITA

MAZE R.S.

LOA — HANKSVILLE

(95)

DIRTY

NOTOM

MT. ELLEN ✕

E

BULL MOUNTAIN

FIDDLER BUTTE

ORANGE CLIFFS

DEVIL

RIVER

(276)

BROWNS RIM

✕P

WAGON BOX MESA

MT. PENNELL

✕ MT. HILLERS
H

HITE

MOUTH OF DARK CANYON

POWELL

(95)

ESCALANTE

✕ H

HITE CROSSING

E

TICABOO

HALL MESA

MT. ELLSWORTH

MANCOS MESA

UTAH

(276)

LAKE

MOODY CREEK

BULLFROG

HENRY MOUNTAINS

ROBBERS ROOST

THE RINCON

LAKE CANYON

NAVAJO MOUNTAIN

SCALE

0   25   50

223

Further Reading

In Search of Butch Cassidy, Larry Pointer, University of Oklahoma Press, Norman, Oklahoma.
Butch Cassidy, My Brother, Lula Parker Betenson, written by Dora Flack, Brigham Young University Press, Provo, Utah
The Wild Bunch at Robbers Roost, Pearl Biddlecome Baker, Abelard-Schuman, 257 Park Ave. So., New York.
Outlaw Trail, A History of Butch Cassidy and his Wild Bunch, Charles Kelly, Devin and Adair, New York.
The Bandit Invincible, William T. Phillips(Introduction by Jim Dullenty and Pearl Biddlecome Baker), Rocky Mountain House Press, P.O. Box 858, Hamilton, Montana.
The Outlaw Trail, Robert Redford, Grosset & Dunlap Publishers, New York.
Robber Roost Recollections, Pearl Biddlecome Baker, Utah State University Press, Logan, Utah.
Trail on the Water, Pearl Biddlecome Baker, Pruett Publishing, Boulder, Colorado.
Rainbow Views, A History of Wayne County, Daughters of the Utah Pioneers.
The Historical Guide to Utah Ghost Towns, Stephen L. Carr, Western Epics, 254 South Main, Salt Lake City, Utah.
Standing Up Country, The Canyonlands of Utah and Arizona, C. Gregory Crampton, Peregrine Smith Books, Salt Lake City, Utah.
Ghosts of Glen Canyon--History Beneath Lake Powell, C. Gregory Crampton, Publishers Place, Inc., St. George, Utah.
Incredible Passage--Through the Hole-in-the-Rock, Lee Reay, Meadow Lane Publications, Provo, Utah.
The Exploration of the Colorado River and its Canyons, John W. Powell, Dover Publications, Inc., New York.
Geologic History of Utah, Hintze, Brigham Young University, Provo, Utah.
Report on the Geology of the Henry Mountains, G. K. Gilbert, 1877, USGS.
Utah Geological Association, #8, 1980, *Henry Mountains Symposium,* M. D. Picard.
Utah Geological and Mineralogical Survey, #2, 1972, *Henry Mountains Coal Field,* H. H. Doelling.
Utah Geological and Mineralogical Survey, #22, 1967, *Uranium Deposits of Garfield County, Utah,* Hellmut H. Doelling.
USGS Professional Paper #228, *Geology and Geography of the Henry Mountains Region, Utah,* Charles B. Hunt.
Henry Mountains Grazing Draft Environment Impact Statement, BLM publication, 1982.
Anthropological Papers, University of Utah, #42, 1959, *Outline History of the Glen Canyon Region,* C. Gregory Crampton.
Anthropological Papers, University of Utah, #54, 1961, *The Hoskinini Papers, Mining in Glen Canyon, 1897-1902.* Robert B. Stanton.
Anthropological Papers, University of Utah, #61, 1962, *Historical Sites in Glen Canyon--Mouth of Hansen Creek to Mouth of San Juan River,* C. Gregory Crampton.
Anthropological Papers, University of Utah, #72, 1964, *Historical Sites in Cataract and Narrow Canyons, and in Glen Canyon to California Bar,* C. Gregory Crampton.
Anthropological Papers, University of Utah, #104, 1980, *Cowboy Cave,* Jesse D. Jennings.
The Archeology of Eastern Utah (Emphasis on the Fremont Culture), J. Eldon Dorman, College of Eastern Utah Prehistoric Museum, Price, Utah.
Canyon Country Prehistoric Indians, Barnes and Pendleton, Wasatch Publishers, Inc., 4647 Idlewild Road, Salt Lake City, Utah.
Canyon Country Geology, Barnes, Wasatch Publishers, Inc., 4647 Idlewild Road, Salt Lake City.
Prehistoric Rock Art, Barnes, Wasatch Publishers, Inc., 4647 Idlewild Road, Salt Lake City, Utah.

Other Books by the Author

Climbers and Hikers Guide to the Worlds Mountains (2nd Ed.), Kelsey, 800 pages, 377 maps, 380 fotos, waterproof cover, 14cm x 21cm x 4cm(5.5" x 8.5" x 1.5"), ISBN 0-9605824-2-8. **US$19.95** (Mail Orders US$20.95).
Utah Mountaineering Guide, and the Best Canyon Hikes (2nd Ed.), Kelsey, 192 pages, 80 maps, 105 fotos, waterproof cover, 15cm x 23cm(6" x 9"), ISBN 0-9605824-5-2. **US$7.95** (Mail Orders US$8.95).
China on Your Own, and the Hiking Guide to China's Nine Sacred Mountains (3rd Ed.), Jennings-Kelsey, 240 pages, 110 maps, 16 hikes or climbs, 14cm x 21cm(5.5" x 8.5"), ISBN 0-9691363-1-5, **US$9.95** (Order this book from Milestone Publications, P.O. Box 35548, Station E, Vancouver, B. C., Canada, V6M 4G8).
Canyon Hiking Guide to the Colorado Plateau, Kelsey, 256 pages, 120 maps, 130 fotos, waterproof cover, 15cm x 23cm(6" x 9"), **US$9.95** (Mail Orders US$10.95).
Hiking Utah's San Rafael Swell, (plus A History of the San Rafael Swell, by Dee Ann Finken), Kelsey, 144 pages, 37 maps, 104 fotos, waterproof cover, 15cm x 23cm(6" x 9"), ISBN 0-9605824-4-4. **US$7.95** (Mail Orders US$8.95).